MW00560358

APOLOGETICS

FOR AN

EVER-CHANGING

CULTURE

SEAN McDOWELL

GENERAL EDITOR

HARVEST HOUSE PUBLISHERS
EUGENE. OREGON

Unless otherwise indicated, all Scripture quotations are taken from the *Holy Bible*, New Living Translation, copyright © 1996, 2004, 2015 by Tyndale House Foundation. Used with permission of Tyndale House Publishers, Inc., Carol Stream, Illinois 60188. All rights reserved.

Other Scripture versions used in this book are listed at the back of the book.

Cover design by Faceout Studio, Molly von Borstel

Cover images © Beautalism, Theus / Shutterstock

Interior design by KUHN Design Group

For bulk, special sales, or ministry purchases, please call 1-800-547-8979.
Email: CustomerService@hhpbooks.com

M This logo is a federally registered trademark of the Hawkins Children's LLC. Harvest House Publishers,
Inc., is the exclusive licensee of this trademark.

Apologetics for an Ever-Changing Culture
Some material previously published in *Apologetics for a New Generation*, with revisions
Copyright © 2009, 2024 by Sean McDowell
Published by Harvest House Publishers
Eugene, Oregon 97408
www.harvesthousepublishers.com

ISBN 978-0-7369-8927-5 (pbk)
ISBN 978-0-7369-8928-2 (eBook)

Library of Congress Control Number: 2024935707

All rights reserved. No part of this publication may be reproduced, stored in a retrieval system, or transmitted in any form or by any means—electronic, mechanical, digital, photocopy, recording, or any other—except for brief quotations in printed reviews, without the prior permission of the publisher.

Printed in the United States of America

24 25 26 27 28 29 30 31 32 / BP / 10 9 8 7 6 5 4 3 2 1

*This book is dedicated to a new generation of apologists.
May you "contend for the faith" in your
generation, as countless others have before.*

Jude 3 esv

CONTENTS

Foreword—David Kinnaman   7

Introduction: Apologetics for an Ever-Changing Culture—
Sean McDowell   11

PART 1: NEW CULTURE

1. A Different Kind of Apologist—Dan Kimball   21

2. Truth Never Gets Old—Brett Kunkle   35

   An Interview with Hillary Morgan Ferrer   47

3. A Fresh Apologetic: Relationships That Transform—
   Josh McDowell   51

4. Apologetics and Culture: Four Challenges of Our Age—
   John Stonestreet   63

   An Interview with Adam Davidson   75

5. Effective Apologetics in the Local Church—Derwin Gray   79

PART 2: NEW METHODS

Introduction to Part 2—Sean McDowell   93

6. Doing Apologetics in the Home—Natasha Crain   95

7. Storytelling and Persuasion—Brian Godawa   105

   An Interview with Lee Strobel   119

8. Capturing the Imagination Before Engaging the Mind—
   Craig J. Hazen   121

9. Emotionally Healthy Apologetics: Understanding Our Ways of
   Finding Meaning and Truth—Mark Matlock   131

10. Making Apologetics Come Alive in Youth Ministry—
    Alex McFarland   143

An Interview with Jeff Myers 153

11. Defending the Faith Online: Becoming a Twenty-First-Century
Online Apologist—ALLEN PARR 155

12. Helping People Through Doubt—BOBBY CONWAY 165

13. Taking the Other Perspective—TIM MUEHLHOFF 175

PART 3: NEW CHALLENGES

Introduction to Part 3—SEAN MCDOWELL 187

14. Urban Apologetics—Two Tensions—CHRISTOPHER W. BROOKS 189

15. Homosexuality: Truth and Grace—ALAN SHLEMON 199

16. Defending Femininity: Why Jesus Is Good News for Women—
JONALYN GRACE FINCHER 211

An Interview with Michael Kruger 225

17. Wading into the Abortion Debate: Making the Controversial Civil—
STEPHANIE GRAY CONNORS 227

18. Critiquing Critical Theory—NEIL SHENVI 237

19. Church of Invisible Diseases: Apologetics and Mental Health—
JEREMIAH J. JOHNSTON 249

20. Engaging the Transgender Debate—KATY FAUST 261

An Interview with John Marriott 273

21. Jesus for an Ever-Changing Culture—JASON CARLSON 277

22. Nothing New Under the Sun: Engaging New Age—
MELISSA DOUGHERTY 287

23. Recentering Biblical Authority—JONATHAN MORROW 297

Notes 309

FOREWORD

David Kinnaman

The book you are holding is timely. Ultimately, it is about passing on the faith—passing on our faith in Jesus to the next generation. Our research at Barna, and perhaps your own experience, shows this to be one of the great challenges facing the church today.

There are few things that spark my personal passion more than *faithfully* passing on the faith. I am grateful that my colleague and friend Sean McDowell has asked me to make a small contribution to this volume. You're about to dive into a treasure trove of stimulating essays from amazing thinkers, apologists, writers, and leaders. Most importantly, you should know that we all love Jesus. We desire to see those closest to us, including our own children and grandchildren, come alive to Jesus in all parts of their lives—heart, mind, body, and soul.

On that theme, I've been reading and rereading 2 Timothy 1, in which Paul reminds his young protégé of some foundational realities. As is true for all of Scripture, I believe we witness something here that is both contextual *and* universal—we see inside the relationship between Paul and Timothy, and we also gain insights about how to think about apologetics for an ever-changing culture.

Following are some of the lessons I notice. What about you?

First, the affection that Paul has for Timothy is on full display. Paul calls him "my dear son" (verse 2 NIV). He discloses his near-constant prayers for Timothy and, in what seems especially rare today from older adults and mentors, Paul says he is *grateful* for Timothy (verse 3). He also recounts with deep tenderness his sadness at their last parting and anticipates joy at their next meeting (verse 4).

If we zoom out, we notice that truth is best conveyed and received in the context of a trusting relationship. Paul cares deeply for this young man and his concerns nearly bleed through the page. Try reading this section of Scripture and fill in the names with those of your own family. Imagine it's a letter you're writing (or receiving) from someone dear to you. It's tough not to feel the same emotional vulnerability Paul expresses toward Timothy.

Second, Paul reminds Timothy of his spiritual heritage and legacy, including his grandmother Lois and his mother Eunice (verse 5). It's fascinating to me that Paul mentions only women in this heritage. And it's a reminder that women generate much of the warmth that young people need to grow spiritually. Our research at Barna backs this up. Don't get me wrong, we need both men and women in the lives of young people. Yet each play a vital role, and we see that legacy from Lois and Eunice.

In verse 5, we also find this: We would do well to help young people—a generation that oozes self-made reliance—realize that the most important things about them (their family, genetics, passions, place in history, and so on) are not chosen by themselves, but by God. Paul communicates this same thing to Timothy. Paul gives him a sense of *place* in the grand story of Jesus. Storytelling, as you'll learn from screenwriter Brian Godawa, is not subordinate to other approaches to apologetics.

Third, directly after this reminder of his background (and c'mon, Paul is giving major don't-make-me-tattle-to-your-mama-and-grandmama vibes), Timothy is asked to recall his ministry commissioning. Apparently, at some earlier point, Paul had spoken words of affirmation and giftedness to Timothy. In verse 6, Paul says to "fan into flames" the passions and gifts the Lord revealed at that special moment in Timothy's life. Paul even laid hands on him and prayed for Jesus to work through him. Here, I think we learn that young people need purpose, and to be part of something as grand and as world changing as gospel work. This involves identifying and calling out gifts, commissioning for work, and continual encouragement to be all they were made to be.

Finally, Paul reassures Timothy with words that clearly convey both contextual and universal potency:

> God has not given us a spirit of fear and timidity, but of power,
> love, and self-discipline (verse 7).

Recently, I was shocked to realize that this incredible verse—one I memorized as a teenager myself—was wrapped in the sage advice of a mentor. The words are not just abstract peace of mind; they were given in the context of the personal relationship Paul had with Timothy. *Don't stress yourself out. You're going to be more than okay! You belong to something bigger than yourself. Your gifts are given for the purpose of advancing the church.*

This verse echoes through the ages to speak to today's culture of anxiety and an "anxious generation." Paul knew that Timothy needed reassurance, and the Holy Spirit knew that we would need the same thing today. In addition to our prayers, our gratitude and our affection, and on top of understanding our place and our purpose, the Word of God reminds us that we can experience peace.

At Barna, we recently launched *The Open Generation* study, a global research project conducted with nearly 25,000 teenagers in 26 countries. We learned, among many other things, that helping teenagers find inner peace is a new apologetic. They are desperate for that kind of peace found only in Jesus. We can help stressed-out, eager-to-please, ambitious young people to be discipled in the way of the Prince of Peace.

We are raising young people in a time of confusion and chaos. Various forces in our society are giving voice to demonic ideas of identity and self-expression. In the face of daunting pressures, we can help the young disciples around us to find quiet, purposeful conviction in Jesus, who is the Way, the Truth, and the Life (see John 14:6).

If we can have a light moment together, 2 Timothy 1 calls to mind a scene from *The Lion King* in which Mufasa appears to his son Simba during a thunderstorm one night. Simba is lost and rudderless after his father's death. The presence of Mufasa rumbles over the savannah in the roiling clouds and whipping winds, encouraging Simba to remember exactly who he is.

The excellent book that you're holding is one way to help us remember who we are and who we serve. This volume enables us to help the young people in our lives as they learn to trust and follow Jesus. I benefitted from the breadth of these essays. And I deeply appreciate the hard-won insights that these writers have shared here. (I was moved to tears as I read the real-life honesty of Josh McDowell's piece.)

When we embody the multitude of lessons in this book, I hope it moves us closer to the kind of model Paul displayed with Timothy—one filled with prayer, exuding warmth, robust in connection and gratitude, that propels toward purpose and peace, and that convinces of the necessity of the gospel mission.

In contrast to merely passing on a dry, dusty, and irrelevant faith, I believe this book will help you, as it did me, to remember who all people are in Christ and our unending need to know Him!

David Kinnaman
CEO, Barna Group
September 2024

APOLOGETICS FOR AN EVER-CHANGING CULTURE

Sean McDowell

People often ask me why I became an apologist. Undoubtedly, having a father as an apologist influenced me profoundly. But as a grad student in philosophy and theology, there were also three things that I believed deeply that steered me toward apologetics. First, I loved working with high school and college-aged students. Second, the students I met had a lot of questions about God, morality, and religion. Third, as far as I could tell, not many people were helping young people address these big questions effectively. The more I reflected, prayed, and sought counsel, the more it became clear that there was a big need for apologetics, *and* I had a passion for doing it. So I became an apologist.

I started by teaching apologetics at a Christian high school in Southern California. At the time, there were many Christians claiming that apologetics was no longer important. Many leaders in the "emerging church" movement made statements like these:

We live in a postmodern era, so apologetics is not important anymore.

Young people no longer care about reasons for the existence of the Christian God. What matters is telling your narrative and being authentic.

New generations today no longer need "evidence that demands a verdict" or a "case for Christ."

Conversion is about the heart, not the intellect.

I have worked with high school students for roughly a quarter century and can say that these sentiments were devastatingly wrong. While culture has shifted radically since the early 2000s, and some different issues have arisen, we need apologetics training in the church today more than ever. Let me say that again, to make sure it sinks in: *We need apologetics training in the church today more than ever.*

To say that apologetics is critical for ministry today is not to say that Christians just continue business as usual. That would be foolish. Our world is changing, and it is changing *rapidly*. But God does not change (Malachi 3:6), and neither does human nature. Humans are thoughtful and rational beings who respond to evidence. People have questions, and we are all responsible to provide helpful answers. Of course, we certainly don't have all the answers and when we do provide solid answers, many choose not to follow the evidence for personal or moral reasons. But that hardly changes the fact that we are rational, personal beings who bear the image of God.

People often confuse apologetics with apologizing for the faith, but the Greek word *apologia* refers to a legal defense. Thus, apologetics involves giving a rational defense for the Christian faith. First Peter 3:15 says, "Sanctify Christ as Lord in your hearts, always being ready to make a defense [*apologia*] to everyone who asks you to give an account for the hope that is in you, but with gentleness and respect" (NASB). Jude encouraged his hearers to "contend earnestly for the faith which was once for all handed down to the saints" (Jude 3 NASB1995). The biblical evidence is clear: All Christians are to be trained in apologetics, which is an integral part of discipleship. This involves learning how to respond to common objections raised against the Christian faith and how to positively commend the gospel to a particular audience.

Christians have certainly made mistakes in the way we have defended our beliefs in the past (as chapters in this book will illustrate), but this hardly means we should abandon apologetics altogether. Rather, we ought to learn from the past and do better today. Beyond the biblical mandate, apologetics is vitally important today for two reasons.

Strengthening Believers

The first reason is to fortify faith. For about a dozen years, I took high school students on apologetics mission trips to engage atheists, Mormons, and Muslims. These trips were first inspired by my friend Brett Kunkle, who still leads numerous apologetics trips with his team at MAVEN (see his chapter "Truth Never Gets Old"). One year, right after returning from a mission trip to Salt Lake City, I got a call from one of my students. He had a tough apologetics question for me. But why was he calling me on a Saturday? Couldn't it wait? Nope! He was in a conversation with two missionaries from the Church of Jesus Christ of Latter-day Saints. His willingness to reach out to them flowed from the confident faith he developed from his training in apologetics.

Apologetics also helps students withstand challenges to their faith. It is no secret that many Christians, including *young* Christians, are leaving the church. According to the authors of *The Great Dechurching*, "More people have left the church in the last twenty-five years than all the new people who became Christians from the First Great Awakening, Second Great Awakening, and Billy Graham crusades *combined.*"[1] This trend has continued to increase since the mid-1990s.[2] While there are many reasons people disengage from the church, one common reason is that people are talked out of believing that Christianity is true. Why sacrifice time and money—and *sleep*—if you think Christianity is a fairy tale?

Christian students are being bombarded with anti-Christian messages on social media, in the classroom, and from their friends. While "deconstruction" can often be a positive way of aligning one's faith more closely with scripture,[3] there is also a significant trend of social media influencers trying to "help" Christians deconstruct *away from the historic Christian faith.*[4] How do we help them resist some of the secular ideas permeating our culture? How do we help them stand strong in their faith and not abandon it?

Apologetics training must be part of our parenting and discipleship with the next generation (for help in this area, see the chapters by Natasha Crain and Alex McFarland).

Reaching the Lost

The second reason apologetics is vital today is for evangelism. The apostles of Christ ministered in a pluralistic culture. They regularly reasoned with both Jews and pagans, trying to persuade them of the truth of Christianity. They appealed to fulfilled prophecy, Jesus' miracles, evidence for creation, and proofs for the resurrection. Acts 17:2-3 says, "According to Paul's custom, he went to them, and for three Sabbaths reasoned with them from the Scriptures, explaining and giving evidence that the Christ had to suffer and rise again from the dead, and saying, 'This Jesus whom I am proclaiming to you is the Christ'" (NASB1995). Some were persuaded as a result of Paul's efforts.

We live in an increasingly pluralistic world today. And yet, there is an openness to Jesus in this generation.[5] Does this mean young people are walking around with deep spiritual questions at the forefront of their minds? Not necessarily. But it does mean that many young people are open to Christianity when motivated in the right way. The key question is how we might use apologetics to engage people to consider the claims of Christ. If done in the context of a relationship, and with the right attitude and approach, apologetics can be one effective means of helping remove intellectual barriers people have to the Christian faith. It is one vital tool for reaching the lost.

Effective Apologetics in Our Ever-changing Culture

Apologetics is clearly important today. But what must characterize apologetics in our current cultural moment? Allow me to offer two suggestions.

Apologetics Today Must Be Motivated by Love

The point of studying apologetics is not merely to gain knowledge. The point of apologetics is not simply to build up our faith. While these are important, the point of apologetics is to better love God and love others. Although it may seem counterintuitive—since apologists often enjoy debate—apologetics is a ministry of loving Christians by helping them build a stronger faith and loving nonbelievers by helping them remove intellectual barriers to faith. Forgetting this goal is what often leads to a failure to honor Christ in our witness.

This is something I try to model on my YouTube channel. While most of my guests are evangelicals, I have also had progressive Christians, agnostics, atheists, Muslims, Mormons, LGBTQ advocates, and many others on the channel. My goal is not to win the argument. My biggest goal is to be loving toward my guest. Sometimes that involves pushing back on ideas, but many times it involves listening well, respecting their views, treating them with kindness, and looking for common ground. I want them to leave feeling truly understood and valued. While there is still need for formal debates, and I engage in them now and then, many people yearn for civil, gracious dialogue across worldview differences. Christians can lead the way by engaging their neighbors with kindness and charity (for a strategy on how to do this, see the chapter by Tim Muehlhoff).

Let me sum it up: If you write an apologetics book but have not love, you have *nothing*. If you get a huge social media following defending the Christian faith but have not love, you have *nothing*. If you defeat non-Christians in an argument but have not love, you have *nothing*. Love is what matters most.

Apologetics Today Must Be Humble

I failed miserably to act humbly a few years ago when getting my hair cut in Breckenridge, Colorado. The hairdresser noticed I was carrying a Christian book, so she asked, "Are you a Christian? If so, how can you explain all the evil in the world?" I had just graduated from Biola and received an A in Introduction to Apologetics, so I was ready with an answer! Unfortunately, I proceeded to give her a ten-minute lecture about the origin of evil, the nature of free will, and the Christian solution. I unloaded my apologetics onto her. My arguments may have been decent, but I lacked humility and sensitivity in my demeanor. I had a slick answer to her every question, but I missed the fact that her needs went beyond the intellect, to her heart. Eventually she started crying—not because she became a Christian but because she was so offended by my callousness and arrogance.

In retrospect, I wish I had responded with a question such as this: "Of all the questions you can ask about God, why that one?" While questions about evil and suffering might be intellectually motivated, in my experience, such questions are often motivated by personal hurt. Was she bullied as a kid? Did her parents recently divorce? Did she have a loved one dying of cancer? Had she experienced church abuse? I will never know because I didn't ask. I wish I could rewind the clock and engage her with more humility and curiosity.

What might it look like to be a humble apologist? Consider a few suggestions. Listen more than you talk. Ask questions more than you make statements. Admit when you are wrong. Don't overstate an argument. Apologize when you offend someone. Be willing to concede if you don't have an answer. Have a prayerful spirit.

>> >> >>

There are many other ways to do effective apologetics today. But there is a reason why you got this book! *Apologetics for an Ever-Changing Culture* is unique. It explores fresh topics from an apologetics standpoint, including mental health, critical theory, deconstruction, and urban ministry. It is also practical. This is not a *why* book but a *how* book. Contributors don't focus on answering difficult questions, but on strategies for doing apologetics with your friends, family, neighbors, coworkers, and online. This book is also diverse. Its contributors include men and women, people from different theological backgrounds, and apologists from different generations, places, and races. This book can be used for individual study, in the classroom, for small groups, or as a discussion starter for church and ministry staff. This book is substantially different from the earlier book *Apologetics for a New Generation*, all the interviews are new, existing chapters have been updated significantly, and there are a dozen completely new chapters.

The Apologetics Renaissance

One final word of encouragement. While there are arguably more people doing apologetics than ever before in history, we need *you* to join the cause. Every apologist matters. Whether it is teaching a class at your church, having a conversation with a skeptic online, or starting a YouTube channel focused on apologetics—every contribution matters. The good news is that we are living during an apologetics renaissance. This can be seen in the number of apologetics conferences that have sprouted up in churches all over the country, the growth in apologetics books and resources, and the explosion of apologetics content on YouTube and other forms of social media. Novel and powerful apologetic works are being published in the areas of the historical Jesus, near-death experiences, philosophical theology, the abortion debate, and the existence of the soul.[6] This is good news because America and the church continue to become more and more secular. And in response, the church desperately needs to be equipped.

Os Guinness is one of my favorite thinkers. One time, while interviewing him for the *Think Biblically* podcast, I asked him this question: "Os, what do you think your legacy will be?" I will *never* forget his response. Without hesitation, he said, "Sean, legacy is a secular idea. All that matters is that God says at the end of your life, 'Well done, my good and faithful servant.'" His response goes through my mind almost every day. Don't worry about results. Don't compare yourself to others. Simply aim to please the Lord. Faithfulness is what matters most. This book is merely a tool to help you be a faithful apologist. Let's go!

Sean McDowell

PART 1:
NEW
CULTURE

1

A DIFFERENT KIND
OF APOLOGIST

Dan Kimball

pologetics is desperately, urgently, and critically needed more than ever before in our ever-changing culture. In my thirty plus years of serving in ministry, I have never seen more confusion and misinformation about the Christian faith among younger generations. The amount of intentional teaching against the historic Christian faith seems unprecedented. Because of all this, we need to be more bold, more clear, more aggressive, and more passionate to see the truths of Scripture be taught to new generations. This isn't the time to back down or avoid engaging the tough theological and sensitive cultural questions of our day. Yet because our culture is shifting so quickly, we must wisely think through our strategy of doing apologetics today. We need to consider this question: What does a new kind of apologist look like for today?

For New Generations to Hear the Truth, Attention to Tone Is Necessary

I once attended a Christian event that included a dialogue with opposing presentations on a vital theological issue. The speaker who represented historic Christian doctrine was correct in his conclusions, but he came across somewhat smug in his tone and attitude, and took an overly confident just-the-facts approach. He also subtly mocked those who believed differently.

The other speaker, who I totally disagreed with, gave some good-sounding arguments and shared the compelling stories of people hurt through their Christian upbringing. His tone was gentle, and he intentionally related to the people in the stories, showing empathy for those who have faith struggles and doubts. He shared that he does not believe Jesus wants to see His followers be divisive, and cause so much pain and hurt in people through "theology." He said, what is now so cliché, that Jesus doesn't want His followers to be known for what they are against or for hurting people with their beliefs. He presented on how Jesus is about love, inclusion, and acceptance, not division and hatred.

The second speaker sure seemed to persuade the hearts of those in the room. After all, who wants to be known for what they stand against, or to be viewed by others as hateful? As I sat there, next to a young church leader who was also attending the conference, he leaned over and said something I will never forget: "I think I agree with that guy [the theologically conservative one], but he's so blunt and mean sounding, I want to go hang out with the other guy [the theologically progressive one], who seems really nice and caring."

Now, the church leader next to me was mature enough to discern that the truth is far more important than the way something is presented and the tone in which it is delivered. Someone can be "nice" but be totally wrong, teaching destructive and evil beliefs. If you have a background in knowing the Scriptures or even studying basic theology, you are more able to easily discern when someone is teaching something contrary to biblical truth. But what about the many individuals in recent generations who can be swayed by emotions and are less biblically trained?

I imagine that quite possibly many in the room that day were more won over by the progressive liberal speaker than the traditional conservative one. I wish it wasn't this way, but many younger generations (and really *all* generations) are more easily drawn to what is attractive and relatable rather than to what is true.

He Made Me Feel that I Am a Stupid Person for Being an Atheist

Another quick example comes from my church. There was a college-age girl who wasn't a Christian, but she was interested in exploring who Jesus is. She was an atheist who was open for discussion. I asked her if she would be willing to read an apologetics book that addresses atheist claims against Christianity. It was a super helpful book to me, so I eagerly wanted her to read it. She said yes, and I enthusiastically gave her the book. However, a week later, she returned the book. I asked her what she thought about it, and she said, "I stopped reading it after a few chapters. The author was basically saying that all atheists are stupid." She shared that the author used negative generalizations of and stereotypes for atheists (which touched her personally), and this made her not want to read any further.

After this girl told me about how the book made her feel, I reread it, but this time through the lens of a non-Christian. Sure enough, I could see what she was saying. The author of the book gave compelling arguments, but it was written to an already-Christian audience. The Christian terminology inside lacked definitions. There was a lot of wording with a "those atheists" type of framing. Although I am sure that the author of the apologetics book didn't intentionally do this, I can see why this young girl was turned off. The tone, attitude, and stereotypes that were used repelled her. Ironically, the book's goal is to help atheists want to follow Jesus, but sadly, the exact opposite happened.

It Is a Time for Clarity, Boldness, and Not Avoiding the Difficult Topics. But...

Now you may be thinking, *Well of course she didn't like what she read. Someone who doesn't believe the truth won't want to hear the truth.* I disagree. She wanted to learn, and we have since had many great conversations. But in today's world, as we use apologetics, we need to understand the cultural changes that have occurred that have caused a shift in what is viewed as important. The minds, emotions, and values of new generations are swayed not only by the truths we have, but *how* we state them. The issue isn't that many are not open to hearing truth; the issue is how we go about speaking the truth to them.

This is very important: When I say "new generations," I am not talking about the youth and young adults in your church who are already Christians or who go to apologetic events. I am not thinking of the teens or college aged in your Bible studies who light up when you start explaining reasons to believe in God, or the Bible, or answering some tough questions. They will enthusiastically welcome apologetic truths that build their confidence.

The new generations I am primarily talking about are those who don't know Jesus yet. Their parents likely have never been part of a church (which is increasingly normal today). These new generations are made up of young people whose only exposure to Jesus and the Christian faith has been through bits and pieces of Christian beliefs. And likely, they are already familiar with Christianity being portrayed on social media through messages like: "How Christians have misused the Bible to control and oppress women" and "The Christian Bible is pro-slavery and filled with violence." I am thinking of new generations who are getting saturated on social media by "ex-Christians" who are very aggressively trying to steer them away from the "evangelical cult" they were once a part of. I am talking about new generations who may have never attended a youth group or a church, but who occasionally hear about a scandal surrounding some Christian leader on the news.

Christians need apologetics as a way to have their confidence boosted in what they believe. We want to be proactively training new generations with ways to respond to the mass of criticism against the Bible in advance of when they hear the arguments. This way, they are prepared and will not be caught off guard when they hear new challenges. Thus, we critically do need to be teaching apologetics in our churches and filling up the church van to drive to apologetics events. But if we also want to be using apologetics with new generations who aren't yet Christians, or with those who may be doubting, or who are leaving the faith due to peer pressure and the teaching of "ex-Christians" on social media, we need to become a new kind of apologist. One which, actually, isn't anything new. It simply means practicing what Peter laid out in the classic New Testament passage beloved by apologists:

> In your hearts revere Christ as Lord. Always be prepared to give an
> answer to everyone who asks you to give the reason for the hope
> that you have. But do this with gentleness and respect, keeping

a clear conscience, so that those who speak maliciously against your good behavior in Christ may be ashamed of their slander (1 Peter 3:15-16 NIV).

In apologetics, we often focus on "Always be prepared to give an answer." We can fully prepare answers to the toughest questions, and we absolutely need to do that. But the verse continues, "…to everyone who asks you." I've never had a total stranger walk up to me on the street and say, "Excuse me, I'd like to know the answer for the hope that you have." So the indication here is that there is some type of trust already present when a person is asking you. And then, of course, Peter says to give our answers "with gentleness and respect." Apologists all know the first part of this verse, but in today's world especially, we need to be paying attention to the whole verse.

It Is Sometimes Harder for Those Drawn to Apologetics to Think Tone Is Important

Due to the nature of apologetics, those often drawn to the discipline (myself included) have temperaments that are primarily facts driven. We are inclined to value the concrete data, the hard facts, the bare truth, and to be able to follow the trail of logic in someone's argument. But we must remember, people are not driven solely, or even primarily, by facts. As time marches forward, an increasing number of people are born into and entirely raised in a culturally post-truth, emotions-led, follow-your-heart world.

There is a common saying: "Facts don't care about your feelings." Which is true! Facts remain true no matter what our feelings are. Yet, in order to share the facts with people in a way that they will truly listen, we need to pay attention to their feelings. The tone we use is one of our most important assets when connecting the truth found in Scripture to someone's feelings.

In New Generations, Social Contagions Rule What Is Considered True and False

We see the madness every day, when social media amplifies the spread of false teaching, false narratives of history, and false theologies. It happens non-stop, and is just one click away. I don't know what else to call it but madness, although I do believe there is an enemy behind the deception that is happening (Ephesians 6:10-11; 1 Peter 5:8-9; Revelation 12:9).

Younger generations who crave community and a place to have identity, are accepted into groups that ignite their beliefs in conformity to the group because it *feels* right. Products are marketed to people by emphasizing how someone will feel if they were to buy it. Feeling the "right" way about something, as determined by the voices around us, is what makes something "true."

Thinking Through a New Kind of Apologist Lens

There is a nationally known college campus ministry that has used a diagram of a train to illustrate that Christians need to be led by the facts and what is true, instead of being led by their feelings.

The facts (the train's engine) are the truths found in Scripture. When we have the facts correct, then our faith (the fuel car) develops from and follows the facts. And that, then, impacts our feelings (the caboose) which are following along the same path as our faith and the facts. The train is laid out like this:

From *Have You Heard of the Four Spiritual Laws?* written by Bill Bright, ©1965-2024 The Bright Media Foundation and Campus Crusade for Christ, Inc. All rights reserved. https://crustore.org/product/4-spiritual-laws/ Included by permission.

However, in a world driven by image, saturated by social media, led by emotions, and influenced by the message to "follow your heart," it becomes our feelings that sway us into believing what is true or not. People are reorienting their lives in a way that structures the train in the reverse order—**Feeling-Faith-Fact**. Individuals are placing their feelings as their engine, while faith and facts follow behind powerless to influence the driving force that has been placed in control—their emotions.

Again, I wish this wasn't the case. And there are still some "just-give-me-the-facts" young people out there for sure. (If you are an apologist type, you likely already hang out with them as well.) But I want to pose the question to you right now: *Which of the two trains would you say you personally relate to more?*

Knowing Who We Are Talking to Is Critical for Apologetics

I was talking to someone who has dedicated their life to apologetics and teaches apologetics at conferences. I asked him some questions about how non-Christians respond to him. He paused, and then he said something fascinating. He reflected that as he has been teaching apologetics, seemingly only Christians show up to the classes and seminars. He hasn't actually been in a relational dialogue using apologetics with a non-Christian in a long time—he couldn't even remember the last time.

Another question for you right now: *As much as you love apologetics, when was the last time you have been in an actual conversation with a non-Christian about the Christian faith?*

If we are surrounded only by Christians in our daily lives, we may become so ingrained that we lose our sensitivity to and awareness of the mindsets of those who aren't believers in Christ. Let's consider three categories of people apologists encounter:

1. Believers in Jesus who trust the apologist and want support for what he or she already believes.

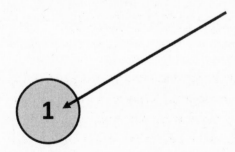

Group 1
The already-Christian group who cheer and applaud when apologetics are applied, and who accept and believe biblical truths.

The people in Group 1 come from a core group of already Christians who have been taught strong biblical beliefs and who hold to a worldview that is generally aligned with Scripture. They will trust the speaker, who is presenting apologetics, and are eager to learn more from them. The apologist can teach on solid biblical truths related to complicated topics, such as religious pluralism, the afterlife, prolife, and sexuality according to Scripture, and the apologist will be cheered on. *Give me the answers!* is the eager sentiment of this group. The apologist can, more or less, get straight to the truths without needing to guard their words too much as this group is already on their side.

2. Those who have some trust in the apologist but may not yet be fully convinced of biblical truths.

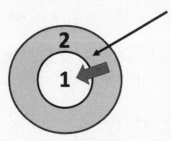

Group 2
The primarily already-Christian group who has some trust in you. They may still be learning or going through doubts, but what you say is welcomed. You desire that they move inward to be part of Group 1, who has full belief of truth with confidence.

In any population—youth, young adult, or adult—there are those who the apologist has some relational equity with, or else they wouldn't be there. Most people in Group 2 are likely already Christians, but they lack maturity in areas. They may have been raised in a church, but are now being influenced by others to reject faith or take on progressive and false teachings about doctrines and ethics. The apologist's hope is that they will move inward, to Group 1.

Common characteristics that can be present in Group 2 are:

- They likely are becoming influenced by "new teaching" regarding the Bible and Christianity on social media, which often undermines biblical views on topics such as sin. Taking on this new view, they can be a "Christian" and not have much of their life clash with culture or their peers.

- Definitions get blurry for them relating to topics such as the nature of the "gospel" or the identity of Jesus.

- Some have experienced disappointment in the church and may be moving toward abandoning their faith.

- They may be struggling with doubts and beliefs. Some are afraid to share the questions they have with those around them because they have heard the voices of their parents or church leaders who have expressed strong negative tones and reactions regarding those who believe differently.

A great way to learn from Group 2 is to survey them and ask what questions they have. This shows them respect, and the apologist can find out if they are presenting apologetics that answer the questions this group really wants to hear about.

3. Those who haven't yet developed trust in the apologist, and who don't know many of the doctrines and beliefs of Christianity.

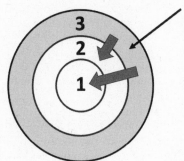

Group 3
New generations who are open to seeking God, but don't have trust in you yet. More likely, they have suspicion of you. They don't have any foundation in or knowledge of Christian beliefs—likely, only incorrect perceptions from media.

In many ways, Group 3 is who apologetics is ultimately for. There are a massive number of young people in this group. This group likely:

- is highly suspicious of Christians and church leaders today.

- is not familiar with most Christian terminology or beliefs, as they likely did not grow up in Christian homes. The apologist must define terms and be careful about assumptions regarding what this group already knows.

Tone really matters most with Group 3. Smugness or condescension are big repellants and discredit the messenger. Group 3 has been bombarded with teaching that is often contrary to historical Christian beliefs, and many of them distrust conservative Christians. This group needs to know that the apologist wants to hear and respond to their questions.

The apologist does not need to hide any beliefs from this group. They can state historical biblical truths with confidence, and most importantly, with clarity. But clarity must have along with it great kindness, gentleness, love, patience, and empathy. The hope with this group is to move them inward to Group 2, where they are hearing more, gaining trust, and surrendering their lives to Christ. Then ultimately, moving them to Group 1, where they will build a solid Christian foundation in the truth.

In the Bible, we see that Jesus' heart broke with compassion for those who did not know Him yet. Christ saw this group (Group 3) as lost sheep without a shepherd, and He wasn't passive toward them. He sent His followers to go to those who do not know Him (Matthew 9:36-38).

》》》》》》

Once, I was at a church gathering where a sensitive topic was talked about during the announcements. It was stated strongly that the issue centered on deception, and there was a kind of "rally-the-troops" tone in the communication about it. There were even people who clapped. I saw a young woman leave the gathering, and I went outside as well, to find out why she had left. I figured it was because of what was said.

I came to find out that she would have fit into Group 2. She had drifted away and was coming back to give "church" a try. And unfortunately, it felt to her that this church was an "us-versus-them" place. I listened with intention and learned that it wasn't *what* was said, but *how* it was said. She headed out the door because of how the topic was spoken about.

This gathering was not a church-leader meeting with only committed, mature Christians. Instead, these things were said in the worship gathering, with drifters from faith and nonbelievers present. If we aren't considering these varying perspectives, we can unintentionally repel those in Groups 2 and 3 from hearing truth simply by the way in which we talk about issues. A new kind of apologist doesn't hold back truth but is strategic and winsome about how they present the truth to new generations.

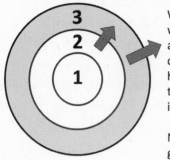 We may have Group 1 cheerlead us on, but if we aren't thinking about how Groups 2 and 3 are hearing what we say, considering their current belief systems, and taking to heart how emotions and feelings work, we can see them repelled backwards—not by the truth itself, but how we communicate it.

Now, we have an amazing opportunity as new generations are open to truth.

Time to Pay Attention

It is not time whatsoever to hold back on speaking the truth. But it is time to pay attention to how we talk about it. As we conclude this chapter, let's consider something especially important. Our focus is on using apologetics to engage new generations, teens and college-aged people who are growing up in a very confusing world and being taught many false and deceptive things. Here is the key: We must have a broken heart as Jesus did—seeing them like lost sheep following false shepherds and teachings. Viewing them in this way transforms our tone and approach.

Our approach to using apologetics will be noticed by new generations. They will see our attitudes and postures, and how we speak about the people we disagree with. They will notice if we are combative or kind. If we truly care about those who don't know Jesus, we don't want to create a new generation of apologists who mainly use apologetics that lack an evangelistic focus. We want to see those who are caught in a world of false truths and sadness to learn about the goodness of God, His grace, and the joys of following Jesus in the way of truth.

I want to mention an important observation that this tone and way of speaking to and with those who aren't Christians is not only about in-person situations. It also matters how we interact online on social media. I see far, far too many Christians into apologetics who type responses to people that are horribly callous and feel uncaring. Please note that the point I am raising here also applies to the words that we type. You may see attacks on our faith and want to respond back (which I think we should), but *how* we are responding online matters. Remember that we should expect critics to sometimes share harsh and mean words about Christians and our beliefs. Non-Christians do not have the Holy Spirit within them and are only thinking naturally through the lens of how the culture has shaped their worldview. I need to realize that if I wasn't a Christian, I would likely have the same questions about and criticisms of the faith. Don't hold back in sharing truth online, but what our fingers type matters.

Allow me to pose another question to you: *Looking at your online social media interactions and what you type, do you see biblical truth paired with kindness and patience, or do you see truth laced with attacks and callousness?* Are you listening to Jesus and His words on loving our enemies, and Peter's words about "gentleness and respect"? Be honest with yourself about what you see when you look back upon the words you type.

The Young Atheist Who Came Back for More

Let me share a positive story that began when I was in an online social media discussion with a young atheist who lived in a different city than I did. We had been communicating for about six months, and it so happened that I was speaking at an apologetics event taking place where he lived. So I told him about it and invited him to meet me there and attend the session I was teaching. I truly wasn't expecting him to go, but I got to the event as it had started (I was speaking later in the day) and he let me know he was already there. He told me that he was sitting in the seminar: "How to Understand the Mind of an Atheist." I got all flushed and was honestly worried, as I didn't want him to be pushed away from the faith in a seminar about atheists. I almost ran as I made my way to the seminar. I wanted to let the speaker know that an atheist I had invited was in the room. I got there too late to talk to the speaker, as the session had already begun. I sat down next to my new atheist friend and was very conscious of every word the speaker was saying.

In this case, the speaker—who didn't know there was an atheist in the room—taught about how to dialogue with atheists and did an amazingly excellent job. I felt a major sense of relief as the speaker consistently reiterated that he respects atheists and even understands why they believe what they do. Though the seminar clearly was about how to respond to atheist challenges against Christianity, he never once stated negativity about an atheist person's value or intelligence. The speaker's approach was that of gentleness, kindness, and respect. He even defined words that a non-Christian, or someone who may be new to faith, may not already be aware of.

When it was over, my atheist friend was quite moved and told me he really learned a lot. Afterward, we ended up talking with the speaker and stayed for an hour with him. My atheist friend ended our talk by saying that he wanted to have more information about Christian beliefs. He had sat through a seminar about why his beliefs were wrong, yet how the speaker talked about atheists with compassion and respect caused this young man to want to learn more about Jesus. The speaker perfectly demonstrated being a new kind of apologist in our current culture.

In closing, of course the Holy Spirit is the One who changes people's hearts. He uses our apologetics to open doors to others with the truth. The most important practice any new, or old, kind of apologist needs to desperately do is to pray. We are partners in a battle against evil for souls and minds, but God is powerful, and He transforms new generations with the truth. We are living in a truly exciting time to be using apologetics.

Dan Kimball is the author of several books, including *How (Not) to Read the Bible: Making Sense of the Anti-women, Anti-science, Pro-violence, Pro-slavery and Other Crazy-Sounding Parts of Scripture.* He is also a vice president at Western Seminary and on the staff of Vintage Faith Church in Santa Cruz, California.

TRUTH NEVER GETS OLD

Brett Kunkle

s there a topic of greater importance to the apologetic project than the nature of truth? "To make a defense to everyone who asks you to give an account for the hope that is in you" (1 Peter 3:15 NASB) and "contend earnestly for the faith which was once for all handed down to the saints" (Jude 3 NASB1995) presupposes that Christianity is true. Therefore, truth is central to our apologetics.

So what is truth? Philosophically speaking, truth is straightforward. The word *truth* describes a relationship between our beliefs or claims and the way the world is—reality. If I say, "The grass is green," or "It's raining outside," or "I am a lifelong Pittsburgh Steelers fan," these statements are true if they match up with the way things really are. It's not merely my believing that makes them true, it's whether they correspond to reality. The word *truth* captures the relationship of correspondence to the objectively real world. In other words, truth is a statement of the facts. Professional philosophers call this the Correspondence Theory of Truth. The rest of us call it common sense.

Now it should be obvious why truth is of utmost importance to the apologetic project and to the larger Christian faith. We are contending for and defending what we take to be the central facts of reality, including but not limited to:

- God exists and is the almighty Creator of the universe.

- God made human beings in His image and loves His creatures.

- All human beings are in moral rebellion from their Creator and are deserving of punishment and death.

- Jesus' sacrificial death on the cross atoned for our sins.

- Two thousand years ago, Jesus rose bodily from the grave to complete His conquest over sin and death.

- Faith in Jesus rescues individuals from their sin and reconciles them to their Creator.

These statements of Christian belief are objectively true—they're true whether anyone believes them or not. They are factually accurate descriptions of the nature of reality. They are the most important truths that can be known! Indeed, every topic covered in the chapters of this book presuppose the truth of the Christian worldview.

But here's the massive problem we face. Culturally speaking, the concept of truth is buried in an avalanche of confusion. Culturally dominant views about the nature of truth displace God as the Author of truth, and in His place elevate the autonomous human individual as the arbiter and supreme authority on matters of truth. As a result, young people's confidence that objective truth exists and can be known is thoroughly undermined. The very framework within which they conceptualize their Christian faith is altogether detached from the objective realm of truth. They don't think of Christianity primarily in terms of its truthfulness. Instead, Christianity turns out to be a private subjective matter of faith, a personal relationship with Jesus that works for me (at least, in the present moment) but which can easily be dispensed with, under the right conditions and with enough pressure. They do not see Christianity as a universally true and binding worldview and therefore, morally obligatory. Rather, it's simply one of many lifestyle choices available.

That is why we must begin our discussion of truth with the surrounding cultural context. We find ourselves amidst cultural conditions that make teaching the truth to the next generation extremely challenging. The gospel is never heard in isolation. Our conception of the Christian life is often shaped by the culture's larger patterns of thought. Specific cultural ideas either help or hinder us. Thus, an accurate assessment of the current culture is vital. If we misdiagnose the problem, our prescriptions will likely be wrong too, and the gospel will suffer.

Cultural Confusions About Truth

For some time, the Western world has been awash in postmodern thought. At its core, postmodernism is a reinterpretation of truth and knowledge. In a postmodernist view, objective truth does not exist and even if it does, we're in no position to know it. Instead, truth is relative. Atheist philosopher Friedrich Nietzsche explains relativism this way: "You have your way. I have my way. As for the right way, the correct way, and the only way, it does not exist."[1] According to Nietzsche, then, who determines what is true? We do. Truth is relative to either the group or the individual. It's up to us. We simply do our own thing. And this postmodern relativism continues to be our culture's default view of truth.

It used to be "Christian cool" to talk about postmodernism and even attempt to marry its central concepts to the Christian faith. Remember the Emergent Church? But Christians have largely moved on from that conversation and some may even object to my assessment here, arguing that postmodernism is dead. "We're in a post-postmodern era," they'll declare. Well, for now we'll leave the debate over postmodernism's official time of death to the scholars. However, even if we are transitioning out of a postmodern era to something else, it seems clear that at minimum, we still suffer from the lingering effects of major postmodern thought in regard to truth. The in-depth Gen Z research George Barna has done in partnership with the Impact 360 Institute only confirms this.[2] An Impact 360 headline summarized their findings this way: "Moral relativism is one of the defining characteristics of Gen Z."[3]

My own experience confirms our culture's relativistic impulse. My work gives me the opportunity to speak with thousands of Christian and non-Christian students and adults across the country every year. When I speak to a typical group of teenagers, I can count on the fact that the majority of them will be religious pluralists and moral relativists, a suspicion that's confirmed almost every time I offer a "truth test" (you'll see it later in this chapter). The only exceptions are those students who have had training in apologetics.

And pop culture offers further proof. Relativism reveals itself in mainstream cultural mantras like "Follow your heart," "Live your truth," or "You do you." These messages litter the pop-culture landscape, from social media to music, to movies and television, to influencers and beyond.

Nonreligious voices have weighed in as well. Prominent secular psychologists Edmund Bourne and Lorna Garano note that moral relativism has come to dominate modern life: "There is no shared, consistent, socially-agreed-upon set of values and standards for people to live by."[4] And make no mistake, ideas have consequences. False views of truth lead to negative outcomes. Bourne and Garano go on to argue that moral relativism is a major cause of anxiety among Americans.

However, rather than recognizing the intellectual and moral bankruptcy of relativism and digging ourselves out of this postmodern hole, we are actually diving deeper into it. Let me illustrate this with two sets of song lyrics from the world of Disney.

In 1998, Walt Disney Pictures released the animated musical action-adventure film *Mulan*. The movie was a hit with audiences, grossing more than $300 million, and its soundtrack was nominated for an Academy Award for best music in an original musical or comedy score. Following good Disney princess tradition, the story revolves around a young girl, Mulan, trying to make her way in the world.

One song in particular, "True to Your Heart," perfectly captures not only a prominent Disney theme but the larger cultural ethos regarding truth. Mulan's heroic adventures have been a success and the movie concludes with this song as a summary of the film's main message. The opening stanza informs us that when life gets tough and you need guidance to get you through, you simply turn inward and let your heart guide you. The chorus then exhorts us to be true to our heart, claiming unequivocally that what we feel in our heart can never be wrong. Later in the song, it's even intimated that we should never question what feels right.

What's the message? Relativism. If you want to navigate the challenges of this world, look inward for the truth. As the song title and lyrics explain, you must be true to your heart. Your own thoughts and desires are all you need for guidance because your heart will never deceive you. Truth is relative to the individual.

Contrast this with another popular Disney film, *Moana*. Eighteen years later, in 2016, the company released this popular animated action-adventure musical, grossing more than $680 million. It was another Disney princess tale about one teenage girl, Moana, who ventured on a coming-of-age quest. At a critical moment of decision, Moana receives advice from her wise grandma in the song "Where You Are." The majority of the song lyrics capture the Motunui villagers' attempt to persuade Moana to stay on the island and lead her people, appealing to their history and tradition. But toward the end of the song her grandma interjects with a contradictory message, not only instructing Moana to follow the voice inside herself instead, but also informing her that the voice is her true *identity*.

First, notice the similar lyrical message we discovered in *Mulan*. Follow the voice inside. Follow your heart. Different movie, same theme. Truth is relative to the individual, so go inward to find it. However, this time, also notice a second message in the sage words from Moana's grandmother—your heart is who you actually are. It's a move that's subtle but insidious. Did you catch it? Not only does your heart guide you and give you truth, but that inner voice and what it tells you defines your identity. It tells you who you are at your core.

This is the relativistic move that further entrenches the next generation in their confusion about truth. It raises the relativistic stakes: *Your* truth determines *your* identity. So what's going on here? Our culture is simply following the progression of postmodern relativism, which says, "I determine my truth," to one logical relativistic outworking: "And my truth defines my core identity." In his important book *Strange New World*, Carl Trueman summarizes it this way:

> The modern self assumes the authority of inner feelings and sees authenticity as defined by the ability to give social expression to

the same. The modern self also assumes that society at large will recognize and affirm this behavior. Such a self is defined by what is called expressive individualism.[5]

Postmodern relativism is now wedded to identity. If relativism is true, you ("the modern self") are the authority on what's true for you. Therefore, in order to live authentically in this world, you must be true to yourself and express your true self socially ("give social expression to the same") and publicly. And what should you expect from everyone around you? They "will recognize and affirm this behavior." Trueman and other social commentators have called this approach to life expressive individualism.

And does not our current transgender moment perfectly and powerfully illustrate these ideas at work in the larger culture? If I feel like a woman trapped inside a man's body, what should I do? I allow my internal feelings to determine what is true for me. I then identify as a woman and begin to transition socially, by wearing women's clothing and acting out feminine qualities, and medically, by removing healthy body parts and attempting to reconstruct a female anatomy. All the while, I demand those around me to unreservedly affirm my transition.

Yes, ideas certainly have consequences (just listen to the thousands of heartbreaking detransition testimonies from young people that can be found online). I hope you feel the weight of the situation. Expressive individualism is a doubling down on relativism. It attempts to lock us in a relativistic prison of our own making, while throwing away the key. And the next generation is drowning in these treacherous postmodern waters.

Restoring Confidence in the Truth

If we're going to turn the tide on relativism, it will take a comprehensive effort. One youth-group talk on truth will not suffice. Reading a book on apologetics is not enough. Our young people have absorbed relativism for years. For their entire upbringing, they have been thoroughly infected and the infection runs deep, even contaminating their sense of who they are at their core.

For those actively engaged in the discipleship of the next generation, it's time for decisive action. This means creating cultures of truth in our homes, our churches, our youth ministries, and our Christian schools. Resisting relativism's corrosive influence is not enough. We need to empower students to be agents of transformation to their generation. But how do we make truth a part of their daily experience? How do we teach them to bring Christ into all areas of life? We need a thorough action plan to restore the next generation's confidence in God's truth.

Diagnose Their Condition

Are your students relativists? To find out, test them. First, be sure they are clear on the difference between subjective truth and objective truth. Give them an analogy to clarify the distinction. Have them consider, for example, the difference between ice cream and insulin. Is there a single flavor of ice cream that is the right flavor? Do we fault others for choosing chocolate over vanilla? Of course not. Ice cream preferences are subjective truths—true for some, but not for others.

Contrast ice cream with insulin. If your doctor diagnoses you with diabetes, does he ask your preference in medicine? Again, of course not. You want the right medicine, and this has nothing to do with your personal preferences. Even if you sincerely believed ice cream could control diabetes, the facts would not change.[6] Regardless of preferences, diabetics still need insulin, not ice cream.

Now for the test. Read the following statements (or come up with your own) and ask students to identify the statement as subjective truth or objective truth:

TRUTH TEST
Ice Cream (Subjective) or Insulin (Objective)?

	Objective	Subjective
1. That guy's shirt is red.	☐	☐
2. Red is the most beautiful color.	☐	☐
3. 2 + 2 = 4	☐	☐
4. Hawaiian vacations are the best vacations.	☐	☐
5. Atoms consist of protons, neutrons, and electrons.	☐	☐
6. Brett can bench-press 350 pounds.	☐	☐
7. God exists.	☐	☐
8. Jesus is the only way to God.	☐	☐
9. Premarital sex is immoral.	☐	☐
10. It is wrong for women to have elective abortions.	☐	☐

The first five are fairly simple. Number six might trip up a few students because it's false even though it is an objective claim. Remember, objective claims are *either* true or false, while subjective claims are *neither* true nor false. Students infected with relativism will either hedge or flatly affirm relativism on statements seven through ten. Then you'll know if your student is a relativist in matters of religion and morality.

Show That Ideas Have Consequences: Relativism Makes Christianity Largely Irrelevant

Listen carefully and you'll notice young people assume, in most areas of everyday life, that truth is objective. No one is postmodern, for example, when balancing a checkbook, reading the directions on a medicine bottle, or simply walking across the street. Gregory Koukl, coauthor of *Relativism: Feet Firmly Planted in Mid-Air,* puts it this way:

> Everyone is already deeply convinced of the truth, even when he denies it. True, our culture is driven by a postmodern impulse, but deep down each of us is a common-sense realist. Those who are not are either dead, in an institution, or sleeping in cardboard boxes under the freeway.[7]

But we are inconsistent here. Most Westerners function with a worldview split in two, what sociologists refer to as the public/private split.[8] In the public sphere, we operate in the realm of rationality, knowledge, facts, and objective truth. Doctors, scientists, corporations, and the state conduct their matters here. In the private sphere are institutions—like family and church—driven by personal preference, opinion, and subjective (relative) truth. Matters of religion and morality are confined to this realm. Accordingly, "Religion is not considered an objective truth to which we submit, but only a matter of personal taste which we choose."[9]

Here's the devastating result. This split effectively severs Christ from our public life—where we live most of our lives—and consigns Him to our private prayer closets. Let me illustrate. Do college students spend four years of study researching family traditions to find the true traditions that should be practiced in society? Of course not. Those "truths" are relative, a matter of personal preference. Rather, those students will study science, medicine, and technology to discover facts that have implications for all areas of life.

Sociologist Christian Smith discovered what happens when religion is relativized and relegated to the realm of personal preference and mere opinion: Religion becomes compartmentalized in the daily experience of most American teenagers. Thus, "religion simply doesn't seem consequential enough to most teenagers to pay close attention to and get right." As a result, American teenagers are "*incredibly inarticulate* about their faith, their religious beliefs and practices, and its meaning or place in their lives."[10] In a word, religion becomes irrelevant, and when this happens, Christ becomes irrelevant too.

Might this explain why youth in our churches are often passionless about Christ? He has been severed from the very things that occupy most of their lives. How can they be passionate about Christ when He seems so inconsequential? Might this also explain why many Christian young people are double minded? Morality is mere preference, and preferences come in all shapes and sizes. That's why you'll see students who, on their social media profiles, identify themselves as Christians who love Jesus, and yet, post sexually suggestive pictures, vulgarities, or even celebrate sinful behaviors. Why? Because their relationship with Jesus is only part of their life—the private part.

For many of our students, Christianity is trapped in the realm of relativism. This prevents Christ from informing every area of their lives. For them, relativism has made Christ irrelevant to the rest of life.

Show That Ideas Have Consequences: Relativism Undermines the Gospel

If relativism is true, there are no objective moral facts that hold true for everyone. If morality is subjective, moral choices are mere preferences. And if right and wrong are simply matters of taste, sin evaporates, neutering the gospel.

Gospel (*euangelion* in Greek) literally means "good news." But *this* good news implies some very bad news. And here, Scripture is very clear. Sin is the disease that is cured by the good news Jesus brings. However, if radical relativism is true, then there is no moral law, no sin, and no good news. The gospel is neutralized, and Christianity loses its voice. C.S. Lewis points out, "It is after you have realized that there is a Moral Law and a Power behind that law, and that you have broken the law and put yourself wrong with that Power—it is after this and not a moment sooner, that Christianity begins to talk."[11] Christianity has nothing to say to young people if they are convinced relativism is true because once sin disappears, grace disappears with it.

The impact this has on students is unmistakable. Students will seesaw between their common-sense moral intuitions and a morally relativistic impulse that prohibits all moral judgments. The vocabulary students commonly use tells the story. Completely absent from their descriptions of the gospel message are terms like obedience, duty, obligation, judgment, and accountability. The reason? Such words only make sense if objective moral truths exist.

Test your own students. Ask them some version of this question: What does it mean to be a Christian? In response, you'll hear talk about relationship with God or following Jesus, important concepts to be sure. Take note, however, whether any of these are missing:

- repentance of sins (Luke 5:32; Acts 3:19)
- atonement for sins (Romans 3:25)
- forgiveness (1 John 1:7-10)
- freedom from God's wrath (John 3:36; Romans 5:9)
- justification before God (Romans 5:16)
- reconciliation with God (2 Corinthians 5:18-20)

Aren't these ideas essential to the gospel? Yet these are the very things that relativism ultimately renders meaningless, stripping the gospel of its transformative truth and power.

Ground Truth in Reality

Fortunately, truth has a powerful ally: reality. If we're going to recapture young minds for truth, they must first understand the nature of truth. And reality is central to that understanding.

Return to the truth test. What makes statements seven through ten objective truths? Reality. They correspond to the way the world really is. Our young people need to be confident that our religious and moral claims are more than mere opinion. "God exists" is an objective claim about the world "out there." It is either true or false. Moral truths are not merely preferences. Real moral laws are grounded in reality and inform our behavior.

Is anything more sobering in life than reality? When our beliefs about the world are false, people get hurt. When relativistic beliefs lead the emerging generation astray, they get injured. But hope finds its beginning in reality. Youth can count on reality when their beliefs are true. And because Christ is true and central to all reality, the emerging generation has the ultimate reason for hope. This is the reality we must constantly bring them back to.

Connect Identity to Truth

Relativism's incursion into our young people's view of identity must be directly, yet gently and lovingly, challenged. They need to see the inadequacy and instability of our culture's proposed sexual identities, represented by the ever-expanding acronym LGBTQIA+. If they attempt to ground their identity in malleable sexual proclivities, their sense of self and well-being will fluctuate with their changing feelings and desires. Their perception of their own value will waver. These false identities cannot provide a stable foundation upon which to build one's sense of self.

Instead, we must help them find their identity in their Designer. We must consistently and joyously proclaim our true identity as God's image bearers (Genesis 1:27). Being made in the image of God is a fact of reality that does not change based on our inner thoughts and feelings. It's not something that can be lost or erased. It's inherent to human beings. Only God's objectively true and good design of humanity will anchor a young person's sense of self and provide a sturdy foundation for their own dignity and self-worth.

Create Opportunities to Engage the World with Truth

Is training in the truth confined behind the walls of the church? It shouldn't be. We can bring the truth to life when we connect students with the real world. Are you teaching your students about world religions? Great. Have classroom instruction, but don't stop there. Bring in your Mormon neighbor or LDS missionaries so students can ask them questions. Take a tour of the local Buddhist temple or engage your friendly Hindu neighbor.

Are you teaching on evolution? Don't confine it to the classroom. Instead, find a science museum in your area and ask the curator for a tour and Q-and-A session. Let the classroom teaching come to life as students engage a real-life evolutionist with the truth.

It's time to get our youth out of the church and into the world. For more than 20 years, I've helped students interact with atheists in Berkeley and Mormons in Utah.[12] We have created hundreds of real-time, real-life experiences allowing them to engage real people with the truth. Nothing I do has been more effective to train students. Every time, they come back more passionate about the truth.

An Old Word About Truth

Above all, we must embody the truth for our young people. Life with Christ is more than a set of true propositions. Note Blaise Pascal, a Christian sage from the past:

> Men despise religion. They hate it and are afraid it may be true. The cure for this is first to show that religion is not contrary to reason, but worthy of reverence and respect. Next make it attractive, make good men wish it were true, and then show that it is. Worthy of reverence because it really understands human nature. Attractive because it promises true good.[13]

When we contend for the truth of Christianity (Jude 3), we show it's not contrary to reason. If our lives also embody Christ's truth, we make it attractive. In so doing, we become full of grace *and* truth, like Jesus (John 1:14). That kind of truth never gets old.

Brett Kunkle is the founder and president of MAVEN. He is the coauthor of *A Practical Guide to Culture: Helping the Next Generation Navigate Today's World* and *A Student's Guide to Culture*.

AN INTERVIEW WITH
HILLARY MORGAN FERRER

Sean: There is a growing interest in apologetics among women. Why do you think that is the case?

Hillary: I can, of course, only speak in generalities, but I have a theory that men often pioneer, but women civilize. Apologetics has had a bit of a "Wild West" reputation where it has been seen as a way of conquering ideas (2 Corinthians 10:5) rather than freeing the people held captive to them (Colossians 2:8). Not very many people—men or women—are interested in ideas merely for the idea's sake. We as apologists often are, and have done, a disservice by presenting apologetics in the way that interested us.

The average woman is not interested in a battle of wits, but rather in knowing how to engage people, the culture, and her children in a way that leads to increased faith in Christ. If a woman doesn't see a tangible need, she will likely put her efforts into more obvious ways of serving and loving. With the internet invading every corner of our lives, anti-Christian ideas have now trickled down from the ivory towers into our children's programming. Your average woman likely knows way more people (and especially youth) whose faith has taken a hit because of faulty worldviews or emotionally haunting objections to the faith. Therefore, I think the average woman is more interested in apologetics now than say, 20 years ago, when anti-Christian rhetoric was largely sequestered within higher education.

Sean: Are there unique approaches or insights that women tend to bring to apologetics? What suggestions do you have for the church to better engage and equip women?

Hillary: My fellow female apologists and I have noticed a trend. When it comes to women's interest in apologetics, the questions are often fueled more by a loved one's doubt than their own. As such, women bring a very missional mindset to apologetics. Furthermore, women with children become voracious readers and learners when they realize how toxic ideas are affecting their child's faith. It's the mama bear instinct; moms will rise up and do whatever they need to do to protect and prepare their kids.

If churches want to equip women, they need to capitalize on these protective and missional instincts. Apologetics shouldn't be presented as a way to "talk people into the faith" (or in many cases, back into the faith). If we want to engage the average churchgoer—and especially the women—we need to emphasize the role apologetics has in preventing people from abandoning the faith in the first place. If churches would emphasize the preventative benefits of apologetics, I think we'd see many more women and moms getting involved. I shouldn't even say that as a hypothetical. We are seeing this happen with women and I have been so honored to be a part of this movement.

Sean: What encouragement would you give to women who want to either become apologists, or just do effective apologetics in their families and communities?

Hillary: First off, ladies: We need more of us! I wasn't aware of this until a few years ago, but there is a large demographic of women who will not interact with ideas unless it's presented by women for women. So get involved! Pick a topic that you are passionate about or a demographic who is largely unreached, and make that your mission.

Secondly, when it comes to discipling your family, much of apologetics will revolve around being able to think critically through an issue. Classic apologetics revolves more around facts and data, but the most pressing issues today are largely cultural. You don't need a scientific study to illustrate how following your heart can be horrible advice. Practice thought experiments. Discuss the unintended consequences of bad ideas. The hardest part will be remembering to stop and discuss an issue when you hear something fishy. After that, it becomes a habit and often your kids will start initiating the conversations.

Next, be comforted by the Fuller Youth Institute study which showed that merely providing a safe environment for question-asking went a long way in preventing kids' future doubts.[1] Nobody needs a PhD to encourage their kids to voice their burning questions about the faith.

And finally, take my dad's advice: "You don't need to know all the answers. You just need to know where to find the answers." There are so many good resources just a click away. You are not alone in your journey.

Hillary Morgan Ferrer is the founder and president of Mama Bear Apologetics®, which provides accessible apologetics resources for busy moms. She is the general editor or primary author of *Mama Bear Apologetics*, *Mama Bear Apologetics Guide to Sexuality*, and *Honest Prayers for Mama Bears*.

A FRESH APOLOGETIC: RELATIONSHIPS THAT TRANSFORM

Josh McDowell

Brace yourself.

Some of the things I will share with you in this chapter may sound strange to you. They may sound contrary to the way you were raised, the way you think, the way you perceive the gospel of Jesus Christ, and the way you typically relate to truth itself. Some of my words may surprise you and may even shock you. But though such a response may be unavoidable, I am not trying to provoke such a reaction. Instead, I want to present you with one of the most important discoveries of my life in the hope that it will transform your life and the lives of many people around you—and even the church itself.

Years ago, I visited a large church in the Midwest to speak to pastors, parents, and many others over the course of a weekend. The church's new facility, surrounded by cornfields and wooded areas, dominated the rural landscape. As I approached the entrance, I couldn't help noticing the enormous banner hung across the front of the church building. The banner announced, in large, bold letters, "We preach the truth—and the truth only!" I felt a wave of sadness wash over me. If that sign truly reflects the attitude of that church, they might as well close their doors now, for they will surely fail.

The Whole Truth

"But, Josh, how can you say that? You've dedicated a lifetime of energy and passion to telling the world the truth! How can you say that a church that preaches 'the truth—and the truth only' is doomed to failure?" This is the reaction I received from the pastor of that church, but by the end of the weekend, he indicated that his attitude had begun to change. I hope and pray that the same thing will happen in all of us for the sake of our children and grandchildren and for all those in our families, churches, and communities who haven't yet experienced new life in Christ.

We live in a culture that is generally uninterested in the truth of the gospel, partly because they are thoroughly unimpressed by those who proclaim it. From 2007 to 2021, those who identified as Christian fell from 78 percent to 63 percent, while those who have no religious affiliation rose from 16 percent to 29 percent.[1] Most interesting though, when Americans were asked about their opinion of Jesus, seven out of ten viewed Him positively. Now why is there such a decline in those who identify as Christians while the general population continues to view Jesus in a positive light? Many factors are at play, but one key answer is found in the gap between the perception of Jesus and the perception of His followers. While 71 percent of the general population have a positive view of Jesus, only 26 percent have a positive view of His followers.[2] More specifically, when those who identified with no faith gave their opinions about those of us who are committed to the truth of the gospel, only *nine* percent had a positive opinion. The number one reason why? *The hypocrisy of religious people.*[3]

So you see, we can preach the truth—and only the truth—from now until Jesus returns and still be met with utter disinterest from those around us because they are not looking for what they see in us. They don't want the truth from us. And that's directly related to our failure to grasp, live, and communicate "the whole counsel of God" (Acts 20:27 ESV).

What Engenders Belief

When the pastor of that church asked me how I could take issue with his church's boast about preaching "the truth—and the truth only," I explained to him that it was not the proclamation of truth that turned the world upside down in the apostles' day or in more recent times.

This is an issue I wrestled with for roughly 15 years of my life: What engenders belief in a young person? In any person, for that matter? In other words, what will cause your children, grandchildren, students, neighbors, friends, and family members to want to hear the truth, know Jesus, follow the Scriptures, and live out the values you yourself treasure?

I think I can answer that question now in a single word: relationships.

You may counter by saying, "No, Josh, it's the Holy Spirit who engenders faith in a person." Yes, of course that is true. But what does the Holy Spirit use? He doesn't work in a vacuum. More than anything else, He will use relationships to stimulate belief.

King David said, "I am always aware of your unfailing love" (Psalm 26:3). Notice he didn't say once in a while or even a couple times a week. He said, "I am *always* aware of your unfailing love." What did that do to David? What did such an awareness produce in him? The rest of the verse provides the answer: "And I have lived according to your truth." David clearly connected his constant awareness of God's love with living according to the truth.

He does much the same thing in Psalm 86, when he prays, "Teach me your ways, O LORD, that I may live according to your truth" (verse 11). That is a prayer that certainly reflects the desire of every godly parent for our children and grandchildren, as well as the kids in our churches, schools, and neighborhoods. I feel as if I prayed this prayer nearly every time I held my son or one of my three daughters in my arms. But notice David's motivation for praying that prayer, the relational foundation that prompted his prayer: "For your love for me is very great" (verse 13).

In 2003, Dartmouth Medical School commissioned a foundational scientific study of young people that is still relevant for today. Rather than generating new research, this project analyzed the results of more than 260 recent scientific studies of young people. The results were so revealing, they prompted the project to be renamed. "A Scientific Study of Young People" became "Hardwired to Connect."[4] Why the change? Because, they said, all the research—not 90 percent, not 95, not even 99 percent, but all of it—showed that from the moment a baby is born, that child's brain is physically, biologically, and chemically hardwired to connect with others in relationships. That's the case not only spiritually and emotionally but also physiologically.

Do you want to pass your values on to young people? Do you want your children to come to know your Savior? Do you want the next generation to grasp and live biblical truth? If so, scientific research says you must do two things: (1) Build loving, intimate connections and relationships with children or they will almost certainly reject the truth you care about, and (2) model that very value or truth in the presence of those young people.

Relationships engender belief. Jesus spent three years with His first disciples, eating with them, laughing and crying with them, traveling with them, sleeping next to them, teaching them, correcting them, and building a relational foundation for the day when He would say to them, "I have given you an example to follow. Do as I have done to you" (John 13:15).

Likewise, Paul established a relationship with people in Philippi, including a merchant named Lydia and her family and a Roman jailer and his family. He and the others in his party lodged with them, ate with them, performed miracles in their midst, and endured persecution with them, providing the relational basis for Paul's words years later: "Pattern your lives after mine, and learn from those who follow our example" (Philippians 3:17).

Jesus and Paul both clearly foreshadowed the model recommended by twenty-first-century scientific research: Relationship engenders belief.

Where Relationship Is Lacking

After the tragic shootings at Columbine High School, which claimed 13 lives, Columbia University commissioned a study. The objective was to find out if (and how) family structure affected a child's involvement in drugs and alcohol, and whether that had any impact on that child's potential for violent behavior. Here is a portion of the study's findings:

- In a single-parent home where the mother is the head of the home, a child is 30 percent more likely to become involved in drugs, alcohol, and violence.

- In a two-parent biological home, but where there is a fairly poor relationship with the father, a child is 68 percent likely to become involved in drugs, alcohol, and violence.

- In a two-parent biological home where the child has a good to excellent relationship with the father, a child is less than 6 percent likely to become involved in drugs, alcohol, or violence.[5]

According to that study, not only the structure of a family but also the strength of the relationships within the family produces the likelihood of certain behaviors. Relationships engender our beliefs. Beliefs then contribute to the formation of our values, which, in turn, drive our behavior:

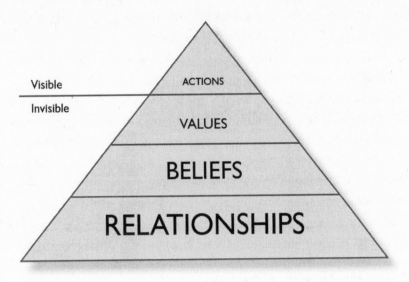

In light of many of the heartbreaking and traumatizing stories of recent mass shootings, some have set out to understand what leads to such destructive and life-altering behavior. One study funded by the National Institute of Justice examined a database of every mass shooter since 1966, and every shooting incident at schools, workplaces, and places of worship since 1999. Their findings indicated a consistent pathway of broken relationships, including early childhood trauma through violence in the home, sexual assault, parental suicides, or extreme bullying resulting in hopelessness, despair, isolation, self-loathing, and oftentimes rejection from peers.[6] Relationships engender the beliefs that form our values and drive our behavior.

Johns Hopkins commissioned two doctors to identify any contributing factors for five diseases or conditions (mental illness, hypertension, malignant tumors, heart disease, and suicide) in people's lives. In other words, would it be possible to say that if *A* or *B* were true in a child's life, that child would be more likely to experience any of these things later in life? After 30 years of research involving 1,377 graduates, they found only one common factor among these conditions. It wasn't diet (thank God). It wasn't exercise (hallelujah!). Remarkably, the sole common link was the lack of closeness to one's parents, especially the father.[7]

Don't feel badly if you find that incredible. I did too at first. So I called Johns Hopkins, and when they couldn't answer my questions, they connected me with the authors of the study, who took only a few minutes to persuade me that the lack of closeness to one's parents—especially to the father—is the common contributing factor to those five conditions. Why? In a word: stress. In other words, they found that a child raised in a loving, intimate family relationship, especially with the father, can handle stress so much better as they grow older. Relationships are the key.

Michael Jackson is well known for his musical achievements and was often referred to as the "King of Pop." In the midst of all his success, he became obsessed with changing his image to appear as a child and live the childhood he never had. More specifically, one who lived like Peter Pan in Neverland. After his death, it became evident that the impact of childhood trauma and lack of healthy relationships greatly affected his well-being. He once shared about something that happened in his first rehearsal as lead singer of the Jackson Five, when Michael was only five years old. During the rehearsal, something went wrong, and Michael turned around and called out, "Daddy!" His father abruptly stopped the rehearsal and sternly said, "I am not your father! I am your manager! And don't you ever forget that." Michael said he never did.

Once, Jackson spoke at Oxford University in England to around 800 students and professors about Heal the Kids, a foundation he started. Just minutes into his talk, he broke down in tears. When he regained his composure a few minutes later, he explained, "I just wanted a dad. A father who showed me love, and my father never did that. He never once said, 'Michael, I love you.'" Relationships engender the beliefs that form our values and, in turn, drive our behavior.

Hugh Hefner, founder of the *Playboy* publishing empire, had given many interviews about his hedonistic lifestyle. Yet I never heard him reference his father, and only once did I hear him talk about his mother. In a cable news interview, he said, "I knew my mother loved me, but she never expressed it. So I had to learn about love from the movies." He seemed to be saying that his belief system and value system lacked a relational foundation.

I've tried to do exactly the opposite in raising my children. Whenever the need for a healthy dose of truth arose with my kids—for example, when some lesson or discipline was called for—I tried to firmly place it in the context of my relationship with them. My first words were always, "Do you know that I love you?" Because, of course, the answer to that question was an all-important antecedent to the effective transmission of truth. Before ever dealing with issues or attitudes in my children, I first cemented the relationship, and only then went on to deal with the problems—still in the context of the relationship. Relationships engender belief.

A Biblical Apologetic

Remember the pastor whose church boasted about preaching "the truth—and the truth only"? When I explained to him that it was not the proclamation of truth that turned the world upside down, he bristled.

"Sure it was," he said.

I smiled and shook my head. "No, it wasn't," I said.

You see, what happened in the first century—and the task we face today, as well—involved far more than a strictly modernist approach, which appeals to the intellect. It also involved more than an extreme postmodern approach, which treats the truth as an irrelevance. Our first-century forebears would be unsatisfied with both modernism, which exalts truth but minimizes relationships, and postmodernism, which minimizes truth and exalts relationships. Truth without relationships is modernism. Relationships without truth is postmodernism. The world we live in—the great host of people all around us—is desperate for truth that is firmly grasped, grounded, and communicated in the context of relationships.

"Preaching the truth is not what turned the world upside down," I explained to that pastor. "It was a thoroughly biblical apologetic, neither modern nor postmodern." It's what Paul referred to when he depicted the process that brought the Thessalonians to a vibrant faith in Christ: "Having so fond an affection for you, we were well-pleased to impart to you not only the gospel of God but also our own lives, because you had become very dear to us" (1 Thessalonians 2:8 NASB1995).

That's what turned the world upside down in the first days of church history! It was an apologetic exemplified in those first Christians' willingness to impart not only the truth but also their very lives. Their apologetic was not "truth only." It was not modernism. Not postmodernism. It was truth in the context of relationships. The way they lived their lives was further proof of the truth of the message (1 Thessalonians 1:5).

Writing to the church at Rome, Paul said, "I will not presume to speak of anything except what Christ has accomplished through me, resulting in the obedience of the Gentiles by word and deed" (Romans 15:18 NASB).

Paul's apologetic was richer than modernism and fuller than postmodernism. It was clearly two-pronged: People were drawn to the gospel by the truth in the context of relationship.

In his book *They Like Jesus but Not the Church,* Dan Kimball dedicates a chapter to discussing "What They Wish the Church Were Like"—that is, what non-Christians and nonchurchgoers say would make the Christian faith attractive and perhaps even irresistible. These are two of the most common answers he discusses: "I wish the church were a loving place," and "I wish the church would respect my intelligence."[8] Both are crucial.

That's My Story (And I'm Sticking with It)

Most people assume I came to Christ through the intellectual route. Certainly, there can't be more than a few people who have documented more evidences for the faith than I have. And yet, all the evidence I have documented—on the reliability of the Bible, the deity of Jesus Christ, and the evidence for the resurrection—never brought me to faith in Christ.

That's right. The evidences did not bring me to Christ. The evidences got my attention, but it was God's love that drew me. It was the love I saw between a group of genuine believers who loved not only Jesus Christ but also each other—and even me!

The evidence got my attention, but love drew me. When I think back to that night when I realized it, I still get chills. It was Saturday night in a university dorm. I was a total skeptic and an absolute heathen. Only God and the Holy Spirit could have shown me that if I were the only person alive, Jesus still would have died for me.

I've said often that I grew up with a father who was the town drunk. I've told how I had to watch him beat my mother. I've shared that I hated him and took my revenge on him when I got old enough and strong enough. But I never shared the following until recently.

Between the ages of six and thirteen, I was severely sexually abused by a man named Wayne Bailey. When I was six years old, he was hired on the farm to be a cook and a housekeeper. Whenever my mother would leave or my folks would go downtown or go away for a few days, my mother would always march me to Wayne Bailey and say, "Now, you obey Wayne. You do everything that he tells you to do or you'll get a thrashing when I get home." So I was at Wayne Bailey's mercy.

When I was nine years old, and again at the age of twelve, I told my mother what had been going on. She didn't believe me. I can't describe the pain and abandonment I felt, on top of the abuse, when my own mother refused to believe me.

Finally, however, at thirteen years of age, I was strong enough. My parents had left for the weekend, and I went into the house and backed this man against the wall.

"If you ever touch me again," I said, "I will kill you."

And I would have. Two weeks later, he left. I remember my mom and dad talking that night around the dinner table. They asked each other, "I wonder what happened? Why did he leave? Why didn't he give notice?"

I sat there thinking, *Why didn't you believe me?*

Wayne was gone, but of course by that time, the damage had been done. I had nothing going for me and everything going against me. A worse-than-absent father. Abandoned by my mother. And horribly abused on top of it all. I should have become the victim of victims.

But when I arrived at Kellogg College in Battle Creek, Michigan, I met a group of Christians who exposed me for the first time to the love of God. Oh, how they loved each other. And I wanted what they had so badly that I would have paid anything for it. I would have pawned my soul to have what they had. That love—and the desire for that kind of relationship—paved the road of faith for me, and thus began my journey of faith.

Some time later, I met the pastor of a tiny church, Factorville Bible Church. I went to him and shared what had happened to me. And he believed me! I can't tell you what that meant. It was like being born again…again. He believed me!

For six months after that, he walked me through Scripture after Scripture, verse after verse, on forgiveness. When he finished and finally said, "Josh, you need to forgive him." I answered, "No way." I wanted him to burn in hell, and I wanted to escort him there.

Obviously, if I had not encountered God's love in that student group at Kellogg College and experienced it again through that pastor's friendship and mentoring, I would have been content to hate Wayne Bailey for the rest of my life. But the truth had taken root in me as a result of those relationships. I'm convinced that all the evidence in the world, all the most powerful arguments and most convincing proofs, would never have gotten through to me if the transforming power of God's love had not reached my heart through that student group and others, including the pastor of tiny Factorville Bible Church. In fact, my mind continued to rebel long after my heart knew what I must do.

But, steeled by that pastor's loving support, one day I found out where Wayne Bailey lived. I drove to his house. I knocked on his door. I introduced myself. And, though I must admit I didn't want to tell him because I didn't want it to be true, I forgave Wayne Bailey and told him that Jesus died for him as much as He did for me.

The Ring of Truth

What was true of the Philippians and Thessalonians—and me—is true of our children, grandchildren, students, neighbors, coworkers, friends, and family members. They are desperate for truth that is firmly grasped, grounded, and communicated in the context of relationships. As Paul said, "If I could speak all the languages of earth and of angels, but didn't love others, I would only be a noisy gong or a clanging cymbal" (1 Corinthians 13:1).

According to the research, that's what our proclamation of truth has sounded like to the world around us: a meaningless noise. Our message is falling on deaf ears to the world around us because we are too often delivering the truth—and the truth only, unfortunately.

We need a new approach, a fresh apologetic, though it's actually as old as the church. It's how Jesus trained His first followers. It's the way Paul won a Philippian merchant and jailer to the faith. It's the route by which Jason and others from Thessalonica were drawn to Christ. And it's the path I took as well.

It's not relationships and it's not truth, not one or the other. It is a thoroughly biblical apologetic: truth in the context of relationships, an apologetic that acknowledges and capitalizes on the fact that truth bears the sweetest fruit when it is planted in the soil of a loving relationship.

Josh McDowell is the author or coauthor of more than 165 books, including *More Than a Carpenter* and *Evidence That Demands a Verdict*.

APOLOGETICS AND CULTURE: FOUR CHALLENGES OF OUR AGE

John Stonestreet

n the spring of 2002, at a small Christian college in eastern Tennessee, a renowned philosopher and Christian apologist announced the end of postmodernism. I was there when he said it. He was, of course, mistaken.

At the time, his argument did not sound as unconvincing as it does now. Because the horrors and evils of the 9/11 terror attacks had been broadcast over and over throughout the world, he thought that most people would no longer find moral relativism plausible. In retrospect, he had underestimated how deeply entrenched relativism had become in the Western cultural imagination. He thought the world would be forced to conclude, "Well, this act of terror was clearly wrong, so moral absolutes must exist." Instead, many concluded, *because* of their relativism, "Those who believe in moral absolutes do this sort of thing." He also overestimated the role of logical consistency in human belief and action.

Friedrich Nietzsche—an Unlikely Prophet

More fundamentally, this helpful and thoughtful defender of Christianity had underestimated the consequences of "unchain[ing] the earth from its sun." This phrase is taken from "The Parable of the Madman," written by the brilliant and troubled nineteenth-century atheist philosopher Friedrich Nietzsche.[1] The parable is one of the two places Nietzsche made his famous announcement, "God is dead."

Nietzsche also announced the death of God in another parable, *Thus Spake Zarathrustra*.[2] That piece, which Nietzsche hoped would become a kind of atheistic counter to holy Scripture, promised the potential of what might be once humans, or at least some of them, evolved beyond religion and took on the role of God in the world. "The Madman" is different. It's more of a warning, written not to those who believed in God but to those who didn't. It has proven more prophetic than *Zarathrustra* and, for that matter, than the apologist's prediction of postmodernism's demise.

"The Parable of the Madman" begins:

> Have you not heard of that madman who lit a lantern in the bright morning hours, ran to the market place, and cried incessantly: "I seek God! I seek God!"—As many of those who did not believe in God were standing around just then, he provoked much laughter. Has he got lost? asked one. Did he lose his way like a child? asked another. Or is he hiding? Is he afraid of us? Has he gone on a voyage? emigrated?—Thus they yelled and laughed.

The optimism of late nineteenth-century secularists was palpable and often took forms of various utopianisms. With the decline of religion's influence, many believed that a bright, scientifically determined future was inevitable. Nietzsche did not share their optimism. He believed that these children of the Enlightenment remained in the dark, that they had underestimated all that secularism entailed.

In response to the ridicule, the madman "jumped into their midst and pierced them with his eyes," and responded:

Whither is God?…I will tell you. We have killed him—you and I. All of us are his murderers. But how did we do this? How could we drink up the sea? Who gave us the sponge to wipe away the entire horizon? What were we doing when we unchained this earth from its sun? Whither is it moving now? Whither are we moving? Away from all suns? Are we not plunging continually? Backward, sideward, forward, in all directions? Is there still any up or down? Are we not straying, as through an infinite nothing? Do we not feel the breath of empty space? Has it not become colder? Is not night continually closing in on us? Do we not need to light lanterns in the morning? Do we hear nothing as yet of the noise of the gravediggers who are burying God? Do we smell nothing as yet of the divine decomposition? Gods, too, decompose. God is dead. God remains dead. And we have killed him.

Nietzsche was not making an *ontological* observation in either of the parables, claiming that God once existed but no longer does. His observations were about dramatic changes that must follow for a world once largely oriented around, but now without, belief in God. He understood that for both individuals and societies, the belief in God is a *controlling* belief, a point of orientation around which the rest of life is defined and ordered.

This was (and still is) the case for the Western world, given the centrality of religious belief and the role of religious authorities and institutions in shaping politics, education, art, architecture, and most other aspects of culture. "How could we drink up the sea? Who gave us the sponge to wipe away the entire horizon?" The death of God is a much bigger deal, Nietzsche believed, than the utopianists understood. In a reference to one of the most consequential scientific discoveries in history, he believed that the death of God had "unchained the earth from its sun."

The Western world had been orientated to God. Without God, life had to be reimagined but without any true north for our collective cultural compass. Specifically, Nietzsche understood that the death of God had incredible implications for *morality* and *meaning*. What is up and down, forward or back, if there is no sun to hold the earth in orbit? What will warm us? What will light our way?

The madman continued:

> How shall we comfort ourselves, the murderers of all murderers? What was holiest and mightiest of all that the world has yet owned has bled to death under our knives: who will wipe this blood off us? What water is there for us to clean ourselves? What festivals of atonement, what sacred games shall we have to invent? Is not the greatness of this deed too great for us? Must we ourselves not become gods simply to appear worthy of it? There has never been a greater deed; and whoever is born after us—for the sake of this deed he will belong to a higher history than all history hitherto.

Religion plays a central role in the making and ordering of meaning. It declares the place humans have in the cosmos and in relationship to each other. In the twentieth century, as the Western world became more secularized, religion was increasingly marginalized from the central place it long held. Though the process of secularization did not necessarily lead to more atheism, it did lead to more "practical atheism." Religious belief was increasingly privatized, and God seen as less relevant to much of life and culture.

The cultural voids leftover had to be filled, and were so by the secular political ideologies of the twentieth century—such as Marxism and Fascism—and the cultural ideologies of the early twenty-first century—such as Critical Theory, some forms of nationalism, and LGBTQ+ identities. It's no accident that contemporary secular ideologies so often resemble medieval religions. There are true believers and heretics. There are, as Nietzsche described, new "festivals of atonement" (Pride Month, anti-racism) and new "sacred games" (pronoun "hospitality," land acknowledgments). And there is much social pressure to participate.

Nietzsche predicted as much, but it wasn't immediately obvious that he was correct. Secular humanists, like the mockers in his parable, promised a better world by dismissing the moral constraints associated with God, Christianity, and the Bible. Salvation was to be found in human progress, through amazing advances of medicine and especially the prosperity, comfort, convenience, and infinite choice delivered through technology. The existentialists promised that each of us could make our own meaning, even if life were ultimately meaningless. Sexual liberation promised unlimited pleasure with no consequences, if sex were untethered from the religious hang-ups of morality, marriage, and children.

From Hypothetical to Real

All of this was, at least at first, largely *theoretical*. Initially, the culture wars were fought in academia, at universities with weapons of competing manifestos and social proposals written by intellectuals and cultural elites. Francis Schaeffer was among a few Christian thinkers to identify how dangerous these ideas would become, even beyond shaping the world wars, once they seeped throughout culture into the popular mindset.

The twentieth-century Christian apologists responded in kind, with theoretical engagement. If God did not exist, many effectively argued, there was no adequate grounding for morality, meaning, or human value. If humans were just animals, as evolutionary scientists had concluded, there was no compelling cause for altruism or compassion. If the world and human beings were merely products of naturalistic causes and processes, without purpose or design, there were no "oughts," only what "is." These arguments and others like them, leveled by Christians at atheistic worldviews, were sound and accurate.

Nietzsche was among the few willing to admit all that his atheism implied. And his predictions were far more accurate than the utopianists who thought religion could be shrugged off and the world would simply move on. Nietzsche embraced a godless future without platitudes or wishful thinking. The strong would survive and dictate new absolutes for a post-human world.

I began teaching comparative worldviews and apologetics in the early 2000s, engaging secular ideas by highlighting the absurd inconsistencies of attempting to make meaning in a meaningless universe. If truth is relative and words have no fixed meaning, I asked my students:

What would prevent someone from claiming a stop sign, in fact, says go?

Could a man claim to be a woman?

Could murder be called healthcare, if committed for the "common good"?

Could not injustice be justified by redefining oppression and justice?

Somewhere in the last decade, many of these hypotheticals were no longer hypothetical. The theoretical became existential. Nietzsche prophesied this too:

> Here the madman fell silent and looked again at his listeners; and they, too, were silent and stared at him in astonishment. At last he threw his lantern on the ground, and it broke into pieces and went out. "I have come too early," he said then; "my time is not yet. This tremendous event is still on its way, still wandering; it has not yet reached the ears of men. Lightning and thunder require time; the light of the stars requires time; deeds, though done, still require time to be seen and heard. This deed is still more distant from them than most distant stars—and yet they have done it themselves."

A building can remain standing, for a while, even as its foundation crumbles. An engineer might examine the building and theorize its destiny. However, the experience is different for tenants of the building, who experience the walls cracking, the floors slanting, and the ceilings falling in.

The Theoretical Becomes Existential—Four Catastrophic Losses

Apologetics in the twenty-first century must reckon with existential realities as much, or perhaps more, than theoretical ones. Many today *feel* the death of God in ways that were predicted long ago but are now all around us. The loss, not only of God but of *any* fixed reference point by which we might know who we are and order our lives, has led to a hyper-subjective inward turn. It's as if we've been left to navigate the wilderness of reality with a compass that always points at us.

Carl R. Trueman began his magisterial work *The Rise and Triumph of the Modern Self: Cultural Amnesia, Expressive Individualism, and the Road to Sexual Revolution*[3] with an illustration that clarifies how much has changed as the theoretical became existential. Writing about the contemporary confusions around gender and identity, he notes that the real question is not why a man would think that he was born in the wrong body. Rather, how did we reach the point as a society that when a man announces he was born in the wrong body, the claim is assumed true, and everyone is expected to embrace the delusion? Even more, how could a society become so unmoored from reality to reorient educational institutions, rewrite laws, and implement public policies according to the delusion?

What Trueman introduced with the scenario are questions of *plausibility*. In different cultural moments, some ideas are taken seriously, others disbelieved, and others simply taken for granted. There is a sociology to what citizens of a particular time and place think, assume, and do. A significant aspect of the existential angst of twenty-first-century life, with which Christian apologists must reckon, are those deep and dramatic changes of plausibility.

That angst is a feature of our cultural moment. A moment in which a deep and pervasive relativism now extends beyond how people think about *morality* to how people think about *reality* itself. This is the experience of living in a world untethered from anything fixed and outside of us, and it can be described as four catastrophic losses.

Catastrophic Loss #1: The Loss of Truth

Truth is that which corresponds to reality. Attempting to redefine truth as that which corresponds to each individual replaces "what's true" with "what's true *for me*." This is, of course, logically futile and quickly devolves into a power struggle as various "truths" collide.

In practice, the consequences of the loss of truth have been incredible, even before the chaos brought on by hundreds of millions of social media accounts, viral deepfake videos, and myriad implementations of artificial intelligence. It's one thing to live in a society in which there is broad agreement about where we are going but many different ideas about how to get there.

It's another thing entirely when a society has no shared ideas of what is real, where we ought to be headed, or what is up and what is down.

The prophet Isaiah wrote, "Woe to those who call evil good and good evil, who put darkness for light and light for darkness, who put bitter for sweet and sweet for bitter!" (Isaiah 5:20 ESV). This confusion can not only infect individuals but entire cultures. Even more, the moral imagination of individuals is cultivated by the cultural contexts in which they live. So for many today, the very idea of a truth that exists outside of themselves is simply unthinkable. Their feet, to repeat a quote commonly attributed to Francis Schaeffer, are "firmly planted in mid-air."

Of course, Christian apologists have been engaging the issue of truth and countering the lie of relativism for decades. Again, this has taken largely theoretical approaches of logical reasoning and exposing how those who deny truth tend to live as if there is truth. This work must continue.

At the same time, on a cultural level the skepticism has deepened. People are increasingly creating and inhabiting alternate realities, especially online. The very notion of truth is constantly undermined in, of all areas, education, as well as in journalism and law. It's one thing to argue that truth doesn't exist. *It's another to experience life in a world built on the lie that trust doesn't exist.* Nietzsche foresaw this world that is, in many ways, now here.

Catastrophic Loss #2: The Loss of Trust

This is an inevitable and extremely disorienting consequence of the loss of truth. In different cultural moments, specific existential questions are more acutely felt. For example, after a natural disaster or act of terrorism, people tend to wonder if God exists, and if so, why He would allow evil and suffering. In the Information Age, we encounter more communication from more sources than any generation that has ever lived. Thus, the Information Age is also an age of competing authorities.

It only makes sense that one of the acutely felt questions of our age is: Who do I trust? Should we trust our pastors or our peers? Our parents or our professors? This news organization or that one? Is anyone really "fair and balanced"? Of course, what most people decide to do is google the questions they have, but even then, how can they trust an ever-changing, profit-driven algorithm?

Adding further complication to the confusion is that so many public figures and institutions have proven *un*trustworthy. In fact, try to name a social institution that *isn't* suffering a credibility crisis right now. Religious institutions, school boards, elite universities, government officials, medical experts, bloggers, Hollywood producers, teachers, coaches, athletes, and influencers are pretty much all in the same leaky boat.

Catastrophic Loss #3: The Loss of Meaning

There was a span of three years prior to the COVID-19 pandemic that was the first period in a century in which the average life expectancy of the American male *declined*.[4] The last time this had happened, there was a world war and the Spanish Flu outbreak. There were no factors like these impacting the population between 2014 and 2019.

Instead, a collection of conditions emerged that earned the name "deaths of despair."[5] With the isolation of pandemic lockdown policies, deaths by suicide and overdose continued to climb, but the trend pre-existed the pandemic, as did spikes in mental illness diagnoses among most demographic groups. Loneliness has been declared a public health crisis. A related set of maladies, which could be called "acts of desperation," also emerged, including young men committing acts of mass violence, people acting out at concerts and on airplanes, and young people mutilating their bodies in a fruitless search for identity.

In the twentieth century, atheistic philosophers like Jean Paul Sartre boldly announced that life had no ultimate meaning other than what we assigned to it. He believed both birth and death were meaningless, calling people to embrace the darkness and courageously forge their own path and purpose. It was a bluff. None of the conveniences and distractions, toys and sexual experimentations, can fill the God-shaped hole in the human heart.

Still, life was lived as if there were meaning to be made. There was the promise of meaningful employment, meaningful relationships, and meaningful stories and myths that contained meaningful morals that could touch the human heart. Not as much anymore.

The twin trends of "deaths of despair" and "acts of desperation" suggest that all the theorizing that concluded life has no meaning has become, for many, a growing sense that *my life has no meaning*. Much of this can be attributed to the isolation and loneliness caused by smartphones, broken families, the cynicism present in political divisions, and the distrust created by constant narratives of oppression. Fundamentally, however, the catastrophic loss of meaning is closely connected to the final catastrophic loss.

Catastrophic Loss #4: The Loss of Identity

"Modern man," sociologists Peter Berger, Brigitte Berger, and Hansfried Kellner declared in 1974, "is afflicted with a permanent identity crisis."[6] They listed a number of contributing factors, both social and technological—consequences of the vast changes brought by modernism. Were they to update the book today, the authors would have far more evidence to support their thesis, much of which is already mentioned above.

Still, one of the most prevalent and unexpected aspects of our culture-wide identity crisis today is a complicated and pseudo-gnostic understanding of the human body.[7] In the twentieth century, Christian apologists spent much time and ink defending the scientific, real-world relevance of the Christian worldview and its emphasis on the supernatural. In an ironic turn, Christians are now among the few defending the biological and relational realities of human beings in a culture that—aided by art and technology—treats our humanity, especially the body, as infinitely pliable and moldable. This follows from the Christian view that the world is fundamentally the good creation of God—a view that stands in direct contrast to the late postmodern view that *everything*, from morality to humanity to reality itself, is socially constructed.

Contra Mundum: Against the World, for the World

Nietzsche believed the church would prove powerless to confront the inevitabilities of the death of God:

> It has been related further that on the same day the madman forced his way into several churches and there struck up his *requiem aeternam deo*. Led out and called to account, he is said always to have replied nothing but: "What after all are these churches now if they are not the tombs and sepulchers of God?"

Here, Nietzsche was wrong, and not only because the church and its influence exploded in growth globally during the century after his announcement that it is dead. Christians know that, ultimately, "The kingdom of the world [will] become the kingdom of our Lord and of his Christ, and he shall reign forever and ever" (Revelation 11:15 ESV). That much is sure. And until it is accomplished by the One who did indeed die but was raised to life again, His people can effectively obey Peter's admonition to "make a defense…for the hope" we have (1 Peter 3:15 ESV), in this unique cultural moment to which we have been called. Following are four ways in which we must do so.

First, in this age of absolutized relativism, we must appeal to created givens. What Paul wrote to the church in Rome is still true: "His invisible attributes, namely, his eternal power and divine nature, have been clearly perceived, ever since the creation of the world, in the things that have been made. So they are without excuse" (Romans 1:20 ESV). While the capacity of fallen humans to suppress truth can never be overestimated, Christians must bear witness, always, to *reality*. Christianity is personal, but it is not private. It is public truth, the best account of the world as we experience it.

Second, in this age of radical subjectivism and dehumanization, we must emphasize the imago dei as the true identity of every human being. This idea is at the core of the biblical narrative, central to understanding and responding to many cultural conflicts, and has been among the most consequential ideas in all of human history. However, many Christians do not grasp its significance for individuals and society.

Third, in this age of progressive disillusionment, we must retell Christian history. In many ways, the modern world continues to live off of what Christianity built. Christianity gave the world human rights, the rule of law, science, hospitals, ordered freedom, and so many other things that are taken for granted today. These goods cannot be sustained apart from their source.

Finally, in this age of loneliness and disconnection, we must recapture the possibility of love. Jesus identified that the greatest commandment is to love: first God, then others. Love is possible and knowable only because of God's love, which offers humankind both forgiveness and reconciliation. There is simply no other source from which relationships can be restored outside the reality of a God who went to such lengths to be restored to His creation. All attempts at love without Him devolve into a sentimentality without substance or, even worse, selfish sensuality. True love is, however, irrefutable.

John Stonestreet is the president of the Colson Center for Christian Worldview. He is an author, speaker, and the host of *Breakpoint*. He is also the coauthor of several books, including *A Practical Guide to Culture* and *A Student's Guide to Culture*.

AN INTERVIEW WITH
ADAM DAVIDSON

Sean: What is your profession and why are you interested in apologetics?

Adam: I am a career journalist. I have been a reporter at NPR (National Public Radio), *The New York Times Magazine*, *The New Yorker*, and elsewhere. I cocreated NPR's *Planet Money*. As a journalist—well, really, starting when I was a kid—I've had enormous curiosity about people who are quite different from me. Growing up in the 1970s and 1980s, the one group that was most hated and least understood in the world I lived in was evangelical Christians. So in college, I studied the history of religion and did my senior thesis on evangelicals, and met many. Since then, I've been fascinated by evangelical beliefs. I find apologetics lays out the belief system clearly, which is quite helpful to me. I have had similar explorations of other groups—I was a Middle East correspondent and got to know Islamic fundamentalists. I also have many Amish friends.

Sean: Is there a perception of Christians in your circles? How are evangelicals viewed?

Adam: I was born in 1970, in Greenwich Village, New York. I've lived and worked in New York, Chicago, Los Angeles, and Vermont. I don't believe I have ever met an evangelical Christian organically. I do have evangelical friends (including you!) who I sought out. But in my day-to-day life, I can't remember ever meeting one. A few friends come from evangelical backgrounds but left, but I'm fairly sure that most of my friends and colleagues have little direct experience with or knowledge of evangelicals. These are two distinct worlds.

In my world, at least as I think about it, evangelicals are among the most disliked groups of people. They (you) are seen as bigoted, closed-minded, ignorant, and fanatic. Most of my friends and colleagues would struggle to describe what evangelical means or who these people are.

One key point: evangelicals just don't come up very often. They aren't a big topic of conversation or concern, except in the political context. There is deep confusion about how evangelicals make political choices and why they seem to prefer candidates who are personally immoral and performatively cruel against immigrants and others. Few of my friends are followers of Jesus in any way—mainline, progressive, evangelical—but the general view would be that Jesus would not encourage this kind of performative cruelty.

Sean: Are there common misperceptions you see Christians having of atheists? If so, what are they?

Adam: I have few evangelicals in my life, and the ones I do know personally are people I sought out precisely because they are open to talking thoughtfully with atheists and others with whom they disagree.

However, I do watch a lot of evangelical Christian YouTube and, boy oh boy, is there deep confusion about atheists. I simply don't recognize the people being described. We have the same mix of moral, amoral, and immoral people. We love and worry about our families. We don't walk around thinking about sinning all the time or hoping to disrupt the lives of believers. We are just people—regular people. Most of us don't care about New Atheists. We're not trying to sell atheism or seeking to disrupt faith.

Sean: What are some common mistakes you see apologists make?

Adam: Most apologists spend most of their time talking to evangelicals. There are very, very few that I see who are meaningfully engaging nonbelievers. Much of what apologists seem to do is flatter believers by presenting weak, straw-man nonsense about nonbelievers. So the vast majority of apologist content is irrelevant to nonbelievers. They describe atheists in a way that no atheist would recognize. They make arguments that are unpersuasive. They assert "truths" and use a language that most nonbelievers aren't familiar with. (If you assume most people are sitting around thinking about Kalam,[1] you are not talking to most people; if you think the Kalam Cosmological Argument[2] is some kind of persuasive mic drop…I don't know what to tell you. Has any single person in the history of the world changed their mind about the fundamental nature of God because of that argument?)

Generally, I see apologists as almost a parody of how *not* to persuade people. Persuasion happens through conversation, through listening to the other side, through modesty about things you can be modest about, through modeling a kind of behavior. Asserting things using in-group language is…not going to persuade anyone of anything.

From my point of view, apologists are doing exactly what I want them to do: They are making weak arguments that flatter the believer and have zero impact on the nonbeliever. I'd be surprised if they have any real impact on anyone in my world. And that's just fine by me.

Adam Davidson is a journalist and economics expert who has served as a staff writer at *The New Yorker*, columnist at *The New York Times Magazine*, and was the cofounder of National Public Radio's *Planet Money* podcast. He is the author of *The Passion Economy*.

EFFECTIVE APOLOGETICS IN THE LOCAL CHURCH

Derwin Gray

I didn't grow up going to church. In my family, Sunday was reserved for worshipping at the altar of Dallas Cowboys' football games. Words like *gospel, pastor, evangelism, discipleship, sanctification,* and *apologetics* would have been so foreign sounding to me I would have thought they were from an alien language. I was born on April 9, 1971, in San Antonio, Texas. My mom was only 17 years old, and my dad, 19. From middle school on, I lived with my grandparents, until I went off to college, in 1989.

Religiously, my grandmother had a complicated relationship with the Jehovah's Witnesses. She had been involved in the organization but was excommunicated. Still, she maintained the major tenets of the organization such as: God is not tri-personal, Jesus is not eternally God the Son—He is Michael the archangel, and salvation can be obtained only through their organization. She taught me that every other religion was false. As I look back now, my grandmother had sort of created her own version of religion.

I'm happy to say, several years before my grandmother passed away, she recognized Jesus as the eternal Son of God, Lord and Savior, and that salvation was by grace through faith in Him alone. I will see her again in the new heavens and new earth with a perfectly healed, glorified, and resurrected body.

Football Was My Functional Savior

Humanity needs four things: unconditional love, identity, significance, and purpose. The human heart will search far and wide to find something or someone to satisfy these four needs. This is what worship looks like in real life. Humanity looks to created things to meet the needs that only the uncreated Creator can meet and satisfy:

> They worshiped and served the things God created instead of the Creator himself, who is worthy of eternal praise! (Romans 1:25).

Starting in middle school, football became my functional savior. When I played well, I received what I thought was *love* because I was good at what I was doing. Football became my *identity*. I was Derwin, the football player. I gained *significance* through my performance on the field. People recognized me as a great football player. Football gave me *purpose*. I could earn a football scholarship and get out of the environment I grew up in.

In 1988, at the end of my senior football season at Converse Judson High School, I was being recruited to play football by Kansas State, Texas Christian University, and Brigham Young University (BYU). I wasn't seriously considering BYU until I went on my recruiting trip. Provo, Utah, was beautiful! The BYU campus was also beautiful. And then, the BYU football recruiting staff took me and the other recruits snowmobiling. After the snowmobiling escapade, I had made up my mind. I accepted a scholarship to BYU. Besides, I knew I would receive an elite education, play on a winning football team, and play for one of the best coaches in America—the late LaVell Edwards. It was truly a great opportunity.

At BYU, I met my wife Vicki, had a legendary career, and made lifelong friends with members of the Church of Jesus Christ of Latter-day Saints, or the Mormon Church. I even have family who are members of the Mormon Church. As a pastor-theologian, I know that historic, orthodox Christian beliefs differ widely from the beliefs of the Mormon Church on essential doctrines such as: the nature of God, the person and work of Jesus, the gospel, salvation, salvation by grace, and the end goal of the saved. But I also know that if I ever want to persuade my LDS family and friends of the gospel, love must lead the way, and patience must closely follow.

On April 25, 1993, my dream of becoming a player in the National Football League came true. I was drafted by the Indianapolis Colts. Soon after that spectacular highlight, my dream morphed into a nightmare when I joined the day-to-day grind of the team. It was a rough transition, emotionally and mentally. I often doubted if I was good enough to compete at the highest professional level.

One of the reasons I wanted to play in the NFL is that I thought the money I earned would help heal some of my family's hurts. Things just got worse. Despite some on-the-field and off-the-field success, like being voted the RCA Man of the Year for my community service (1994) and having Indianapolis Mayor Stephen Goldsmith declare October 14, 1996, "Derwin Gray Day," I knew something was missing.

By my third season with the Colts, I had become a good professional football player. I was one of four team captains. On the outside, I was a portrait of success. But on the inside, where life really is lived, I couldn't love my wife the way she deserved to be loved, and I lived with fear because I knew the NFL stands for *Not for Long*. Who would I be if I didn't play football? My identity and my football career were united in an unholy bond.

Despite my success, I felt abandoned by my father. The dysfunction of my family of origin was painful. I had a deep ache in my soul. Ultimately, I knew I needed forgiveness for my sins. So many of the "good things" I was doing were really an effort to wash away the bad things I did. But the more I tried to scrub away my sins, the more I became aware I was a sinner. And, in 1997, God, in His grace, used one of my teammates to lead me to Christ. His name is Steve Grant, better known as the Naked Preacher.

The Naked Preacher

Every day after practice, the Naked Preacher would take a shower, dry off, wrap a towel around his waist, and ask my teammates, "Do you know Jesus?" And in my mind, I was like, *Do you know you're half naked?* In my rookie year, I asked the veterans on the team, "What's up with the half-naked black man walking around asking: 'Do you know Jesus?'" They said, "Don't pay any attention to him. That's the Naked Preacher!" After practice one day, he began walking toward me. He asked me a question that changed my life: "Rookie D Gray, do you know Jesus?" From those initial words a five-year relationship began, one in which the house of cards I built my life upon collapsed under the weight of God's grace.

On August 2, 1997—my fifth year in the NFL—through the influence of the Naked Preacher, I met Jesus personally in a small dorm room. The Indianapolis Colts were doing a training camp at Anderson University in Anderson, Indiana. After lunch on that day, I walked back to my dorm room with what felt like a Grand Canyon-sized hole in my soul. I called my wife and I said, "Sweetheart, I want to be more committed to you. And I want to be committed to Jesus." That is when I was born again. That's when I met Jesus. I knew He loved me with a love that is forgiving and lifegiving. I was a new man.

Immediately, I wanted Jesus more. I wanted to know Him well, so that naturally led me to reading the Bible. I just couldn't get enough of Jesus. Later, in 1998, my wife and I moved to Charlotte, North Carolina, because I signed a contract to play with the Carolina Panthers. I played in three games before I injured my knee and broke my leg. This forced me to miss the rest of the season. All I could do was rehab my knee and read the Bible. The more I read the Bible, the more the Holy Spirit was rehabbing my soul. The Lord was working on my sanctification.

Dr. Norm Geisler—My Friend and Mentor

In 1999, through my first pastor, I met Norm Geisler. My pastor saw that I had a deep hunger for theology and apologetics, so he told me, "I want you to meet a friend of mine. You two will get along great." The first time Dr. Geisler and I met, we talked about theology and apologetics for two hours. We barely mentioned football. After our initial conversation, Dr. Geisler became my professor, my mentor, and my friend. I graduated magna cum laude from the seminary he founded, with a Master of Divinity degree, and a concentration in apologetics.

Dr. Geisler was essential to my spiritual formation as a husband, father, pastor-theologian, and apologist. Dr. Geisler wrote, "Apologetics is the discipline that deals with a rational defense of Christian faith. It comes from the Greek word *apologia*, which means to give a reason or defense."[1] He not only taught me the importance of apologetic preaching and teaching from the pulpit, but he also taught me the value of being a godly husband. He was married for 64 years! He taught me to love Jesus' church and all her diverse expressions. He gave me an appreciation for the church fathers and Thomistic philosophy. He taught me to heed these words of Paul, and to pour my life into others:

> Be strong through the grace that God gives you in Christ Jesus. You have heard me teach things that have been confirmed by many reliable witnesses. Now teach these truths to other trustworthy people who will be able to pass them on to others (2 Timothy 2:1-2).

As Dr. Geisler's health declined, and he was moving toward eternity, I would spend time with him at his house. Later, at his going-home celebration, his wife, Ms. Barbara, told me how much he loved when I would come over to hang out with him. I loved spending time with my friend. In the new heavens and new earth, we shall gaze at the beatific vision together, enjoying perfect knowledge of the Father, the Son, and the Holy Spirit. Dr. Geisler also wrote,

> This ultimate knowledge of God will be perfect (1 Cor. 13:9-10); our partial knowledge will turn into whole knowledge; our incomplete understanding will be transformed into complete understanding. Whatever we can know about God, we will know, and we will know it perfectly. This does not mean we will know God infinitely. Because we will always be finite, so will our knowledge be finite. Only God has an infinite knowledge of the infinite; in heaven our knowledge will be finite. We will perfectly apprehend God, but will never completely comprehend Him. God will always be ineffable.[2]

I am looking forward to that day.

Key Ingredients to Effective Apologetics in a Local Church

I was fortunate to be shaped by a preeminent apologist, Norm Geisler—a man anchored in the love of Christ Jesus and rooted in theological rigor, with apologetic and philosophical underpinnings. The overflow of his ministry in my life helped my wife and me plant and form Transformation Church. Along with a team of people, we planted the church on February 7, 2010, in Indian Land, South Carolina. Because of Norm's influence, there are three key ingredients that we have implemented to have an effective apologetic culture in our local church.

Recognizing God's Kingdom Matters

First, effective apologetics in the local church starts with a biblical, gospel-centered vision, rooted in God's glory through Christ Jesus by the Holy Spirit's power. For example, Transformation Church's vision is this: We are a "multiethnic, multigenerational mission-shaped community, that loves God completely (Upward), ourselves completely (Inward), and our neighbors compassionately (Outward)."[3] Our vision is anchored in the Great Commandment:

> "You must love the LORD your God with all your heart, all your soul, and all your mind." This is the first and greatest commandment. A second is equally important: "Love your neighbor as yourself." The entire law and all the demands of the prophets are based on these two commandments" (Matthew 22:37-39).

And the Great Commission:

> Jesus came and told his disciples, "I have been given all authority in heaven and on earth. Therefore, go and make disciples of all the nations, baptizing them in the name of the Father and the Son and the Holy Spirit. Teach these new disciples to obey all the commands I have given you. And be sure of this: I am with you always, even to the end of the age" (Matthew 28:18-20).

And, it is empowered by the great grace of God:

> My old self has been crucified with Christ. It is no longer I who live, but Christ lives in me. So I live in this earthly body by trusting in the Son of God, who loved me and gave himself for me (Galatians 2:20).

Our vision belongs to King Jesus; it's His vision for human flourishing and the embodiment of God's kingdom.

Because of the gospel, because of all that is true about Jesus, He bestows on His followers righteousness and power through the Holy Spirit simply because we are in Him. Our past, present, and future are incorporated into Jesus' grand eternity.

> God has united you with Christ Jesus. For our benefit God made him to be wisdom itself. Christ made us right with God; he made us pure and holy, and he freed us from sin. Therefore, as the Scriptures say, "If you want to boast, boast only about the LORD" (1 Corinthians 1:30-31).

Imagine with me, for a moment, how beautiful the world would be if we loved God, ourselves, and our neighbors—of different ethnicities, generations, and social statuses—through the indwelling life of King Jesus by the Spirit's power. Heaven would invade earth! Light would push back the darkness! Love would conquer hate! Those in our spheres of influence would know the Father sent the Son because of the way Jesus' multiethnic followers love each other (John 13:34-35). This is God's heartbeat for humanity.

> God's purpose in all this was to use the church to display his wisdom in its rich variety to all the unseen rulers and authorities in the heavenly places. This was his eternal plan, which he carried out through Christ Jesus our Lord (Ephesians 3:10-11).

The grandeur of God's vision for humanity realized in King Jesus must be theologically taught, faithfully lived out in the Spirit's power, and apologetically defended with love. Satan and his legions of dark powers are masters of deceit, disseminators of disinformation, and liars of the highest order. Sound doctrine and apologetics are necessary for practical Christian living.

> We use God's mighty weapons, not worldly weapons, to knock down the strongholds of human reasoning and to destroy false arguments. We destroy every proud obstacle that keeps people from knowing God. We capture their rebellious thoughts and teach them to obey Christ (2 Corinthians 10:4-5).

Love Matters

Second, to have effective apologetics in the local church, there must be a clear definition and understanding of discipleship. A *disciple* is an apprentice of Jesus who, through the power of the Holy Spirit, is progressively learning to love God and their neighbor more as they join with Jesus on His mission to reach the world with the gospel. A disciple is one who is allowing the Spirit of God to form them into the likeness of the Son of God, for the glory of God.

> All of this is a gift from God, who brought us back to himself through Christ. And God has given us this task of reconciling people to him. For God was in Christ, reconciling the world to himself, no longer counting people's sins against them. And he gave us this wonderful message of reconciliation. So we are Christ's ambassadors; God is making his appeal through us. We speak for Christ when we plead, "Come back to God!" For God made Christ, who never sinned, to be the offering for our sin, so that we could be made right with God through Christ (2 Corinthians 5:18-21).

A defense of the Christian faith without a life that bears witness to the loving-kindness of Jesus is a false defense that does more harm than good. Even the classic scripture in 1 Peter 3, one of the places where we get the term *apologetics* from, is written in the context of suffering for doing good:

> You must worship Christ as Lord of your life. And if someone asks about your Christian hope, always be ready to explain it. But do this

in a gentle and respectful way. Keep your conscience clear. Then if
people speak against you, they will be ashamed when they see what
a good life you live because you belong to Christ (verses 15-16).

The life of the suffering follower of Jesus arouses questions from those
around them about why they live the way they do. Peter sought to encourage those he was discipling by reminding them of Jesus' suffering that was
motivated by His love. Discipleship and apologetics go together like good
friends walking down the street side by side.

The word "explain" in the translation above is from the Greek word *apologia*. A disciple of Jesus, reborn with resurrection life, filled with the Spirit, and
motivated by the glory of the Father is gentle and respectful in their explanation of why they follow Jesus and embody His kingdom. Apologetics are not
weapons wielded to slash the hearts of those hostile or indifferent to Christ
and His gospel. Apologetics are holy shears that prune dead branches away
so that people can clearly see Christ, who hung on a bloody cross for their
sins. Love still works, friends.

A servant of the Lord must not quarrel but must be kind to everyone,
be able to teach, and be patient with difficult people. Gently instruct
those who oppose the truth. Perhaps God will change those people's
hearts, and they will learn the truth. Then they will come to their
senses and escape from the devil's trap. For they have been held
captive by him to do whatever he wants (2 Timothy 2:24-26).

The Body of Christ Matters

Third, effective apologetics in the local church must come from the pulpit, small groups, Sunday school, and classes. In other words, it needs to
be incorporated into all aspects of biblical teaching! Just as eating a healthy,
well-balanced meal is important to our physical and mental health, so is eating a healthy, well-balanced spiritual meal for the body of Christ, the church.
Sound, exegetical biblical theology and Christo-centric preaching—shaped
by the gospel, apologetics, and practical application—provide a nutritious
meal for the body of Christ to grow strong in love. Paul tells us,

> We will no longer be immature like children. We won't be tossed and
> blown about by every wind of new teaching. We will not be influenced
> when people try to trick us with lies so clever they sound like the
> truth. Instead, we will speak the truth in love, growing in every way
> more and more like Christ, who is the head of his body, the church.
> He makes the whole body fit together perfectly. As each part does
> its own special work, it helps the other parts grow, so that the whole
> body is healthy and growing and full of love (Ephesians 4:14-16).

Serving as one of the lead teachers of Transformation Church, I include
apologetics in the annual preaching calendar. For example, a few years ago, I
did a sermon series called, "The Bible Says What?!"[4] Topics included the following: "Is Jesus Really the Only Way to God?," "Should Women Be Silent in
the Church?," "Is God Anti-Science?," and "Does the Bible Support Slavery?"
This sermon series, as well as a sermon on taking a Christian view of sexuality, was given to our high school students when they graduated, an extremely
formative time for them. I also regularly incorporate apologetics insights and
truths into my weekly messages. And I try to share regularly about apologetics and evangelistic encounters I have with others, to model for my congregation how to lovingly and wisely engage others.

In the rhythm of feeding God's sheep, over the years, I have invited trusted
apologetics speakers to come in and teach on various apologetic topics. I recommend that local churches have an apologetics curriculum that matches the
rhythm of their spiritual formation. Local church leaders should decide on
the topics they cover, and develop systems and pathways to root their people in apologetics.

We know the church matters to Jesus because He died for her (Ephesians
5:25). The body of Christ is a chosen people, a family of royal priests, a holy
nation, the very possession of God (1 Peter 2:9) who now have the mission
of displaying the goodness of God and shining His light into the darkness.
Let us be like Jude, and recognize the urgency in this:

> Dear friends, I had been eagerly planning to write to you about
> the salvation we all share. But now I find that I must write about

something else, urging you to defend the faith that God has entrusted once for all time to his holy people (Jude 3-4).

This people, this mission, this gospel, is worth defending!

Derwin Gray played professional football in the NFL for six years. He and his wife, Vicki, are cofounders of Transformation Church, where Derwin serves as lead pastor. He is the author of several books, including *Lit Up with Love: Becoming Good-News People to a Gospel-Starved World* and *How to Heal Our Racial Divide*.

PART 2:
NEW
METHODS

INTRODUCTION
TO PART 2

T he world is changing faster than ever. We are confronted daily with unfore-
seen challenges to our faith and witness. While heroes of the faith provide immeasurable wisdom from the past, we need to have the courage
to engage contemporary issues with clarity and conviction. We must wrestle
with questions like these: How do we defend the faith online? How do we
help people through painful seasons of doubt? In an age of social media and
distraction, how do we teach truth to the next generation?

These are critical questions that every minister today must intentionally
consider. Yet these are only a few of the issues discussed in this section. The
bottom line is this: *Apologetics in our ever-changing culture must be about taking
timeless truths and applying them to timely issues and challenges.* We can do this
with the right methods and approach. If you have an open mind and a willing heart, each of these writers will guide you down a path that could lead to
a transformation of your ministry. They will help you to wrestle with creative
and practical methods for reaching a new generation. Are you ready to go?

Sean McDowell

DOING APOLOGETICS IN THE HOME

Natasha Crain

O ver my years of speaking to parents about the importance of teaching their children apologetics, one question has come up more than any other. After I finish a presentation and offer to take audience questions, the first person to raise their hand will almost invariably ask, "What book should I give my kids so they can learn all of this?"

While I appreciate the heart behind the question, it also betrays a common misunderstanding that parents have about the nature of teaching apologetics. It's seen as something too difficult and time consuming for the parent to learn, so they want resources they can give to their kids that are from the "experts." But teaching apologetics shouldn't be a one-time event where you provide your child with a fancy book and call it a day. Done well, it should be as much a part of ongoing discipleship as everything else we do to raise kids who know and love the Lord.

In this chapter, we'll look at two important principles to keep in mind as parents seek to make apologetics training an ongoing reality in their home. Then we'll explore the four key knowledge areas that such training should encompass.

Foundational Principles

Having the right mindset is a critical starting point for raising kids with an understanding of apologetics. To that end, the following two principles should inform all we do.

1. Apologetics Should Be a Long-Term, Integrated Part of Discipleship

If you didn't grow up studying apologetics in your own home or church, it can be tempting to think of it as an "extracurricular" faith subject—one that's nice to learn but isn't mission critical. Indeed, depending on when and where you grew up, learning apologetics may not have seemed particularly urgent in your own life. But the world has changed a lot since today's parents were kids. As has been well documented, young adults are leaving the church in unprecedented numbers.[1] Culture has become increasingly secular, and with the advent of the internet and social media, kids are (or will be) exposed to faith challenges on an ongoing basis. Using your own upbringing as a litmus test for whether apologetics knowledge is necessary for a robust faith ignores the fact that today's cultural landscape is radically different. Given the importance of this knowledge, apologetics can't be relegated to the realm of optional, or even the realm of occasional. The knowledge areas outlined in this chapter should form a long-term, integrated component of Christian discipleship.

2. The Time We Give to Teaching Apologetics Should Be Seen as an Investment, Not a Purchase

On the other side of the spectrum from parents who see apologetics as an optional, extracurricular subject are parents who see apologetics as a tool to guarantee their kids will not walk away from their faith. However, when we envision certain outcomes for our children based on the effort we put into their spiritual development—apologetics training or otherwise—it can result in frustration and even anger when it doesn't seem to be "working." When we pursue results, as if we could *purchase* those outcomes with the currency of our efforts, we will often be sorely disappointed. Instead, we should approach discipleship as *investors* who are free to do the job God has given us without the burden and illusion of control. With an investor mentality, we put in all we've got, then pray that God will take it and make it grow.

Once parents have the right mindset in place, understanding the two foundational principles outlined here, the next step is to have a content plan: What, exactly, is it that kids need to know?

Developing a Content Plan

There are four interrelated knowledge areas that parents should be mindful of in developing their kids' understanding of apologetics over time:

1. What the Bible teaches

2. Why believe it

3. What others believe

4. Answering challenges

What the Bible Teaches

The first part of this content plan sounds obvious. Nearly every committed Christian parent assumes that their kids are learning what the Bible teaches at church (if not additionally at home). But when I say kids need to understand what the Bible teaches, I mean much more than the Sunday school basics that Noah built the ark, Joseph had a multicolored coat, Moses parted the Red Sea, Jonah was swallowed by a large fish, and Jesus died for our sins. Knowing these things is, of course, very important. *However, knowing individual biblical accounts is not the same as understanding the theologically rich narrative that stretches across God's Word.* And it's very often a misunderstanding or mischaracterization of this broader Christian theology that skeptics (especially former Christians) promote today.

An example will be helpful in fleshing out the distinction. In a viral deconversion post I saw recently on social media, a former Christian wrote in detail about how Christianity caused her to be self-loathing. She said, "I was [trapped] in a vicious cycle of self-hatred, shame, guilt, and repentance. Bible verses such as 'your heart is deceitful and desperately wicked' combined with 'you are fearfully and wonderfully made' gave me spiritual whiplash."[2]

Thousands of people "liked" and shared her post, presumably finding it to be an accurate critique of Christianity. Yet, there's nothing at all contradictory about the biblical teaching that humans are fearfully and wonderfully made *and* that our hearts are wicked. How we are made is a fact about our value, and the state of our hearts is a fact about our moral inclinations. Although the woman who shared the post said she had spent her whole life in church, she seemed baffled at how these two truths could fit together.

So how can parents help kids get beyond the basics and to an ability to discern the error in biblical misunderstandings like this one? A few strategies are particularly beneficial:

- *Focus on reading the Bible with your kids rather than devotionals.* Devotionals can be helpful with the youngest kids, but they shouldn't develop into a substitute for Bible study. Reading the Bible itself is critical for helping kids mature into independent Bible readers who understand how to approach and study the text. You don't need a curriculum. Just set aside time each week, pick a book of the Bible, read, and discuss.

- *Equip your kids to ask good questions while reading the Bible.* The first question we tend to ask when reading Scripture is, "What does this passage mean for me?" But a better set of questions to teach kids (and ourselves!) is this: "What does this passage say about who God is, who I am, how I should relate to God, and what implications there are for my life?" Learning to think in this way challenges kids to see a bigger theological picture.

- *Teach your kids how to search the Bible for answers to their questions.* When your child asks a Bible question, don't just give them the answer. Show them how to find answers directly in God's Word. Aside from giving them basic Bible study skills, this demonstrates that they should never just accept what another person tells them the Bible says—including you!

- *Provide your kids with examples that demonstrate common misunderstandings of what the Bible teaches.* Whenever you see a social media post, news article, or anything else that mischaracterizes biblical teachings, proactively bring it to your child for discussion. Show them what it claims the Bible says, then show them what the Bible actually says. Their discernment will steadily grow over time.

Why Believe It

The first part of this content plan focused on accurately and deeply understanding what the Bible teaches. But you can accurately and deeply understand what all kinds of religions teach without believing that those teachings are *true*. That's where the second part of the plan comes in: *Why is there good reason to believe Christianity is true?*

When parents become interested in apologetics, they often jump to wanting to teach their kids how to answer challenges to the faith. (That's important, and we'll get to it shortly!) But if kids don't have good reason to believe Christianity is true in the first place, there's little reason to believe they'll even *care* to defend it.

To guide this process, I recommend using the following four-question framework to establish how to think through the case for the truth of Christianity (it's outside the scope of this chapter to provide answers to these questions, but answers are readily available in numerous apologetics books). Parents can start introducing kids to these questions when they are very young, emphasizing that God didn't just leave us to guess if He's there and if Christianity is true; He has provided much *evidence*. As kids get older, each question can be revisited repeatedly, with more detail learned each time.

1. *What evidence is there for God's existence?* Answering this question involves considering the objective evidence for God's existence outside of the Bible. Popular arguments toward this end include the cosmological argument, the design argument, and the moral argument. Despite their academic-sounding labels, each of them is accessible at an introductory level to even preschool-age kids using everyday examples.[3]

2. *Can multiple religions be true?* This is a simple but necessary logical point that connects the first and third questions. It's possible that

God exists, and no religion is true (in the case that He never revealed Himself); and it's possible that God exists, and one religion is true (in the case that He did reveal Himself). But it's not logically possible that multiple religions are true because different religions make logically contradictory claims about the nature of reality.

3. *What evidence is there for the resurrection of Jesus?* Once it's established that all religions can't be true, but it's possible that one is, we're ready to ask if Christianity could be the one true religion. First Corinthians 15:14 tells us how to know if Christianity is indeed that: "If Christ has not been raised, our preaching is useless and so is your faith" (NIV). In other words, the resurrection is the truth test for Christianity. Parents should emphasize this point and teach the historical evidence for the resurrection accordingly.

4. *What evidence is there for the reliability of the Bible?* It's not enough to teach kids what's *in* the Bible; they must also learn *about* the Bible if they're going to trust it as an authoritative source. This includes answering critical questions such as: How were the books of the Bible selected? Why were books left out of the Bible? How do we know we can trust the Bible's authors? And how do we know the Bible we have today says what the authors originally wrote?

What Others Believe

In the years I've been speaking, there's nothing I've received more push-back on from parents than the advice to spend a significant amount of time on this knowledge area—teaching kids what others believe. Parents often respond with something to the effect of, "I'm going to focus on teaching my kids truth! They'll hear enough lies from the world around them...why would I devote *more* of their time to teaching falsehoods?" They then appeal to the frequently repeated idea that federal agents don't learn to spot counterfeit money by studying the counterfeits; they study genuine bills until they've mastered the real thing. The idea is that once you know truth, you'll automatically be adept at spotting falsehood.

That sounds good, but it's a poor analogy. There's an enormous difference between studying a small, concrete bill and studying something as large and complex as a worldview. Now, there are certainly *some* falsehoods that will be obvious to kids merely because they've been taught what's true. For example, if an atheist says, "There's no evidence for God's existence!," it's quite clear that claim conflicts with what the Bible teaches. But many of the lies dominating culture today are not so blatant. Kids whose parents and churches have taught them truth for years quickly buy into secular falsehoods like "follow your heart," "be your authentic self," "you need to do what makes you happy," "love is all that matters," and many more. Many Christian *adults* don't realize why these statements are in conflict with biblical teaching; it's highly idealistic to think that children won't be fooled as long as you've taught them truth.

There are several effective ways to help kids learn what others believe.

First, study other world religions. Five of the largest religions in the world other than Christianity include Islam, Hinduism, Buddhism, Sikhism, and Judaism. Work with your child to create a chart comparing and contrasting other beliefs with Christianity. Emphasize that while there may be some commonalities, those commonalities in no way suggest that all religions are basically the same (a popular belief). The contrasting beliefs in your chart should make that clear.

Second, discuss secularism as a worldview. The predominant worldview in most Western cultures isn't one of the world's major religions, but rather, secularism—a worldview based on the authority of the individual to determine what is true, rather than the authority of any particular holy book. As I detail in *Faithfully Different*, a worldview built on the authority of the self has four basic tenets: feelings are the ultimate guide, happiness is the ultimate goal, judging is the ultimate sin, and God is the ultimate guess (meaning secularists generally believe no one should be able to claim a more confident knowledge of who God is than anyone else).[4] Teaching kids these four tenets will help them identify secular views as they encounter them.

Third, get your kids thinking about the logical implications of any given worldview. It's one thing to understand the beliefs that form various worldviews, but another thing to understand how those beliefs shape a person's life. Discuss how a person's view of God, for example, will be the driving force behind their view of morality. If a person believes a higher power of some kind exists but has not revealed himself/herself/itself, their authority for determining what is right or wrong will be the individual. But if a person believes in a God/god who *has* revealed His/their moral will in some kind of Scripture/revelation (the Bible, the Book of Mormon, the Qur'an, etc.), they'll look to that book for their moral instruction.

Fourth, proactively show your kids examples of other worldviews. Once your kids have a basic understanding of major worldviews (including secularism) and their implications, encourage them to bring you examples when they see them, and proactively bring them examples that *you* see. Once you get your kids thinking in this way, they'll have a "worldview radar" that will consistently help them discern the underlying belief systems they encounter.

Answering Challenges

Last, we get to the knowledge area that most people think of when they hear the word *apologetics*—answering challenges. As is clear from the preceding discussion, understanding apologetics is necessarily more than being able to answer a handful of challenges to Christianity. You can't defend what you don't understand (hence the importance of the first knowledge area); you won't care to defend something you don't think is true (hence the importance of the second knowledge area); and you'll know how to defend more effectively when you understand the worldview from which a given person is presenting a challenge (hence the importance of the third knowledge area).

The goal of teaching kids how to answer challenges to Christianity is to frame it as such that whatever challenge they will encounter in the world is some version of what they've explored before with you. Now, that might seem like a daunting task; after all, the challenges culture poses to Christians today can seem infinite. But it's not as hard to accomplish as you might think. While challenges may come *packaged* in a wide variety of rhetorical ways, the challenges themselves are quite predictable. Think of this task like helping your child study for a test. You might not be able to discuss every imaginable question they'll face, but you can make sure they know (1) the subject areas they'll encounter, and (2) how to think critically about the most common questions that arise in those areas. In other words, this is a test that can be studied for.

Note that this doesn't mean that you should equip yourself just so you can stand by, ready to go if your kids happen to ask a question. Preparing them to encounter challenges requires *you* to prompt *them* with the questions that skeptics pose, and then discuss biblical answers. As one resource, I've provided references in this endnote for my three apologetics books for parents, which cover 100 such challenges and answers.[5] An easy way to incorporate this kind of training is to pick a night each week, and at dinner, read a question and discuss it as a family.

While all of this can admittedly seem overwhelming to parents who are just getting started, remember that a parent's role isn't to be an expert, but rather, a knowledgeable guide. You can't give your kids an understanding that you yourself don't have, but at the same time, there's no need to wait until you've achieved some kind of critical knowledge mass to teach them *something*. Start by learning about just one topic from a book, podcast, or video—however you learn best!—and then use that knowledge to equip your kids in the same way. Continue the process consistently over time, and your kids will eventually grow up to be prepared to make a defense to anyone who asks them for a reason for the hope that is within them (1 Peter 3:15).

That's an *investment* with eternal significance.

Natasha Crain is a speaker, author, blogger, and podcaster who equips Christians to think biblically in a secular world. She is the author of three apologetics books for parents, *Faithfully Different*, and *When Culture Hates You*. She writes at natashacrain.com and hosts *The Natasha Crain Podcast*.

STORYTELLING AND PERSUASION

Brian Godawa

love apologetics. I've studied issues of defending the faith for more than 30 years. In fact, my Christianity has been shaped within an apologetic context. I've learned a lot of biblical doctrine by seeing how it contradicts various cults and worldviews. I've come to understand the nature of the faith "once for all delivered to the saints" (Jude 3 ESV) in terms of rational defense of its propositions. I've defined my doctrinal beliefs through systematic theological objections to false doctrines. One might even say I've been obsessed with apologetics and rational inquiry.

I found in the Bible a justification for my love affair with reason. Paul persuaded people to repent (Acts 18:4), and the Greek word for *repent* means "to change the mind." God's revelation appeals to logical laws like those of identity (Exodus 3:14), antithesis (Exodus 20:3), and noncontradiction (Exodus 20:16), so often it's not even debatable. Oh, and by the way, Jesus used logic too (Matthew 21:24-27).

In my pursuit of rational discourse I came to love propositions.[1] They seemed to be so clarifying, so neat and tidy, in my quest to discover truth and reality. Scripture makes propositional truth claims. God is eternal, immortal, and invisible (1 Timothy 1:17). God is love (1 John 4:8). God knows all things (1 John 3:20) and works all things after the counsel of His will (Ephesians 1:11). These are just a few of the hundreds of propositional truths about our triune God in the Bible.

I have become proficient using one of the most common approaches to defending the faith with unbelievers:

1. Prove the existence of God using the teleological, ontological, or other arguments for God's existence.

2. Prove the Bible is reliable history.

3. Prove the resurrection of Jesus Christ from the Bible.

I thought that being rigorously logical, empirically probable, and calmly rational was the most biblical means of persuading unbelievers. Of course, the Holy Spirit is the one who convicts and saves people, but my task was to provide for them the rational and empirical foundation upon which to rest their faith in a set of doctrinal propositions and historical facts.

Gradually, through an inordinate emphasis in my faith on logic and empirical and rational proofs, I had transformed my Christian faith into the scientific method. Rather than allowing my fear of the Lord to be the beginning of knowledge (Proverbs 1:7), human knowledge acquired through empirical observation and rational inquiry was the beginning of my faith. I had become a Christian Mr. Spock, preferring syllogism over story, proposition over metaphor, science over symbol, logic over emotion. All those messy metaphors, all that ambiguous figurative language, imprecise terminology, and unscientific poetic hyperbole in the Bible got in my way of clear and distinct ideas. Emotions seemed irrational and irrelevant because as all good logicians know, the appeal to pity (emotion) is an informal logical fallacy, and emotions cannot be trusted. Never mind that Jesus appealed to pity to persuade people (Luke 10:29-37). Never mind that God constantly uses an appeal to pity throughout the Scriptures (Jonah 4:10-11).[2] The appeal to emotion may be logically invalid, but it is biblically valid, and that haunted my intellect for years.

I came to realize that what I was lacking in my understanding of the faith and defense of it was story and imagination. I surveyed the Bible and found that about 30 percent of it is propositional truth, and about 70 percent of it is story and imagination (that is, narrative, metaphor, symbol, image, and poetry).[3] Yes, Scripture contains propositional and doctrinal truth, but these are communicated through story, not systematic theology or scientific discourse. Yes, the Bible includes rationality and empirical facts, but these are embedded within a more primary emphasis on storytelling. The Bible is essentially one big story about how God will redeem His people through election, exodus, exile, and eschatological return under Messiah. Jesus didn't come to teach us abstract doctrines of individualistic salvation like a wandering sage. He came to embody the climax of God's story of redemption of His people.[4]

I looked closer at Jesus' ministry. Did He teach dogmatics from a pulpit? No. Jesus taught about the kingdom of God mostly through parables—sensate, dramatic stories. To Him, the kingdom was far too deep and rich a truth to entrust to rational abstract propositions. He chose stories of weddings, investment bankers, unscrupulous slaves, and buried treasure instead of syllogisms, abstraction, systematicness, or dissertations. Jesus could do abstraction. He preferred not to. And He remained an enigma to the unbeliever. He did not explain His imaginative stories and metaphors to those who did not have ears to hear.

Indeed, stories and parables may be superior means of conveying theological truth than propositional logic or theological abstraction. As N.T. Wright suggests, "it would be clearly quite wrong to see these stories as mere illustrations of truths that could in principle have been articulated in a purer, more abstract form."[5] He reminds us that theological terms like "monotheism" "are late constructs, convenient shorthands for sentences with verbs in them [narrative], and…sentences with verbs in them are the real stuff of theology, not mere childish expressions of a 'purer' abstract truth."[6]

I discovered Kenneth E. Bailey, an expert on Middle Eastern culture, who explains that "a biblical story is not simply a 'delivery system' for an idea. Rather, the story first creates a world and then invites the listener to live in that world, to take it on as part of who he or she is…In reading and studying the Bible, ancient tales are not examined merely in order to extract a theological principle or ethical model."[7] Theologian Kevin Vanhoozer agrees that doctrinal propositions are not "more basic" than the narrative, and in fact, they fail to communicate what narrative can. He writes in his book *The Drama of Doctrine*, "Narratives make story-shaped points that cannot always be paraphrased in propositional statements without losing something in translation."[8] Claiming that the "ultimate meaning" of the parable of the Good Samaritan is simply that we should love or help the marginalized does not contain the full truth that comes only with telling the story with all its characters and emotions. If you try to scientifically dissect a parable, you will kill it, and if you discard the carcass once you have your doctrine, you have discarded the heart of God.

Because of my modern Western bias toward rational theological discourse, I was easily blinded to the ancient biblical emphasis on dramatic storytelling. I considered stories to be quaint illustrations of abstract doctrinal universal truths. But God uses stories as His dominant means of incarnating truth. And as I began to look at the Bible with this different paradigm, I saw what I did not see before with my modernist mind-set. Even New Testament apologetics is story driven.

If It's Good Enough for the Apostle Paul...

In Acts 17:16-34, the apostle Paul engages in the only detailed example of New Testament apologetics in a pagan context. So it stands to reason (pun intended) that this should be a strong model for Christians who would defend the faith. In fact, this passage has been claimed by every school of apologetics, from evidentialism to presuppositionalism, in an attempt to justify its approach. One thing most of these differing viewpoints have in common is their emphasis on Paul's discourse as rational debate or empirical proof. What they all seem to miss is the narrative structure of his presentation. An examination of that structure reveals that Paul does not engage in dialectic so much as he does in storytelling. In essence, Paul retells the pagan Stoic story within a Christian framework, and in so doing, he subverts the Stoic story and captures it for the lordship of Christ.

Paul is speaking to poets and philosophers at the Areopagus in Athens. This setting was famous for drawing cultural leaders of the day to debate their philosophy through oration, poetry, and plays. The modern-day equivalent of Athens could arguably be Los Angeles or New York as the centers of media communications in the world. The Areopagus was also the name of the judicial body that formally examined and charged violators of the Roman law against illicit new religions.[9] Narratively, Luke casts Paul as a reflection of Socrates, someone with whom the Athenians would be both familiar and uncomfortable. It was Socrates who Xenophon said was condemned and executed for being "guilty of rejecting the gods acknowledged by the state and of bringing in new divinities."[10] Socrates's death was a shame upon Athens's history. Luke suggests that memory of shame by using a similar phrase to describe Paul when he conveys the accusation from some of the philosophers against Paul in verse 18: "He seems to be a proclaimer of strange deities" (NASB). This technique of narrative analogy (Paul as a Socrates) is one of the ways in which storytelling persuades. Rationalists would consider that rhetorical tactic manipulative, but the Holy Spirit–inspired author Luke obviously did not.

Most apologists are aware that Paul explicitly quotes some Stoic poets in this passage (verse 28), but what many of them miss is that Paul is not merely quoting doctrinal propositions from a couple authors in order to be relevant to his audience. He is following, in his own presentation, the implicit structure of Stoic storytelling about the universe itself. A comparison of Paul's oration with the Stoic Cleanthes's *Hymn to Zeus* will yield an almost point-by-point reflection. In the interest of space and time, I will simply chart Paul's statements[11] along with narrative elements of other Stoic or Greek philosophers that Paul is also reflecting.

> **Paul:** "Men of Athens, I observe that you are very religious in all respects" (verse 22).
>
> **Sophocles:** "Athens is held of states, the most devout."
>
> **Pausanias:** "Athenians more than others venerate the gods."[12]

> **Paul:** "The God who made the world and all things in it, since He is Lord of heaven and earth, does not dwell in temples made with hands" (verse 24).
>
> **Zeno:** "Temples are not to be built to the gods."[13]
>
> **Euripides:** "What house fashioned by builders could contain the divine form within enclosed walls?"[14]

Paul: "Nor is He served by human hands, as though He needed anything, since He Himself gives to all people life and breath and all things" (verse 25).

Seneca: "God seeks no servants; He himself serves mankind."

Euripides: "God has need of nothing."[15]

Paul: "And He made from one man every nation of mankind" (verse 26).

Seneca: "Nature produced us related to one another, since she created us from the same source and to the same end."[16] "All persons, if they are traced back to their origins, are descendants of the gods."[17]

Dio Chrysostom: "It is from the gods that the race of men is sprung."[18]

Paul: "...to live on all the face of the earth, having determined their appointed times and the boundaries of their habitation" (verse 26).

Epictetus: "How else could things happen so regularly, by God's command as it were? When he tells plants to bloom, they bloom, when he tells them to bear fruit, they bear it...Is God [Zeus] then, not capable of overseeing everything and being present with everything and maintaining a certain distribution with everything?"[19]

Paul: "...that they would seek God, if perhaps they might grope for Him and find Him, though He is not far from each one of us" (verse 27).

Dio Chrysostom: "Primeval men are described as 'not settled separately by themselves far away from the divine being or outside him, but...sharing his nature.'"[20]

Seneca: "God is near you, He is with you, He is within you."[21]

Paul: "For in Him we live and move and exist, as even some of your own poets have said, 'For we also are His children' " (verse 28).

Epimenides: They fashioned a tomb for thee, 'O holy and high one' / But thou art not dead; 'thou livest and abidest for ever,' / For in thee we live and move and have our being.[22]

Aratus: All the ways are full of Zeus, / And all the market-places of human beings. The sea is full / Of him; so are the harbors. In every way we have all to do with Zeus, / For we are truly his offspring.[23]

Paul: "We ought not to think that the Divine Nature is like gold or silver or stone, an image formed by the art and thought of man" (verse 29).

Epictetus: "You are a 'fragment of God'; you have within you a part of Him…Do you suppose that I am speaking of some external God, made of silver or gold? It is within yourself that you bear Him."[24]

Zeno: "Men shall neither build temples nor make idols."

Paul: "Therefore what you worship in ignorance, this I proclaim to you…Therefore having overlooked the times of ignorance…" (verses 23, 30).

Dio Chrysostom: "How, then, could they have remained ignorant and conceived no inkling…[that] they were filled with the divine nature?"[25]

Epictetus: "You are a 'fragment of God'; you have within you a part of Him. Why then are you ignorant of your own kinship?"[26]

A few important observations are in order regarding Paul's reference to pagan poetry and non-Christian mythology. First, it points out that, as an orthodox Pharisee who stressed the separation of holiness, he did not consider it unholy to expose himself to the godless media and art forms (books, plays, and poetry) of his day. He did not merely familiarize himself with them, he *studied* them—well enough to be able to quote them and even utilize their narrative. Paul primarily quoted Scripture in his writings to believers, but to unbelievers here, he quotes from and uses unbelievers' writings.

Second, this appropriation of pagan cultural images and thought forms by biblical writers reflects more than a mere quoting of popular sayings or cultural references. It illustrates a redemptive interaction with those thought forms, a certain amount of involvement in and affirmation of the prevailing culture in service to the gospel. Paul's preaching in Acts 17 is not a shallow usage of mere phrases, but a deep structural identification with Stoic narrative and images that align with the gospel. He is not engaging in logical dialectic but is telling a story within a subversive Christian framework of convergences with Stoicism. The list of convergences can be summarized like this:

STOIC NARRATIVE	VERSES IN ACTS 17
The incorporeal nature of God	24-25
God's self-sufficiency	25
The "oneness" or brotherhood of mankind	26
Providence over seasons and habitations	26
Humanity's blind groping	27
Pantheism and immanence	27-28
Zeus and Logos	28
Humans as God's offspring	28
Divine nature is not gold or silver	29
Wisdom versus ignorance	23, 30
Justice	30-31

Look again at this list of Stoic beliefs and their quotes to which Paul refers. They are not mere philosophical propositions about reality, knowledge, and ethics. They constitute a distinct narrative that is a progression of events, a Stoic *story* of redemption. Zeus created all things and deserves to be worshipped. In fact, Zeus exists because he exists within mankind. We are his children. But mankind does not understand this god's nature, so they build temples and seek to serve him as if he needs them. And they are also ignorant of their own nature as having the spark of divinity, being one with the gods. But this ignorance of deity without and within humanity results in our lack of harmony with nature, with each other, and with Zeus (also called the Logos). We end in blind groping for wisdom that is right there within us all along. When we discover our brotherhood of all mankind within this deity, we become enlightened and strive to attain our wisdom and virtue. That is the Stoic *story* of Creation, Fall, and Redemption.

It is instructive to notice what Paul does *not* do as much as it is to notice what he does do. Paul uses language that Stoics and other Athenian pagans would recognize, yet he does not qualify it with distinction from the Christian worldview until the very end of the story. When Paul quotes the pagan poetry, he does not differentiate Yahweh from the Zeus of the poems. When he speaks of God's immanence, he does not deny the pantheism that Stoics would surely be assuming. He doesn't distinguish his "oneness in Adam" from the pantheist "oneness in the gods." He doesn't delineate biblical willing ignorance from the Stoic metaphysical ignorance. Paul may communicate scriptural truth, but here, he never quotes the Bible as a source. He quotes pagan sources, much to the chagrin of modern fundamentalists. And when he does reference Jesus, he never uses Jesus' name, something he would no doubt be condemned for by modern evangelists. So, just what is Paul up to?

> **Paul:** "God is now declaring to men that all people everywhere should repent, because He has fixed a day in which He will judge the world in righteousness through a Man whom He has appointed, having furnished proof to all men by raising Him from the dead" (verses 30-31 NASB1995).

Here is where the subversion of Paul's storytelling rears its head. Everything is not as it seems. Paul the storyteller gets his pagan audience to nod their heads in agreement, only to be thrown for a loop at the end. Repentance, judgment, and the resurrection, all antithetical to Stoic beliefs, form the conclusion of Paul's narrative.

Ben Witherington concludes this about Paul's Areopagus speech:

> What has happened is that Greek notions have been taken up and given new meaning by placing them in a Jewish-Christian monotheistic context. Apologetics by means of defense and attack is being done, using Greek thought to make monotheistic points. The call for repentance at the end shows where the argument has been going all along—it is not an exercise in diplomacy or compromise but ultimately a call for conversion.[27]

The Stoics believed in a "great conflagration" of fire, where the universe would end in the same kind of fire out of which it was created.[28] This was not the fire of damnation, however, as in Christian doctrine. It was rather the cyclical recurrence of what scientific theorists today would call the "oscillating universe." Everything would collapse into fire and then be recreated again out of that fire and relive the same cycle and development of history over and over again. Paul's call of final, linear, once-for-all judgment by a single man was certainly one of the factors, then, that caused some of these interested philosophers to scorn him.

The other factor sure to provoke the ire of the cosmopolitan Athenian culture shapers was the proclamation of the resurrection of Jesus. The poet and dramatist Aeschylus wrote what became a prominent Stoic slogan: "When the dust has soaked up a man's blood, once he is dead there is no resurrection."[29] Paul's explicit reference to the resurrection was certainly a part of the twist he used in his subversive storytelling to get the Athenians to listen to what they otherwise might ignore.

Subversion Versus Syncretism

Some Christians may react with fear that this kind of redemptive interaction with culture is syncretism, an attempt to fuse two incompatible systems of thought. Subversion, however, is not syncretism. Subversion is what Paul engaged in.

In subversion, the narrative, images, and symbols of one system are discreetly redefined or altered in the new system. Paul quotes a poem to Zeus but covertly intends a different deity. He superficially affirms the immanence of the Stoic Universal Reason that controls and determines all nature and men, yet he describes this universal all-powerful deity as personal rather than as abstract law. Paul agrees with the Stoics that men are ignorant of God and His justice, but then, Paul affirms that God proved that He will judge the world through Christ by raising Christ from the dead—two doctrines the Stoics were vehemently against. Paul affirms the unity of humanity and the immanence of God in all things, but he contradicts Stoic pantheism and redefines that immanence by affirming God's transcendence and the Creator-creature distinction. And most revealing of all, Paul did not expose these stark differences between the gospel and the Stoic narrative until the end of his talk. He was subverting paganism, not syncretizing Christianity with it.

Subversive Story Strategy

By casting his presentation of the gospel in terms that Stoics could identify with and by undermining their narrative with alterations, Paul is strategically subverting through story. Author Curtis Chang, in his book *Engaging Unbelief,* explains this rhetorical strategy as threefold:

1. entering the challenger's story

2. retelling the story

3. capturing that retold tale with the gospel metanarrative[30]

He explains that the claim that we observe evidence objectively and apply reason neutrally to prove our worldview is an artifact of Enlightenment mythology. The truth is that each epoch of thought in history, whether medieval, Enlightenment, or postmodern, is a contest in storytelling. "The one who can tell the best story, in a very real sense, wins the epoch."[31]

Chang affirms the inescapability of story and image through history even in philosophical argumentation: "Strikingly, many of the classic philosophical arguments from different traditions seem to take the form of a story: from Plato's scene of the man bound to the chair in the cave to Hobbes's elaborate drama of the 'state of nature,' to John Rawls's 'choosing game.'"[32] Stories may come in many different genres, but we cannot escape them any more than we can escape the use of reason.

The progression of events from creation to fall to redemption that characterizes Paul's narrative reflects the beginning, middle, and end of linear Western storytelling. God is Lord, He created all things and created all people from one (creation), and He determined the seasons and boundaries. People then became blind and were found groping in the darkness after Eden, ignorant of their very identity as His children (fall). Then God raised a man from the dead and will judge the world in the future through that same man. Through repentance, people can escape their ignorance and separation from God (redemption). Creation, fall, redemption; beginning, middle, end; Genesis, Covenant, Eschaton. These are elements of narrative that communicate worldview. And worldviews are ultimately *stories*.

Does this retelling of stories simply reduce persuasion to a relativistic standoff between opposing stories with no criteria for discerning which is true? Scholar N.T. Wright suggests that the way to handle the clash of competing stories is to tell yet another story, one that encompasses and explains the stories of one's opposition, yet contains an explanation for the anomalies or contradictions within those stories:

> There is no such thing as "neutral" or "objective" proof; only the claim that the story we are now telling about the world as a whole makes more sense, in its outline and detail, than other potential or actual stories that may be on offer. Simplicity of outline, elegance in handling the details within it, the inclusion of all the parts of the story, and the ability of the story to make sense beyond its immediate subject-matter: these are what count.[33]

Paul tells the story of mankind in Acts 17, a story that encompasses and includes images and elements of the Stoic story but solves the problems of that system within a more coherent and meaningful story that conveys Christianity. He studies and engages in the Stoic story, retells that story, and captures it with the gospel metanarrative. Paul subverts Stoic paganism through storytelling with the Christian worldview.

Another Example of Subversion

Earlier, I referred to Los Angeles and New York as a strong analogy to the influence of the Greek poets. I would like to conclude with an example of a Hollywood movie that uses subversive storytelling in a way similar to Paul on the Areopagus. *To End All Wars,* a movie that I wrote, was based on the true story of Ernest Gordon, an Allied prisoner of war under the Imperial Japanese in World War II. The story is about how Ernest and the other prisoners dealt with their suffering from atrocities inflicted on them by their captors. When Ernest arrives in the camp, he seeks to survive by protecting himself. As he experiences the sacrifice of a fellow Christian in the camp, he learns how to love his neighbor as himself. And by the end of the story, he and his campmates are faced with the dilemma of what it means to love their enemy when the tables are turned.

The film explores the Eastern, Japanese mind-set as a collectivist culture that denigrates the value of the individual, which results in grave punishment for disobedience to hierarchy. The Western mind-set, as illustrated in the Allies, is a Darwinian individualist culture that elevates the individual at the expense of the community. Survival of the fittest is its ethic. But rather than a typical East-meets-West story, where one of the views is considered superior, *To End All Wars* illustrates that both East (collectivism) and West (individualism) are wrong extremes. A higher kingdom unites the one and the many, the community and the individual, with a proper unity and balance. That kingdom is the kingdom of God.

The kingdom of God subverts both the Eastern and Western worldviews by drawing upon the value that each contains in the group (East) and the individual (West). So Ernest and the Allies learn the value of the community and sacrifice of the individual, and the Imperial Japanese, with their understanding of self-sacrifice, are shown to have access to the gospel in a way that even the Westerners do not. And forgiveness is achievable for all.

A Los Angeles faith-based initiative, Cloud and Fire Ministries, has been showing *To End All Wars* to incarcerated at-risk youth in detention centers in Southern California. The initiative is federally funded, so workers are not allowed to proselytize for their faith. But they are allowed to show the movie, which communicates the gospel and forgiveness through story to the kids in a way they will listen to. They might not pay attention to the same gospel message from some middle-class Christian preacher or suburban volunteer. As they identify the Bushido warrior code of the movie with their own gang codes on the street, they are drawn into the story that transcends all our differences and subverts the system, drawing their souls toward forgiveness. Storytelling can persuade and unify where rational debate and cultural differences only divide.

The conventional image of a Christian apologist is one who studies apologetics or philosophy at a university, one who wields logical arguments for the existence of God and manuscript evidence for the reliability of the Bible, or one who engages in intellectual debates about comparative religions or current scientific skepticism. These remain valid and important endeavors, but in a postmodern world focused on narrative discourse, we need also to take a lesson from the apostle Paul and expand our avenues for evangelism and defending the faith. We need more Christian apologists writing revisionist stories about godless deities such as Darwin, Marx, and Freud; writing for and subverting pagan TV sitcoms; bringing a Christian worldview interpretation to their journalism in secular magazines and news reporting; making movies that undermine both Western and Eastern cultures, as does *To End All Wars*; and writing, singing, and playing subversive industrial music, rock music, and rap music. We need to be actively, sacredly subverting the secular stories of the culture and restoring their fragmented narratives for Christ.

Storytelling is not just a second-class citizen in apologetics that is merely acceptable but subordinate to rational dialectic and empirical observation. Storytelling is the dominant means that the Bible uses to communicate and persuade because storytelling is at the heart of human identity created in the image of a storytelling God.

Brian Godawa is the screenwriter for the award-winning feature film *To End All Wars* and author of *Hollywood Worldviews: Watching Films with Wisdom and Discernment*. This article was adapted from his book *The Imagination of God: Art, Creativity and Truth in the Bible*.

AN INTERVIEW WITH
LEE STROBEL

Sean: You've been doing apologetics in the church for a long time. How have you seen strategies and questions change?

Lee: These days, churches are more attuned to the need for apologetics than in the past. We're facing an increasingly skeptical and even hostile culture, where belief in God has plummeted to an all-time low of 81 percent.[1] Nevertheless, there's an underlying spiritual hunger, which offers great opportunities for the gospel.

Churches still need to create safe spaces where spiritually curious people can investigate the claims of Christ. Specific questions may have changed over the years—with more emphasis on such cultural issues as same-sex attraction, abortion, and gender topics—but what hasn't changed is that many people only want to come to God on their terms, not His. More than ever, we need to help them see that following Christ is the very best way to live.

Sean: How important is apologetics training today?

Lee: It's more needed than ever because people are being inundated with objections to Christianity from the Internet. We need to address objections with *accurate* responses, since half-baked arguments for faith are sure to backfire and can do immeasurable damage.

Sean: What do you think are the biggest barriers nonbelievers have in becoming followers of Jesus today?

Lee: Some objections, such as why God allows suffering and hypocrisy in the church, remain problematic for a lot of people. But to be honest, often these are smokescreens. Many people don't want to follow a God who doesn't conform to their views on social issues or who hinders their chosen lifestyle—and frankly, when you don't want to believe, any objection will do.

Skeptics are applauded by society these days and evangelical Christians are often seen with disdain, so there's a cultural pull toward disbelief. And I do think there's a connection between the rise in fatherless families and the increase in spiritual skepticism. Whether they recognize it or not, many people shy away from embracing a heavenly Father when their earthly father has abandoned or disappointed them.

Sean: What are some of the most effective ways to do apologetics in our current cultural moment?

Lee: Relationships are key. I'm encouraged by the growth of spiritual discovery groups—small settings where a pair of Christians engage in candid conversations with half a dozen nonbelievers over a period of time. Thanks to the ministry of Mark Mittelberg and Garry Poole, we had 1,100 non-Christians in these groups, and 80 percent came to faith in Christ. Younger generations especially like to talk about spiritual matters, so let's seize that opportunity, not to preach at them but to engage them in discussions where they ultimately come to recognize the truth of our faith.

Sean: What encouragement would you offer to younger apologists and evangelists?

Lee: The gospel still works! "Let us not become weary in doing good, for at the proper time we will reap a harvest if we do not give up" (Galatians 6:9 NIV). God is still transforming lives and eternities—and now, more than ever, society needs the hope that only Jesus can offer.

Remember the biblical admonition to be gentle and respectful but represent Christ with confidence. Let your life reflect His love and grace, and keep your words grounded in Scripture. Evangelism and apologetics are the "unexpected adventure"—don't miss it!

Lee Strobel is the founding director of the Lee Strobel Center for Evangelism and Applied Apologetics at Colorado Christian University. He is the author of more than 40 books, including *Is God Real?* and *The New York Times* bestselling book *The Case for Christ*.

CAPTURING THE IMAGINATION BEFORE ENGAGING THE MIND

Craig J. Hazen

vividly remember a short play I had seen performed in a church one evening many years ago, when I was in my early twenties. I had been a Christian for only a short period of time and had begun reading works in Christian apologetics that were recommended to me by theologically astute friends. The play dealt with a theme in Christian apologetics and although I can't recall the titles or content of books I was reading at the time, I definitely remember the play.

Five or six men dressed in bedraggled New Testament-era clothing were sitting around a campfire warming themselves and speaking to one another in hushed voices. The faux first-century campfire dialogue had to do with a group of the apostles of Jesus Christ cooking up a story and colluding with one another about what they would tell the world concerning the identity, death, and supposed miracles and resurrection of Jesus. The dialogue among the actors that night went something like this:

There is nothing ridiculous in dying for nothing at all. And why should we dislike for no good reason undergoing scourging and bodily torture, and if need be to experience imprisonment, dishonor, and insult for what is untrue? Let us now make this our business. We will tell the same falsehoods, and invent stories that will benefit nobody, neither ourselves, nor those we deceive, nor him who is deified by our lies.

None of us must fail in zeal for it is no petty contest that we dare, and no common prizes lie before us—but most likely the punishments inflicted according to the laws of each land. We will face bonds, of course, torture, imprisonment, fire and sword, and wild beasts. We must greet them all with enthusiasm, and meet evil bravely, having our Master as our model. For what could be finer than to make both gods and men our enemies for no reason at all, and to have no enjoyment of any kind, to have no profit of our dear ones, to make no money, to have no hope of anything good at all, but just to be deceived and to deceive without aim or object?

The reason the play has stayed with me all these years is because it so effectively made a crucial apologetic point. When a skeptic brings up the objection that the closest followers of Jesus probably made up the miracle stories and the account of the resurrection, this dramatic presentation demonstrates in an unforgettable way just how ludicrous that idea is. Why would any of these "deceivers" face tremendous loss and death to maintain a lie that didn't benefit them, their families, or their friends whatsoever? Well, they wouldn't. And seeing this acted out by an amateur troupe did more to lodge this in my understanding than the writing of any heavyweight apologist I was reading at the time.

There is one other interesting aspect to this story. They probably mentioned this to the audience viewing the little performance at the time, but it didn't sink in for me until later. This dialogue was very ancient in origin—probably written before AD 311—and authored by one of the top thinkers and historians from the earliest church, Eusebius of Caesarea.[1] And Eusebius was by no means the first to use this effective technique.

Using creative elements to hammer home an important apologetic point is as old as the gospel itself. Although Jesus was not normally engaged in what we call apologetics, He was certainly an amazing trendsetter in illustrating His points with pithy, memorable stories. How many books have been written around the globe and through the centuries analyzing Jesus' parables—and not just the content or interpretation of the parables, but also analyzing why His parables are so memorable and effective? Jesus was obviously tapping into something very deep and powerful in the human soul when He used stories to communicate the great truths of the kingdom. Those who are called to defend the faith in this generation would do well to pay attention to Jesus (in a preeminent way, of course) as well as other successful storytellers as they use narratives to connect with and carry their hearers and readers to conclusions about the most important issues in life—including the truth of the gospel and the Christian view of the world.

The Tough-Minded and the Tender-Minded

Apologists most frequently use rational and evidential argumentation to demonstrate and reinforce the truths of Scripture. I personally have an inclination toward this kind of discourse. Arguments presented in this way were very influential on me and my coming to love God with all my mind. However, not everyone, indeed probably not most people, are moved toward religious truth in this way. Indeed, my former teacher John Warwick Montgomery divided the audience for apologetics into two basic groups. The first he called the "tough-minded"—those who found logic, propositional argument, and hard evidence to be very persuasive. The second group he called the "tender-minded"—those who are persuaded more by artistic, subjective, and emotional vehicles than by strict rational argument. Of course, he had various gradations in these categories, but he thought different approaches were warranted if you could get a fix on the basic category from which the person with whom you are interacting belongs.

Deep Myths and Archetypes

In practical terms, Montgomery never did much more than sketch out what a "tender-minded" approach to apologetics might look like. He left that to great modern exemplars of this method like C.S. Lewis and J.R.R. Tolkien. However, Montgomery, and others, did attempt to articulate why this tender-minded approach was important and effective—there was a substantial theoretical base to it, which I will not cover here. But to simplify it all, Montgomery illustrated the tender-minded approach by using one of the most familiar fairy-tale formulas known by most of us in Western culture because of Mother Goose and Disney animation.

> In the common folktale of "Sleeping Beauty," a Princess is put into a deathlike trance by the machinations of an evil Witch; impenetrable brambles grow up around the Princess's castle; and all is restored only when, in fulfillment of a prophecy, a Prince comes and raises her up with the kiss of love; this is followed by a marriage feast and the declaration that "they lived happily ever after."[2]

The archetypes are striking in this story for those of us who affirm the Christian view of the world. The princess represents the human race, fallen and unable to save herself. The witch is the devil, who wants to destroy this beauty who is adored by the king (God the Father). The prince represents a savior who overcomes the brambles and barriers to reach the fallen princess, driven only by love. The prince raises the princess with a kiss to happiness evermore. We know this story well. But so do other cultures who have never heard of Sleeping Beauty, Mother Goose, or Disney. The names for the characters might be different, but the archetypal roles they play are not. Are there certain basic characters, themes, and stories built into all of us in some way? Given the pervasive evidence, it appears that there are. But it seems that a more specific conclusion might be warranted. The basic *gospel story* itself might very well be imprinted on us at some sublevel of awareness.

The famous twentieth-century Christian author and scholar J.R.R. Tolkien (The Lord of the Rings series) took time to reflect not just on his own fiction writings, but on the culmination of the timeless myths and folktales of the past in relation to the gospel writings. Tolkien said,

The Gospels contain...a story of a larger kind which embraces all the essence of fairy stories. They contain many marvels—peculiarly artistic, beautiful, and moving; "mythical" in their perfect, self-contained significance; and at the same time powerfully symbolic and allegorical; and among the marvels is the greatest and most complete conceivable eucatastrophe [happy ending]. The Birth of Christ is the eucatastrophe of Man's history. The Resurrection is the eucatastrophe of the story of the Incarnation. This story begins and ends in joy. It has pre-eminently the "inner consistency of reality." There is no tale ever told that men would rather find was true, and none which so many sceptical men have accepted as true on its own merits. For the Art of it has the supremely convincing tone of Primary Art, that is, of Creation. To reject it leads either to sadness or to wrath...Because this story is supreme; and it is true. Art has been verified: God is the Lord, of the angels, and of men—and of elves. Legend and History have met and fused.[3]

Tolkien's friend, C.S. Lewis of Oxford (author of The Chronicles of Narnia), came to a similar conclusion in his essay "Myth Became Fact." Wrote Lewis,

The heart of Christianity is myth which is also a fact. The old myth of the Dying God, *without ceasing to be myth*, comes down from the heaven of legend and imagination to the earth of history. It *happens*—at a particular date, in a particular place, followed by definable historical consequences (emphasis Lewis's).[4]

The timeless formula that we have come to know with regard to folktales is that they begin with "once upon a time" and end with "and they lived happily ever after." It appears that there is a deep and not-so-subtle longing in each of us to reach this end, but we are trapped and in need of a prince from outside our castle-prison to storm the walls and to set us free. But in the case of the Christian faith, the great myth has been realized. We no longer look to the ever-indefinite line "once upon a time," but rather, we see the myth become reality in knowable time and space. The New Testament writer Luke began his record of the greatest story ever told by fixing it firmly in history: "Now in those days a decree went out from Caesar Augustus, that a census be taken of all the inhabited earth. This was the first census taken while Quirinius was governor of Syria" (Luke 2:1-2 NASB). Or as the apostle John wrote, "The Word became flesh and made his dwelling among us. We have seen his glory, the glory of the one and only Son, who came from the Father, full of grace and truth" (John 1:14 NIV). The great myth, that which seems too good to be true, has become part of history. It is *our* story.

If it is true that the combined weight of collective dream life, visionary encounters, and the great myths and stories emerging from human experience point toward a deeper story that captures our problem and the solution at the most fundamental level, then it is not surprising to hear some of the greatest thinkers in human history say, along with Saint Augustine, "Thou hast made us for thyself, O Lord, and our hearts are restless until they rest in thee."

The Power of Imaginative Expression

Apart from this grand and powerful theory regarding some inherent human archetypes and stories, there are other more practical issues that make appeals to the imagination a potent apologetic tool. Madison Avenue and Hollywood producers create trends and alter the way people think about important issues by wrapping their views on reality and ethics inside of compelling stories that, over the long haul, are effective at moving public opinion on these matters.

I guess a picture really is worth at least a thousand words and a word-picture or story is the next best thing to an actual visual. As Douglas Wilson put it, we need to learn to "know poetically"[5] and, of course, to communicate poetically as well. He meant by this that perfect reasoning only belongs to God. Given our finitude, we will always be dependent on the metaphorical to explain great truths and make connections with our audience. Because this is the case, we should do our best to maximize our metaphorical impact. However, the danger of going this direction is that doing bad poetry or creating impoverished metaphor is always a possibility.

We should certainly recognize the danger, but it should not dissuade us. I have no doubt that there are many among the true disciples of the Lord Jesus Christ who have anything but a "tin ear." I have contact regularly with brilliant novelists, musicians, painters, composers, sculptors, directors, screen-writers, actors, and essayists among the saints of God who have not enter-tained in a serious way how their creative impulses could best serve Christ and His kingdom. It seems we lack a tradition of imaginative expression in evangelical churches such that those with high-level talents aren't sure how they fit in or where.

The great challenge today seems to be to find a way to allow serious Chris-tian artistic, literary, and musical expression flourish without diluting or altering the essential truths of Scripture. If this fusion can come forward in a robust way, the benefits for the kingdom will be immense and longstand-ing. So how do we do it?

At this point, you likely will be waiting for a grand prophetic word from me on the matter—a word that will set a course for a new generation of Christian influence on a lost and godless culture. I will certainly disappoint you with regard to a true prophetic word, but not on the issue of setting a course for an energized synthesis of imagination and truth. My words will not be prophetic because this "wheel" has already been invented. Indeed, the very best engineers have even tinkered with this wheel over the centuries so that it spins truer than ever. Eusebius, Lewis, Tolkien, Handel, Michelan-gelo, Milton, Rossetti, Paley, and others have already shown us the way to have perennial impact.

In terms of integrating the imagination with the basic tasks of apologet-ics, what can we learn from the past masters? What special adjustments do we need to make for the peculiarities of our own time and place? I will offer a few observations in the words that follow.

Know the Primordial Story Intimately

As Christians, we are in possession of the key to God's grand designs and our place in the great drama. Know it well. It can be summed up in three (very rich and weighty) words: *creation*, *fall*, and *redemption*. Because we have access to the Scriptures, we have a distinct advantage over the world—we know the key secrets about how the story begins, the central conflict, and most impor-tantly, how the story ends. We have been able to read the conclusion before everyone else, and hence, can make decisions about how to proceed with real knowledge. Not only that, but we know our fellow travelers well. From the standpoint of Scripture, we can peer into the human psyche like no one else. We certainly don't have all the answers, but we have deeper and more profound clues about what motivates people, what sin has done to us, what people are seeking, and what they long for to fill the vacuum in their souls.

The Creative Product Has to Be Good

The influence Christians create needs to be good, but not in the sense that it makes people feel happy. Even dark music, visuals, and screenplays can move people in God's direction. Take the film *The Exorcism of Emily Rose* (2005), for example. It was startlingly frightening at certain points. But it was cowritten and directed by a thoughtful Christian, Scott Derrickson, who used the horror genre to point intentionally toward a true nonphysical reality among us: demonic powers. Even films about bad things such as drugs, prostitution, and traitorous behavior can be good if they show the true consequences of sinful behavior. I remember years ago seeing a spy movie called *The Falcon and the Snowman* (1985), which captured the deep personal pain of getting too far into illegal activities. The movie would have been a great antidote for anyone contemplating criminal activity. It was good in that it was real—it did not whitewash the results of sin.

Let me address "good" briefly from another angle. Both films mentioned above had to be good in another sense. They had to be stories that would capture people's attention, and they needed to be carried out with the technical proficiency at, or pretty close to, the standards of the profession. That is *good* used in the same way that people use the word when recommending a movie they like to a friend: "It was good; you really should see it." In order for our creative products to be impactful, they need to meet this standard. However, here is an important caveat: I am not saying that a film, book, composition, or something else needs to be "great" or "classic." I say this so that we do not get dissuaded in attempting these important creative works. It is unlikely that you will be the next C.S. Lewis, but if you have gifting or desire to express truths that reflect parts of the gospel, you should give it a try. It is risky, but as Alister McGrath concluded, "Happily, the rewards often enormously outweigh those risks. They are profoundly worth taking."[6]

Don't Wear the Gospel on Your Sleeve

One huge advantage of articulating Christian ideas in creative new ways is that you have a chance to avoid stereotypes that often shut down the unbelievers' attraction to the things of God. There are many thousands of people who responded to the gospel message at Billy Graham crusades. But what we forget is that there are many, many more who don't respond, or worse, would never dream of darkening the door of an arena holding such an event like that. The evangelistic formulas and images we use most often are easily recognized by unbelievers in our culture and they generally find it easy to sidestep them. The creative arts have the power to draw them in and give unbelievers a fresh view of what the gospel means beyond the stereotypical ideas they have been clinging to for years.

If you are writing a novel or screenplay, find a compelling element or two of the Christian worldview to weave into the story. Use a "side door" to introduce and unpack these elements. Put the most profound comments in the mouths of unbelievers or those who would not be considered pristine, Christian heroes. Have discoveries about true, eternal things made in unusual ways by characters the reader would not expect. All I'm saying here is break the stereotypes, avoid the formulas, and be creative.

Have Something to Say

In my view, this is the most difficult of my suggestions because it requires a lot of hard work beyond the creative craft that you might love. We need to have something to say, and the more timeless, the more salient, the more penetrating, the better. There is only one way to have something to say that meets these kinds of criteria and that is to read, hear, view, and experience the greatest works and ideas that have come down through the ages.

There is a reason why the stories in C.S. Lewis's The Chronicles of Narnia series have moved people at many different levels for several generations—Lewis had a lot to say. Most who are more than 20 years of age know that these are not just children's stories meant to entertain, although they accomplish that with great flair. For instance, because Lewis knew the intellectual controversies of his own day, he was able to address them in creative ways, not just in his erudite essays, but even in his children's stories. In the Narnia book

The Silver Chair, Lewis incorporated a marvelous refutation of a philosopher named Ludwig Feuerbach, who had helped set the stage for the atheism of Sigmund Freud and Karl Marx. Using a dialogue between a witch, a prince, and a couple of children, and calling upon a little backstage help from Plato, Lewis shows the absurd nature of Feuerbach's idea that God is not real, but rather a "projection" of our deepest desires. This would not have been possible for Lewis had he not had familiarity with intellectual controversies in his own day and a knowledge of timeless ideas through thinkers such as Plato.

I am not saying we all need to go out and do graduate work in classics or philosophy. Mastering some key ideas to incorporate into creative works of Christian apologetics is not as daunting as it might seem. Anytime I feel like I don't have anything to say, I start to read the works of some excellent thinkers—whether they be contemporaries or classical. I am always amazed how stimulating it is to do this, how ideas and new conceptual connections come flooding in.

If you have creative gifts, a passion for Christ and for lost people, and you are willing to drink deeply at the well of timeless Christian knowledge, the impact of your fresh apologetic work will be felt far and wide, and perhaps for generations to come. We need you to go for it.

Craig J. Hazen is a professor of Comparative Religion and Christian Apologetics, founder and director of the Master of Arts Program in Christian Apologetics, and director of the Master of Arts degree in Science and Religion, all at Biola University. He is also the editor of *Philosophia Christi* and the author of the apologetics novel *Five Sacred Crossings*.

EMOTIONALLY HEALTHY APOLOGETICS: UNDERSTANDING OUR WAYS OF FINDING MEANING AND TRUTH

Mark Matlock

I n 2001, David Kinnaman—CEO and strategic leader of Barna Group—helped me launch a research project examining the beliefs and behaviors of American teenagers. One of the most significant trends we observed was that students with a set of seven basic doctrinal beliefs stood apart from the rest of the crowd of self-professed Christian teens, teens who regularly attended church, and teens who passed a simple two-question litmus test regarding why they considered themselves Christian.[1]

Later, we conducted another survey examining the supernatural beliefs of students and found similar results.[2] Students who held to a core of seven basic doctrinal beliefs differed profoundly from their peers when it came to beliefs in the supernatural and experimenting with occult activities.

Correlation does not always imply causation, but I couldn't help but believe that students with a solid understanding of core doctrines held a healthy worldview that empowered them to live better. My practical conclusion: Teach doctrine. Why not?

But as I set out to teach basic doctrine to students in small groups, in one-on-one situations, and in larger group settings, I noticed something intriguing. Some students readily absorbed truth presented rationally but, for others, it didn't seem to penetrate their being. This made me curious. What factors differentiate those who readily absorb, versus those who repel, rationalistic explanations of biblical truth?

I began several less scientific, more casual experiments with students and found that it had little to do with whether they were introverted or extroverted, abstract thinkers or concrete. In fact, it didn't even seem to matter if they were initially open or hostile to Christianity. Rather, those who were able to absorb propositional statements of doctrinal truths best were those who were emotionally healthy.

I shared these findings with a doctor friend, and in response, he dropped Daniel Goleman's book *Emotional Intelligence: Why It Can Matter More Than IQ* on my doorstep and said I might find some interesting leads between the covers. Needless to say, I did. Goleman's work triggered a series of inquiries into groundbreaking research in neurobiology. These helped me understand more about Jesus' messages, the way He conveyed truth, and how we can communicate truth and love in community.

Hardwired to Connect

In 2003, the YMCA, Dartmouth Medical School, and the Institute for American Values hosted a symposium of specialists to ask why violence and depression were noticeably increasing among children and adolescents.

Their report, "Hardwired to Connect," looked at a broad overview of research in various fields, including new understanding coming from the expanding field of neurobiology.[3] What they concluded was nothing short of amazing, and I'm still shocked by how few youth pastors and church leaders have heard of the study or its findings.

The principal finding of this study was that neuroscience is increasingly demonstrating that the human person is hardwired to connect. We need close attachments to other people, beginning with mothers and fathers, then family, and then the larger community we live in. Also, we are hardwired for meaning, born with a built-in capacity and drive to search for purpose and to reflect on life's ultimate ends. If these two needs are not met, children cannot be expected to be healthy and to develop emotionally.

This is quite a statement from a group representing diverse fields of academia! What is more, the study shows that primary nurturing relationships influence early spiritual development, that spirituality significantly influences well-being, and that the human brain appears to be organized to ask ultimate questions and seek ultimate answers.

Because you are reading this book on apologetics, I'm sure these conclusions are hardly surprising to you. We know most people are searching for truth in some fashion because we engage people in these conversations every day. In fact, the need is so real that people will believe the most ridiculous things to have these needs satisfied. (For example, just consider some of the reactions to the Hale-Bopp comet in 1997.) But have we considered the role relationships and emotional health play in that quest for truth? The "Hardwired to Connect" report, provides scientific evidence for a biological need to address these issues, and that is significant to apologists for several reasons.

Some Emotionally Unhealthy People Cling to Apologetics and Abuse It Relationally

At the time of this writing, a preponderance of books address the subject of human irrationality as it relates to decision making. Few people make decisions based on sound arguments as opposed to gut feelings. Emotions can be tricky, but that doesn't mean we should ignore them as we employ apologetics.

As a teenager who was fascinated with apologetics, I sometimes used my arguments to announce the judgment of God and not to lovingly invite people to come follow Christ. I spoke truth, but I had convinced myself the goal was to win others over to my way of thinking, not to restore their relationship to a holy God.

So, we need to be aware of the possibility of apologetical abuse in our own lives, and we should guard against it in those we disciple as well. This abuse and the emotional unhealthiness of many apologetically bent believers have caused others to dismiss good thinking and solid evidence for our faith as undesirable. Nothing could be further from the truth!

Emotionally Healthy Relationships Help People Accept and Grow in God's Truth

Think of a time when you had a spiritual breakthrough, an experience that you might label as a spiritual transformation. It may have been your moment of salvation or a subsequent step of growth. Reflect on that event. What brought it on? It was most likely a result of a relationship with another person.

For me, when a church I formerly attended suffered a split, I was challenged in many positive ways by people to mature in my faith. The experience of mentors in my life has also led to great moments of change. For whatever reason, God uses healthy relationships in our lives to help us grow. But what if those relationships do not exist or are unhealthy?

A big conclusion in the "Hardwired to Connect" report is the need for the restoration of what the authors call "authoritative community":

> Authoritative communities are groups that live out the types of connectedness that our children increasingly lack. They are groups of people who are committed to one another over time and who model and pass on at least part of what it means to be a good person and live a good life.[4]

Morality, values, and faith are passed on through relationships, and today's breakdown of community has caused emotional blocks that keep people from receiving truth. In a later section, I'll further expound on how unhealthy relationships act as filters that keep us from experiencing God.

Some Aspects of Current Postmodernism May Be Symptoms of This Epidemic Relational Fracture in Our Society

Relativism is clearly a very real phenomenon in our culture. This shift in philosophy and epistemology could be the result of the breakdown in community, not a rejection of the concept of truth. If my conjecture has any merit, we will not solve the problem of relativism with sharp arguments only, but with well-constructed arguments *and* healthy communities that care for one another. The letters to the early church are chock-full of direction for developing proper doctrine *and* for building healthy community (particularly James's epistle). Could it be that the healing experienced by members of the early church was the result of biblical community as well as sound doctrine?

Recognizing the Holism in Our Ways of Knowing

The research supporting "Hardwired to Connect" got me thinking about how we connect to meaning and truth in a much more holistic manner than merely through the logical mind. The report speaks of "attachments," and that led me to an inquiry into attachment theory.

In the early 1900s, infants placed in foundling institutions died in extremely high numbers. John Bowlby observed that the infants in these facilities were managed very efficiently with various caretakers rolling through their shifts to make sure the children were fed and changed appropriately. But the caretakers were not assigned to particular children. They were assigned simply to the caretaking tasks, regardless of the children involved. Bowlby hypothesized that the children were dying because they were not bonding with caretakers in the way a child would with a parent.

By helping caretakers to establish more individualized relationships with children, foundling homes were able to drastically lower the mortality rate of infants. Indeed, we have a biological need for close relationships! We die without them. Since Bowlby's time, psychologists, sociologists, and neurologists have built on his initial work and are learning how the biology of relationships works.

Some of the most significant findings have led to attachment theory. The basis of this theory is that we all need to make secure attachments with others. That begins with our first caretakers—usually our parents—and then includes relationships in the larger community around us. If we can't make secure attachments, we make insecure ones, and that can negatively impact our emotional health.

These secure and insecure attachments shape the way the brain interprets life and creates meaning. This shaping occurs before the age of two, when our autobiographical memory kicks in—before we are even biologically capable of remembering anything about ourselves! Even though these patterns are formed early in the mind, they can be altered over time, but this is not easy to do.

Dr. Todd Hall at Rosemead School of Psychology has done some interesting work applying attachment theory to our relationship with God.[5] If insecure human attachments keep us from healthy connections with others, couldn't they keep us from connecting with God as well? Dr. Hall's research has helped us understand that if we are not securely attached to humans, yes, we will struggle to have a secure attachment to God.

Instantly this made sense to me. Some of my students were incredibly intelligent and even showed an interest in Christ, but they never seemed to make the breakthrough. I was trying to convince them of the evidence for Christ, and they just couldn't get it. Looking back, I realize many of those students were emotionally wounded (or even abandoned) individuals who simply could not connect to what I was saying. I now wonder if a biological barrier kept them from understanding the truth. I wasn't able to see the barrier at the time, and maybe I was too emotionally immature to offer them the love and acceptance they needed.

Two Ways of Knowing

In the first debate between John F. Kennedy and Richard Nixon, an interesting phenomenon occurred. Those who heard the debate on the radio tended to feel Nixon made the stronger appeal. But among television viewers, Kennedy was favored. Nixon had been ill, didn't wear makeup for the recording that night, and didn't look good. The difference in post-debate perceptions was skewed by the fact that, on the radio, appearances made no difference and only the words of the candidates influenced listeners. Whereas those watching the debate made judgments based on appearances as well.

This debate and a host of other media examples continue to reinforce what neurobiologists now understand biologically. We actively call on two systems of knowing to create meaning in our world. Dr. Dan Siegel in *The Developing Mind* offers this simple framework of explicit and implicit knowing.[6]

Explicit knowing is what we are most familiar with. This knowing involves our verbal language, is logical and linear, searches for causes and effects, uses words to describe the world, and is typically what we use in our right-and-wrong thinking. Explicit knowledge is what is often referred to as left-brain thinking.

Implicit knowing, on the other hand (or other side of the brain), happens without much conscious thought, and it often influences our thinking most. Implicit knowledge contrasts with explicit knowledge because it is nonlinear, holistic, and nonverbal.

Implicit knowledge drives our relationships because it processes automatically and is not under our direct control. Explicit knowledge is important, but we must integrate it with implicit knowledge if we are to love God and others fully.

In apologetics, we typically deal in the realm of explicit knowledge when we make an argument. But what is happening on the implicit level is also important if we want our message to be heard. People assess how much we sincerely care about them when we present a message, and they are quickly able to determine whether the message we offer seems to be true in our own lives. We cannot simply have good arguments; our lives must reflect the presence of the Holy Spirit's life in us.

Once, I watched two young men reenact a skit they saw my friends The Skit Guys perform. It was horrible! These two students had used exactly the same script as the seasoned performers, yet nobody laughed. Why? They possessed the explicit information (the script) but had not yet mastered the implicit information of character, timing, body movement, and interpersonal chemistry that the professionals had already acquired. In fact, The Skit Guys do some material that works only because the majority of people at an event already have a relationship with them. Take out the relational history, and the material wouldn't work. A lot more is happening than the script alone can contain.

Sometimes I feel that this has hurt us when we use apologetics to witness. We borrow the script from our favorite authors, but we don't have the lifestyle and relationship to back it up when we recite it. The arguments are solid, but the message never makes it past the messenger. As we train young people to use apologetic arguments, we must also be sure they are ready to engage others with the same love and respect Jesus displayed. We need to make sure that they have internalized the message themselves.

Two Ways of Remembering

Just as there are two ways of knowing, Dr. Siegel also described two types of memory that fit into the explicit and implicit systems.[7]

Sometimes we explicitly know we are remembering something, but sometimes we remember things without conscious awareness. Phobias are often associated with memories we have consciously forgotten long ago. But when something triggers that memory implicitly, we can experience deep and powerful feelings without understanding why.

A student I worked with refused to go to church. She would attend a home Bible study, but she would never come to a service at church. Some friends finally convinced her to attend, and I watched her as the service progressed. She was tense and fighting back tears. Eventually she got up and left.

I knew something was going on in her, but I completely misread the signals and interpreted her actions to mean that she was hostile to God. After all, she was indeed rough around the edges and having a hard time accepting the gospel in her life. Still, she kept hanging around and never completely rejected it.

In my immaturity, I never realized that her history involved some abuse by a deeply iconic religious member of her family. She wanted to believe God was good, but something in her implicit memory system triggered different feelings. She wasn't necessarily consciously thinking about the abuse when she was having the reactions, but her past and present got interwoven in those moments.

Can these implicit memories impact our understanding of truth? Dr. Hall thinks so, and he talks about attachments forming a filter that keeps us from connecting to God, to others, and to meaning.[8] Dr. Hall performed a series of studies comparing people's explicit behaviors (such as reading their Bibles, going to church, and spending time in prayer) to their implicit relational filters to determine their effect on spiritual health.[9] What he found was interesting: People with unhealthy connections to God were just as likely to engage in the same explicit Christian behaviors as those with healthy relationships to God. This means that we often measure the wrong actions when trying to determine true spiritual health.

Emotionally Healthy Apologetics

When asked to update this chapter for the new edition of this book, I was wrapping up a three-year project with Pete Scazzero and his Emotionally

Healthy Discipleship team. The project explored what it would take to turn Pete's bestselling work *Emotionally Healthy Spirituality* and its ancillary components into a teen edition. Having worked on this project with more than 40 youth pastors and their teens, it became apparent that the need to take an emotionally healthy look at apologetics was essential.

Since the first edition of this book came out, maybe one of the most rapidly emerging generational shifts has been the destigmatization of mental health. As new generations emerge, not only is there more transparency about anxiety, depression, and the use of medications to treat a wide range of clinical diagnoses, but the vocabulary and lexicon around such issues has developed as well. Yet Gen Z is widely known as being the most anxious generation worldwide. Knowing both the prevalence of mental health awareness and the anxiety present in this generation, any practice of apologetics amongst this generation that doesn't take into consideration mental health and emotional wellbeing will, best case, appear culturally tone-deaf and irrelevant and, worst case, cause us to miss a meaningful spiritual connection with a young person that would give them the opportunity to experience Jesus.

While working on the Emotionally Healthy Discipleship for Teens project, several important observations were made:

1. Many youth pastors and leaders are being asked to disciple the next generation and haven't been discipled themselves. While standing in front of a room of some of the country's top youth pastors, I asked how many of them felt they had been discipled as they were growing in their faith. Just a little more than half raised their hands. When I asked if they could name those who had discipled them, about 15 percent of the raised hands fell. This explains the discipleship crisis in our churches today. We can't make disciples if we haven't experienced discipleship ourselves. We must remember that while apologetics is a defense of Christianity, discipleship is the goal, and we are better when it's presented in this context.

2. Older generations are often having to "correct" their spiritual upbringing but younger people are still in the process of being formed. Pete Scazzero and his wife Geri have been an amazing

gift to the church, as they've revealed the painful realities of their own struggling marriage and personal deficiencies while pastoring a very successful multiethnic mega church in New York City. By all typical standards, they were a ministry to be modeled; however, there wasn't any spiritual health in their lives. The reason so many have read their books and taken their courses is that they see their own lives and ministries reflected. But a teenager or college student hasn't lived long enough to be able to always see the emptiness and link it to their lack of spiritual and emotional health. They are the glass half full, and we have the opportunity to fill it. But we cannot just fill it with content; we must form it in their lives.

3. While older generations have typically coped with their lack of emotional health by narrowing the bandwidth of their feelings and developing self-reinforcing strategies to avoid and deflect experiencing pain, teenagers and emerging adults are just beginning to understand their emotions and feelings. With adults we are trying to help them feel more; with teens we are often helping them learn to regulate their feelings and not be overwhelmed by them.

In *Faith for Exiles*, David Kinnaman and I discuss the impact of what we call "digital Babylon" on emerging generations, and why young people who stay in church do. Not surprising, two of the five practices we saw that contributed to resilient discipleship were "experiencing Jesus" and "meaningful relationships." Our research has consistently found that less than 10 percent of young people in the US, who at some time in their life considered themselves to be a Christian, met the definition of a resilient disciple. David and I wrote two words that profoundly describe the crisis today. Those words are "screens disciple." I'll illustrate this and the above points by sharing this story:

I recall a young man in my small group, a senior in high school, who one night challenged me on the existence of God. And he'd really done his homework.

Now, I had been at that church for several decades, so I'd seen this young man come to church for the first time in a stroller, and I witnessed his growing up. One thing I knew was he wasn't knowledgeable enough to argue with me on the level that he was. So where was this coming from? I noticed that he used some unique phrases, so I wrote them down and googled them later. Sure enough, it appeared he'd been going to a webpage about how to debate a theist and absorbing all he could to challenge his parents, and me as well.

Screens disciple.

What did I do? At one time, I would have jumped right in and leveled him with my amazing apologetic training. But I was wiser now, and hopefully a little more emotionally and spiritually healthy myself. First, I wondered how I could have failed this young man. He had grown up in our church. I interacted with him almost every week. How had I not been more aware of his journey?

Then, rather than answer the question he asked, for which I had an answer, I responded with an admiration of his pursuit.

"Wow. I wasn't expecting this from you. It appears you have been thinking about this quite a bit, given it's the first time you've mentioned this. I apologize if I've not noticed that you were having such doubts. Can you tell me more about your journey to this point?"

Instantly the tone changed. I didn't feel challenged, nor did I feel defensive. This young man began sharing where the seeds of his doubt emerged and how hard it was to be thinking about these things when he knew his parents would explode on him if he tried to talk to them about it. Turns out he'd been coming to my Bible study small group to "test me," to see if I was a safe person to talk to. (Phew! I can't always say I have been.)

I asked him if he had ever experienced closeness to Jesus in his life, and he shared that he hadn't. I then asked if he had ever trusted Jesus for his salvation and followed Him. He hadn't! (Imagine going to church your whole life and never wanting to follow in the way of Jesus.) I asked him if he would like to become a follower of Jesus, and he wasn't sure as he had some doubts. And at this point, the apologetic discussion began, and in a much healthier way than if I'd responded to his initial arguments.

I know some will feel that I'm putting too great an emphasis on the touchy-feely, but to reach this generation, we must change our approach. This doesn't mean we are less intellectually rigorous in our study and defense of Christianity. It simply means we must be emotionally healthy in our approach as well.

As we face times of greater uncertainty, there is a danger that the study and practice of apologetics can be a coping mechanism for our own lack of spiritual and emotional health. The confidence and certainty realized when we work apologetic questions to satisfying answers can be a petri dish that cultivates our own lack of health. It is important that we see apologetics properly in the context of spiritual formation and discipleship so that it has an effect in this rapidly changing world.

As we pursue the study and application of apologetics in the twenty-first century, we must be even more mindful that this truth we speak of is about a relationship with God that also results in a relationship with the body of Christ. We live in a broken and disconnected society where relationships are shattered. So for many people, the explicit truth of our message is not enough in itself. They will hear it only when we are also concerned about and aware of their emotional well-being. This means integrating both the explicit and implicit knowledge systems so the message of Christ can be fully heard.

Mark Matlock is currently serving as the executive director of Urbana with InterVarsity. He is also a senior fellow with Barna. Mark coauthored *Faith for Exiles* with David Kinnaman and is the author of *Faith for the Curious*.

MAKING APOLOGETICS COME ALIVE IN YOUTH MINISTRY

Alex McFarland

The gospel never changes, but the questions about the message do.

The gospel reflects the truths of the Bible. It is God's message for the ages—in fact, for every age and era. Questions about God, truth, life's purpose, and the Bible reflect society's shifting opinions and social ethic. The world, in its searching, will always have new questions. The Bible will always have eternal answers.

We have a unique window of opportunity to influence the next 50 years of Christianity and world history. The worldview of this generation will be crafted either by Christians who stand on a solid biblical foundation, or it will be drafted and shaped by social influencers with no morals, no absolutes, and no answers.

In approaching the subject of evangelizing and discipling students amidst an ever-intensifying battle of worldviews, let us say this from the outset: *Children and teens are more spiritually attuned and aware than adults may assume, and they absolutely do care about truth.*

There is a reason their generation is the prime target of the enemy of our souls. They are assaulted in their schools, on social media, and at every critical junction and social construct. The organization I am a part of has been privileged to receive well more than 200,000 survey responses from teens on spiritual, moral, and social issues. The contexts have included conferences, camps, church events, campus open forums, live radio and podcast interactions, and online questionnaires.

A robust discipleship program for young adults should have a goal of leading them to biblically informed convictions about the key issues of life and eternity: God's existence, His attributes, Jesus Christ, prayer, sin, salvation, creation and human origin, sex, gender, economics, government, marriage/family/childbearing, heaven, hell, morals, truth, church involvement, citizenship, the Great Commission, other religions, and practical Christian truth about life's purpose, stewardship, and priorities.

The students God has entrusted to you may hold positions on these topics that range from scriptural to vague to wildly unbiblical (even among youth who claim to be born again). Yet, despite times of confusion or ambiguity, I am absolutely convinced that youth want to know what is true and real—especially about God. Let's look at some ways to seize the great opportunity for spiritual mentoring that lies before us!

"Hey, Have You Ever Tried This? It Worked Pretty Great for Us!"

Before forming Truth For A New Generation Ministries and renting auditoriums for apologetics conferences, I spent 11 years as a local-church youth pastor. It was always helpful to meet with friends in similar ministries to encourage each other and swap ideas.

We used to jokingly call our gatherings the "whine-and-brag sessions." Meeting with fellow youth people, we would celebrate what God was doing in the lives of our students, pray and plan together, and generally commiserate. But some of the best takeaways were strategizing together—discussing what went well, what we could do better, and reaffirming each other in the labor of love to which we'd been called.

Allow me to share some of the practical suggestions we've used (and still do) in the quest to incorporate apologetics into local-church youth programs:

1. The vision to equip and evangelize through apologetics must be held by the ministry leadership. Leaders and volunteers should agree together on the value of apologetics for teens; there should be a commitment that apologetics will be presented, promoted, accepted, and taught within your church's youth ministry. The goal is to help teens become more committed followers of Christ and integrate their faith into all areas of thinking, learning, and doing.

2. Overcome resistance or fear of change. Don't tell yourself, *Some kids might be bored*...If you don't do apologetics, some kids may be lost!

3. Communicate the need for apologetics. Staff, volunteers, and youth must understand why knowledge of apologetics is necessary.

4. Inform students of the biblical mandate for a defense of the faith. Share verses like 2 Corinthians 10:5; 2 Timothy 2:15; Titus 1:9; 1 Peter 3:15; and Jude 3. Remind your flock of scriptures like Matthew 28:18-20 and Mark 16:15, in which God instructs believers to present the message of Jesus Christ to every age group of people.

5. Educate parents and youth on the benefits of apologetics. Share examples of well-known leaders who have been reached because of the evidence for Christianity. As you utilize apologetics-based content in the lives of teens, testimonies from your own group will become plentiful.

6. Present apologetics-oriented messages. Teach a lesson on apologetics in general or on specific topics. Lead an apologetics-oriented teaching series. Here are some teaching ideas and styles that can be tailored to best meet the needs of your group:

   - *Lecture.* This is effective when addressing large groups.

   - *Lecture with discussion.* You may want to prepare one or two questions and individuals ahead of time to get the discussion rolling.

   - *Video.* There are so many great videos out there, by countless numbers of effective apologists God has raised up. Utilize their work!

- *Panel of experts.* You may wish to host such a panel on a quarterly basis. Invite three to five people to be available and tackle a topic.

- *Open forum.* This can be a very memorable and productive approach for outreach and teaching. Planning this will be contingent upon having access to one or more persons who can competently answer the questions. A neutral facilitator or moderator should control the mic and should gently prevent any one person in the audience from dominating the discussion.

- *Small-group study and discussion.* This is a great format because the small size allows participation from everyone.

- *Case studies.* Biblically analyze a topic, individual, issue, or current event. Examples could include formulating a Christian response to Islam, researching how professed atheists left their Christian faith, discussing and critiquing the resurgence of atheism, or providing a Christian response to news items.

- *Role playing.* This can be a serious exercise with ample opportunity for learning. Have students research and argue a point with which they don't agree. Have another student respond, critiquing the other's position or defending the Christian view.

- *Reports.* Allow the teens to study a topic and give a presentation on a certain date. These assignments worked especially well with a Sunday school class of middle schoolers my wife and I led for several years. Eventually, even the most reluctant participants were *asking* me to assign them an apologetics topic that they could share with the class! Allow room for the teens' creativity in the presentations. PowerPoint presentations or drama skits can add a lot, and kids really "buy in" when they are allowed to use their creativity!

- *Worksheets and surveys.* These allow teens to communicate freely without being influenced by others.

- *Guest speakers.* Allocate a budget for bringing in local and national apologetics speakers. Several church youth groups could share the cost of one large event.

- *Apologetics conference.* Plan your own apologetics event, invite a well-known apologist to speak in your church, or consider hosting a regional event. More options to do this are available than ever before. Your church can become a venue that impacts countless numbers of youth and adult leaders!

- *Debates.* This can be an effective means of engaging your community, provided certain parameters are observed. Invest much time in prayer before committing to a debate, and make sure the right parties are invited. The person representing Christianity should be a positive witness, consistently gracious, and of course, intellectually credible. Treat the debate opponent in a loving and Christlike manner at all times. I have hosted and participated in many apologetics debates with positive results. For a debate, my personal preference is that the selected venue be a school or local auditorium and not the church sanctuary.

7. Maximize on what's happening in the culture. Whether it is in movies, trends on YouTube, or cultural or religious issues, help students engage the big issues of the day.

8. Make apologetics practical. Explain how apologetics fosters intimacy with God. Ask these types of questions with each lesson: "Why does this truth matter?" "How does truth shape the way I relate to God and others?" "How can I live differently in light of this truth?"

9. Evaluate existing ministry programs. Consider how apologetics may be integrated into existing programs. Remember: Young people *do* care about truth!

10. Identify teens and adults who have the ability and willingness to assist. Appoint an individual with leadership skills and apologetics interest to serve as your point person.

11. Identify, utilize, and invest in youth volunteers (and you'll also be

helping them to hone their leadership skills). You may be amazed at the level of spiritual depth and apologetics knowledge held by some of the teens God has put in your church.

12. Send teen and adult leaders to apologetics and biblical-worldview training seminars or camps. More options are available than ever before.[1]

13. The most important thing is to cover the teen apologetics ministry in prayer!

How can kids give their lives to the Lord Jesus when they may not even believe God exists? Youth may have a very twisted view of the heavenly Father due to painful experiences with an earthly father. Factoring apologetics and worldview content into our presentations of the gospel is now a necessity.

Common Attitudes of Young Adults Without a Biblical Foundation

Youth are growing up amidst a tragedy of *truth*, an absence of *identity*, and a crisis of *context*. They are ambivalent toward (or distrust) history. The moral and spiritual grounding known to previous generations is absent. Teens frequently describe feeling anxious, resentful, and alienated. Impersonal government (rather than family, church, friends, or neighbors) is expected to ensure solutions, security, and fairness for all.

Such summations—while generally accurate—can prompt angry pushback from teens: They are hurt and feel misunderstood by adults who "don't care." Yet, at the same time, they feel invaded when their shallow beliefs are questioned and "labeled" when adults (accurately) assess their values and morals, or lack thereof.

Adolescence is emotionally and psychologically volatile for almost everyone. That is why a biblical worldview is so crucial: It provides a stable sense of *self* and *life context*. Without God's foundational truths on which to stand, many teens today live with inner turmoil. They fear not being a part of a group, yet are resentful of being "lumped in" with a group. If *conflicted* were a political party, today's teens would hold the majority in both houses. They already have the majority in many homes and churches.

How the Questions Have Changed: "Is God Good?"

In recent decades, the Western world has witnessed changes in the most common questions and objections associated with youth apologetics. Most of our organizations, churches, and ministries have a statement of faith itemizing and defining the core truths we hold sacred and essential. Each person reading these words might phrase the core truths differently, but regardless of the denomination or church tradition, the most fundamental essential of Christianity remains the same: *Jesus, the only Son of God, died and rose for our sins, and we come to Him in repentance, faith, and a life of obedience for His glory.*

Even if many Christian teens would not use the term *apologetics*, they seek the results that good apologetics is meant to provide. In my experience, teens want to know why Christians believe what we believe. It's funny—in all those surveys, camps, and conversations at altars, I've never heard a teen say, "My generation cares more about relationships than *truth*." Never once. And yet, this is what I hear adults—often decades removed from actual interaction with young people—teach. Likewise, none of the approximately 1,250 teens who attend our annual summer worldview camps ever say, "Feelings are what convinces me of a point; evidence doesn't matter at all."

Last, a word for those who assume that good teaching in youth ministry "must not get too deep for the kids." Let me state this clearly: We *never* have students say, "Alex, please stop! Don't you know that people our age aren't smart enough to understand Christianity?"

We should not underestimate the fact that kids are thinking about dozens of theological issues. From elementary ages on up, they are capable of grasping even the most profound of biblical truths. It's almost as if the One who created their minds is the same One who wrote the Bible He so longs for them to understand. Youth are capable of understanding, eager to be challenged, and perhaps, more than any generation before them, thirsty for the truth!

Which Apologetics Issues Should You Tackle in Your Youth Ministry?

Here is a starting point: Allow teens to anonymously submit a list of their "If you could ask God anything…" questions. You'll probably come away with many months' worth of thought-provoking lesson ideas. Here are a few (of the hundreds) our staff has fielded during recent events. Some are not really questions but more observations that beg a response. All are informative:

- *How can God really hear the prayers of so many people?*

- *If homosexuality is genetic, why are Christians so opposed to gay people? Are you against people being the way God made them?*

- *Why are Christians pro-life when the world is already so overcrowded?*

- *Who decided which books would be included in the Bible?*

- *Will we know our loved ones in heaven?*

- *I know non-Christians who live lives that are as good as (or better than) professed Christians.*

- *Has science disproven God?* or *Does science prove God? Can you believe in the Bible and evolution?*

- *I am a spiritual person on my own, and I really don't appreciate anyone judging me.*

For the busy youth leader, one of the perks of ministering in these times is that there is no shortage of content ideas. If you teach on only one question per week, address the resulting questions, and apply the answers to current events, you already have around six months of lesson material! Clearly, some questions deal with spiritual issues, while others are more motivated by how a youth feels about some external circumstance. Many of their questions and observations touch on the need for providing basic biblical information about the Christian worldview.

The volume of teaching options related to apologetics is almost limitless. I believe that the spiritual darkness of our times means that today's church is ministering in the golden age of apologetics. Recent decades of apologetics momentum have brought potent resources like this one to the body of Christ for all age groups. We have witnessed the emergence of several generations of first-rate scholars. Incredibly anointed, Christ-following communicators and thinkers have emerged from all corners of the church. The platform for the truth has never been bigger and the audience has never been more ready!

The overlap of apologetics and evangelism is (finally) being recognized, and every conceivable question or objection has been (and is being) substantively addressed. Like Peter says, "We have not followed cunningly devised fables, when we made known unto you the power and coming of our Lord Jesus Christ" (2 Peter 1:16 KJV).

The Christian gospel is objectively true. We are not asking youth (or anyone) to have blind faith. As Francis Schaeffer articulated many decades ago: God is there. And He is not silent.[2] There are three main types of questions:

1. **Evidential questions:** Evidential questions can be answered from history, archaeology, facts, and undisputed historical evidence, both biblical and secular. Evidential questions include: *Have the manuscripts of the Bible been preserved without changes?*, *Did Moses and the exodus really happen?*, *Does Israel have a divine right to the promised land?*, and *Did Jesus physically rise from the dead?*

2. **Emotional questions:** Emotional questions deal more with how the question (and the answer) make a person feel, rather than whether it is fact or fiction. Examples include: *If God loves me, then why am I hurting?*, *How could a loving God...?*, *Why doesn't God prevent...?*, *Is it fair when God...?*, and *What happens when we die?*

3. **Existential questions:** When I say existential questions, I am describing questions for which the world without God's Word has no answers and no tools to find them. They ask the questions and formulate materialistic, relativist, and experiential quasi-answers in their many attempts to discover and explain two things: *Can reality even be known?* and *Is God good?*

Your Enlistment In a "Little Platoon" that Influences Youth

Chuck Colson (1931–2012) was decades ahead of most leaders in discerning that America and the West are deeply embroiled in a struggle over *worldviews*. Quoting the eighteenth-century, Irish-born philosopher Edmund Burke, Colson would challenge believers not to underestimate the good each of us can do in our "little platoons."

Within our families, churches, and communities, people of all ages are poised to be used by God. It is time we see ourselves as soldiers of the cross, ready to make a difference alongside other believers, youth pastors, and parents in the "little platoon" in which we have been providentially placed.

Leading Teens to a Biblical View of Life

I wish you and I could fellowship together over coffee today and talk about how to reach more youth with the gospel. If we were together, I'd love to hear about how God is leading you and using you. Even though you and I haven't met, I am absolutely certain of a few things:

First, you're making a solid impact for the Lord. You are! (Please read 1 Corinthians 15:58.)

Second, those in your circle view you more highly than you might realize. I urge you to "keep on keeping on." You have no idea how significant your stand for Christ is in the eyes of some impressionable person following you.

Last, let's remember that we not only *do* apologetics, but for God's glory our life is to *be* an apologetic evidence (cf. 1 Peter 2:15). Some teen is evaluating whether Christianity is true by observing how real it is in your life. No pressure! Okay, actually…*pressure!* The battle for our youth is a spiritual battle. Evangelism and spiritual breakthrough among *any* demographic must begin with prayer. And that begins with us. Let's live what we preach, stay on our knees, and intercede for this generation.

Alex McFarland's passion is growing the body of Christ and instructing Christians on how to stand strong while facing ever-diminishing morals, ethics, and values. He has researched and written on youth culture for two decades and was the youth apologetics director for James Dobson at Focus on the Family. Alex is heard on the American Family Radio Network's show *Exploring the Word* and on *The Alex McFarland Show*, which airs on NRB TV and YouTube.

AN INTERVIEW WITH
JEFF MYERS

Sean: What topics and issues seem to be especially relevant to young people today?

Jeff: Since you and I first talked about this 15 years ago, Summit Ministries has trained 600,000 young people in worldview and apologetics through its courses and curriculum. Students' number one question today is the same as it was then: *Why would a good God allow evil?* But our approach to that question (and all other questions) has expanded. Instead of immediately launching into a logical apologetic, we first ask, "What kind of world do we live in?" "Did God really create?" "Did Jesus really rise from the dead?" We use apologetics to help students see that a biblical worldview is plausible. Then we demonstrate how thinking biblically allows us to provide plausible solutions to the existential crises of our times.

We also make it personal. In the last 15 years, I've experienced a lot of turmoil and suffering. I've learned that God doesn't *send* us into the desert of life to abandon us but *brings* us into the desert of life to be with us. God hangs out in the desert. God strengthens us in the desert, shaping us into the image of His Son.

Sean: Do you think we need to make substantial changes in our approach or content when presenting apologetics to this generation?

Jeff: Seventy-five percent of students say they do not have a sense of purpose that gives meaning to their lives. And more than 50 percent have struggled with anxiety and depression.[1] There is nothing theoretical about their doubt. But where do they go for answers? The culture tells students that they can only find truth inside themselves. This sounds empowering, but it is terrifying. They know how inadequate and lost they feel.

Youth need a biblical worldview that is rational, but also one that makes sense in terms of their hopes and dreams, and their fears and disappointments.

Truth and relationship must intertwine. We teach our Summit Ministries staff to picture truth and relationship as two strands of a DNA double helix. Jesus connected truth and relationship by communicating truth while walking alongside His disciples—literally. We want our students to see—from our teaching and from the way we care—that a biblical worldview isn't just another alternative. It makes sense of everything, for everyone, everywhere.

Sean: Christians sometimes have a posture of defensiveness and fear towards the culture. When doing apologetics, what kind of posture should we take and why?

Jeff: Defensiveness and fear come from a deep-seated belief that if we don't have an answer *right now* then we must forfeit our beliefs and adopt the views of our critics. I'm encouraging students to take on a posture of patient curiosity. Jesus asked hundreds of questions in the Gospels. We can do the same by treating faith challenges as God's invitation to grow. This frees students from needing to have a snappy "drop the mic" answer to every question, and to become lifelong learners.

Sean: What is one lesson you have learned from teaching and speaking that relates to apologetics and worldview that you wish you knew when you first started out?

Jeff: When I first started out, I thought that it was my job to call students back to a purer, simpler time of innocent belief. I no longer think that way. I don't want to turn back the clock. I'm interested in identifying Scripture's core convictions that lead to blessing and flourishing even in a complicated world in crisis.

Jeff Myers is president of Summit Ministries, which equips the next generation in leadership development from a Christian worldview. He is an educator, entrepreneur, and the author of many books, including *Understanding the Faith*, *Understanding the Times*, *Understanding the Culture*, and *Truth Changes Everything*.

DEFENDING THE FAITH ONLINE: BECOMING A TWENTY-FIRST-CENTURY ONLINE APOLOGIST

Allen Parr

The internet started to become popular in the early 1990s. Between 1993 and 1996, the number of websites sprouted from 130 to more than 100,000.[1] The ability to communicate with people across the world instantly through electronic mail (email) quickly became a fascinating phenomenon. And businesses were able to freely market themselves and sell their products by simply using a website.

However, with freedom comes choice. Sadly, around that time, pornography websites quickly exploded as the enemy exploited this newfound tool called *the internet* to further his own demonic agenda. The reality is that the internet, like many other things, is a tool that can be used for good or evil purposes. Thankfully, there are many churches and individual Christians who have decided to use the internet to spread a different message—the message that Jesus can both save and sanctify.

Three Reasons for Engaging People Online

In this chapter, I want to provide you with some helpful tips on how to go about communicating Jesus' message so you can be an effective online apologist. I'll conclude by providing some best practices—"beatitudes"—for online ministry. But first, let's begin by asking the simple question: Why should Christians use online platforms to spread and defend the gospel? Let's consider three reasons.

1. We Expand Our Reach

By posting biblical content online, you make your content available 24 hours a day, seven days a week, 365 days a year. The traditional model has been to require people to attend church in order to be able to receive the Word of God. Having biblical and apologetic content online makes these resources available at *any time*. It also makes them available to *anyone*. By having an online presence, your edifying content can be accessed around the clock, all around the globe. This expands your reach from the four walls of your church to the four corners of the world. And we, as Christian content creators, trust the Holy Spirit to make sure that our content gets into the hands, hearts, and minds of the people who need it most.

A few years ago, I hopped on a Zoom call with a lady who had some questions about our online ministry. While on the call, she said, "Brother Allen, do you know how I found you?" I replied, "No, but I'd love to know. Tell me more." What she said next was shocking! She told me that she was the mother of 28-year-old twin daughters. However, recently, one of her daughters had sadly committed suicide. Everyone in her church was telling her that suicide was *the* unforgivable sin and that her daughter would rot in hell. According to them, she would never see her daughter again.

Grieved, this mother turned to the internet for answers. She typed in: "Is suicide the unforgivable sin?" and through the sovereignty and providence of God, one of my videos showed up near the top of the search results. She watched the video and was comforted that her daughter, who was a Christian before her death, could be forgiven and be in heaven! *That* is the power of online ministry. When we publish content, we have no idea who we are helping. By making ourselves and our content available for the world, we vastly increase our reach.

2. We Obey the Biblical Mandate

The Bible says, in Matthew 28:19-20,

> Go, therefore, and make disciples of all nations, baptizing them in the name of the Father and of the Son and of the Holy Spirit, teaching them to observe everything I have commanded you. And remember, I am with you always, to the end of the age (CSB).

The internet has now made it possible for us to make disciples of all nations with greater reach than ever before. With the range of new online tools, we can meet with people across the world and aid them in their discipleship.

3. We Extend the Cultural Mandate

The *message* of Christianity must always remain the same. However, the *methods* by which we share Christianity with the world must shift as the culture is shifting. Church attendance, especially among the younger generations, is declining. Many young people are quickly turning to Google, YouTube, and other social media apps for their information rather than a trusted spiritual leader at a church. For that reason, we need more online apologists to flood the internet with trusted and credible resources for people to consume. Quite obviously, people around the world are increasingly shifting their lives to ones lived online. This trend will only continue. As a result, we must shift to meet them where they are.

Five Principles for Effective Ministry

Here's the bottom line: *We must change our approach from "Come to us" to "Let's go to them."* So how do we do this effectively? Let me suggest five principles that will guide us in becoming effective online apologists.

Principle #1—Clarity

The more clarity you possess on who you are trying to reach, the more you'll be able to target your message to speak directly to a specific group of people. This does not imply that your content cannot or will not be consumed by those outside of this target group, but it gives you a good starting point for the type of content you want to create. You want to try as best you can to get into the minds of the people you are trying to reach. What are their pain points? What questions are they asking? What are their biggest struggles? What are their failures? What are their biggest fears? What problems are they currently facing?

For me, I seek to target Christians who are lacking teaching or who were taught false doctrine. For that reason, I focus my YouTube channel around answering questions that I know many Christians have. From my own personal journey, I know Christians are asking some of these questions because they don't know how to ask, or perhaps, they don't know where to get answers that reflect a Christian worldview. So I address questions like "Is masturbation a sin?," "Should Christians live together before marriage?," "How do I overcome a pornography addiction?," "What does the Bible teach about life after death?," and "How do I share my faith with my unbelieving friends?," to name a few. Finding clarity on who you're trying to reach is critical because it will prepare you for the second guiding principle.

Principle #2—Content

Now that you're clear on who you are trying to reach, it's time to start creating content. But how do you do this? Let me introduce you to what I call "the content sweet spot." This is the place where passion, proficiency, and popularity collide. Here, the first question you must ask is, What am I passionate about? In other words, what are the topics that excite you the most? Create a list of those subjects. Second, ask yourself, What am I proficient in? Or you may ask, What can I become proficient in relatively quickly? There are many subjects you could discuss online, but the ones you will be best at addressing are the areas in which you are a SME (Subject Matter Expert). Once you're clear on your passion and proficiency, it's time to consider the third question, which is: What is most popular to my audience? In other words, what are they hungry to know about?

Now, allow me to caution you on two very critical mistakes that many content creators make. The first one is we either err on the side of passion or on the side of popularity. Neither is ideal to reach the people you want to reach. Let me explain.

If you focus exclusively on your passions, it may result in your content being irrelevant and disinteresting to your audience. For instance, if I do a one-year study on the book of Haggai in the Bible (sorry, Brother Haggai), there may be a subset of my audience who would be interested, but the majority don't see understanding Haggai as a pain point in their lives.

On the contrary, if you focus solely on what's popular, then you run the risk of creating content that chases vanity metrics such as views, downloads, subscribers, ad revenue, etc. While these metrics are necessary to track the growth of your online ministry, they should not be used exclusively to drive your content creation decisions. You must be led by the Holy Spirit as you select and create your content. There will be times when you'll create content you're not very passionate about, but it is popular. There will also be times when you'll create content that is not very popular, but it's something you're passionate about and proficient in and people just need to hear it. Your ideal content will develop when passion, proficiency, and popularity are in balance.

The second caution to consider about content is whether or not it is value-added. When people see your video, listen to your podcast, read your blog post, or otherwise view your online content, do they immediately think, *Ooo, this is really going to help me*? Content that communicates value for the audience is ideal.

Principle #3–Creativity

Now that you've chosen the content you want to deliver to the world, it's time to package and produce it well. How your message is packaged and produced can make all the difference in how it will be received. Is it delivered in such a way that it will maintain the attention of your viewer, reader, or listener? Let me give you an example of this. Not too long ago, on my YouTube channel, I did a series in which I taught through the book of 1 Corinthians. Now, I could have titled it "A Study on 1 Corinthians," but I knew that may not have attracted my audience. So instead, I entitled it "Church Gone Wild: A Modern-Day Look at the Wildest Church Ever!"

Your packaging is essential! This is where online and offline ministry diverge. When people attend church, they choose to pass through the doors and, more than likely, will stay until the end, even if the sermon is bad. Not so with online content. People have an infinite number of choices in terms of what content they will consume. And even when they *start* to consume it, they can always decide to click it off or simply browse to a different website or video. This is why we must work even harder to be creative in our approach to online apologetics. Be creative with the title, the thumbnail(s), the pacing, the editing, etc. This is especially important if your audience has a shorter attention span. You'll need to work hard at being creative in your approach.

Principle #4—Commitment

This principle is not unique to online ministry, but it's critical, nonetheless. One of the reasons many online ministries fail is because the online minister is oftentimes not truly committed to doing the necessary work that is required to grow themselves and their ministry. This becomes evident when creators don't experience the explosive viral growth they initially hoped for. Oh, how thankful I am that didn't happen to me. Why? Because what I learned during the process of growing is priceless!

In my first year on YouTube I published 52 videos (one a week). After one year, I had amassed a whopping 1,564 subscribers. I earned $0 in revenue and most of my videos were averaging around 100-200 views. Had I not been committed to what I knew God had called me to do, I would have given up right then and there, especially with the temptation to compare myself and my growth to other online ministers. But this is why it's critical for you to get back to your proverbial *why?* Why did you get started with your online ministry to begin with? For me, it wasn't to go viral, but to create a library of content that would be available online for many generations to come for all who would need it.

So instead of focusing exclusively on vanity metrics and online growth, what should we be committed to? Video content is quickly becoming the fasting growing online content. For that reason, let me suggest a few things you should commit yourself to. Focus on choosing better topics that interest your audience. Focus on becoming a better speaker in front of the camera (even if your primary media is not videos). Focus on being more creative in terms of how you package your content. Focus on how you can improve the quality of the content you publish (audio, video, research, writing, editing, etc.). Focus on being more consistent with publishing content to your platform of choice. Focus your commitment on these things and you'll have a higher likelihood of seeing growth in your online ministry.

Principle #5—Connection

Now that you are a content creation machine, it's time that you focus on making a genuine and authentic connection with those who consume your content. This is not an essential step, but it is extremely helpful. In the world of marketing, there is something called the Know-Like-Trust factor. The more people *know* you, the more they begin to *like* you, and ultimately grow to *trust* you. One of the ways you can increase the KLT factor is through the content you post on social media. Mix in some personal content so that the people who consume your platform content see you as a real person that they actually *like*. When they like you and you've established yourself as an authority, it increases the possibility that they will be longtime supporters of your online ministry and trust you to deliver content to them that will help them in their spiritual growth. You can do this through personal posts online; taking prayer requests; responding to comments, direct messages (DMs), and emails; doing live streams, Q-and-A sessions, webinars, personal testimonies, and Ask-Me-Anything sessions (AMAs); and so much more.

Helpful Attributes to Take to Heart

Now that I've identified reasons to engage people with the gospel online and provided some helpful principles for becoming an effective online apologist, let's briefly consider some best practices, or "beatitudes" for online ministry.

Be Prepared

When you create content, specifically online content, you are opening yourself up to a world of criticism—literally. For that reason, make sure you are well prepared to defend your position because the critics will surface. I've found that people are much bolder online than they would ever be offline. You will be called names. People will make content in response to your content. You will oftentimes be misrepresented by others who don't agree with you. This is why it is extremely important that you are thorough in how you present your content. Anticipate the questions people will ask. Think ahead about the potential pushback that will be launched from those who don't agree with your position and how you can address that in your content. Be prepared!

Be Gracious

As important as it is to be prepared, I encourage you to be gracious and kind to those who disagree with you. I have had to apply this principle countless times in my online ministry. The temptation will be to respond to negativity in a way that is not godly. I mean, we are all human, right? We take our content seriously and work hard at our craft, and it's difficult when people online seek to attack you, your character, and your ministry. This is when you must respond in love and grace.

I love Peter's advice found in the signature verse on apologetics in the New Testament. He said, in 1 Peter 3:15-16,

> You must worship Christ as Lord of your life. And if someone asks about your hope as a believer, always be ready to explain it. But do this in a gentle and respectful way. Keep your conscience clear. Then if people speak against you, they will be ashamed when they see what a good life you live because you belong to Christ.

As apologists, we love to focus on verse 15, but verse 16 is essential if we want to be heard. We must respond in a gentle and respectful way. If we don't, we've already lost the critic's heart.

Another reason responding in love and grace is critical is because it models for those who may see your responses how you should respond to negativity as a Christian. People who are both inside and outside of your audience are watching. Every time you respond to a negative comment, you have the opportunity to model patience, love, and gentleness.

Be Humble

When you begin to experience a level of "success" as you build and grow an online platform, it's easy to start getting a big head. It's easy to start deriving your identity from the success you're experiencing. It's easy to think, *Because*

I got one million views on this single video, I must be the best! It's also easy to think that you are always right, and that there is no more room to grow in your understanding. *Always* remember that whatever "success" you may have is because God allowed you to experience it. And, as the Bible reiterates, in James 4:6, "God opposes the proud but gives grace to the humble."

Be Grateful

One of the pitfalls we all must be aware of is the pitfall of comparison. I've personally struggled with this in my own online ministry. Instead of focusing on what God is doing in and through my own ministry, I am tempted to take my eyes off Him and look to what God is doing (or what I perceive He's doing) in other people's ministries. The quickest way to experience discouragement and even, at times, depression in relation to your online ministry is to compare yourself to others.

The writer of Ecclesiastes warned us against this when he said,

> I observed that most people are motivated to success because they envy their neighbors. But this, too, is meaningless—like chasing the wind (Ecclesiastes 4:4).

Be intentional about spending some time thanking God for the reach and the impact He has given you with your online ministry. Learn to celebrate every milestone with gratitude and joy. I have more than 1 million subscribers today (by the grace of God), but I celebrated just as much when I passed the milestone of my first 100 subscribers.

Be Flexible

The Bible says, "Blessed are the flexible, for they shall not be bent out of shape," *right?* Well, maybe the Bible doesn't say that, but it's a good principle to live by. Be willing to adjust your strategy as you gather more information and gain more experience. As you learn more about the platform you're posting on, what your audience is interested in, what your interests are—whatever the case may be—be willing to make changes.

Also, be sure to pay close attention to your analytics so you can create content that will perform well, maximize your reach, and strengthen your impact. Be open to experimenting with different types of content. Don't get so committed to what you're doing that you remain closed to trying new things.

Be Balanced

Burnout in ministry is a real thing. I encourage you to be wise and balanced in how you approach your online ministry. As you begin to see explosive growth, the temptation will rise up to make this the number one priority in your life. And you'll justify it because, after all, it's for the kingdom. Be sure that other areas of importance receive the attention they deserve. Nothing is more important than your relationship with God and your family. And you need to be at your best physically, emotionally, and spiritually to lead others. For that reason, guard yourself against burnout.

》》 》》 》》

Becoming an effective online apologist in the twenty-first century requires knowledge, the right skills, a commitment to excellence and progress, and a heart that is committed to the Lord and advancing His kingdom through online media. I encourage you to remember that we are all on a continuum of growth. Where you are at today should not be where you're at a year from now. First and foremost, continue to grow and progress in your relationship with God and let that trickle over into your ministry, because ministry is at its best when it's done out of the overflow of your time with God and not on your reserves.

> **Allen Parr** is an author, speaker, YouTuber, and former pastor. He cofounded Let's Equip with his wife, Jennifer, and his YouTube channel is *The BEAT* with Allen Parr. He is the author of *Misled: 7 Lies That Distort the Gospel (and How You Can Discern the Truth)*.

HELPING PEOPLE THROUGH DOUBT

Bobby Conway

oubt can hurt and doubt can help. Doubt can hurt us if we doubt the truth. And doubt can help us if we doubt untruth. So doubt can be good and doubt can be bad. Doubt is good when it leads us to truth, and doubt is bad when it leads us away from truth. There is a type of doubting that blinds us to truth, and a type that opens our eyes to truth.

Doubt is common. According to a recent Barna study, 52 percent of US adults and teens have experienced religious doubt in the past few years.[1] If you're currently cast under the spell of doubt, you want to be under the *right* spell. One where your doubts lead you to truth. But even in that space, where our doubts are directed toward truth, they can still sting. That's because doubt splits the mind as it seemingly drives a wedge between us and God. Doubt is ruthless and no respecter of persons as it bores a deep hole of confusion into our once-vibrant trust in God. There's a viciousness to doubt that, left unaddressed, can cause us to experience all sorts of mental, emotional, physical, and spiritual torment. Unchecked, doubt can ultimately undo us, sapping us of all hope and leading to despair.

That is why doubts can be so torturous.

Yes, doubts can be a straight-up doozie, especially when you can't get past them—when you remain stuck, or even worse, when you find yourself sinking deeper into the suffocating quicksand of losing your faith altogether. *For some people, doubts come and go, but for others, doubts come and grow.* And this is where doubt can really do its number on the doubter, wearing them flat out and vexing them *beyond belief.* That's because as doubts multiply, the doubter can feel like their faith is slipping away. Like a disease that metastasizes, doubt spreads itself out and seeks to render the final deathblow of apostasy to the once fervent-hearted believer.

If you've never heard the agony of a doubter and despair of a near apostate, I would like to provide you a glimpse. In 2013, I received an email from Jane,[2] a teenage girl in the final stages of doubt—marked by depression, despair, and nearly ready to depart. Here's what she wrote:

> Hello Bobby, my name is Jane Doe. I'm a seventeen-year-old Christian. I've been a Christian for many years. I've always had God inside of me keeping me comforted. There's always been that comfort inside of me. But lately, I've been in what I would call a "crisis of belief." Lately, I've been having doubts in my head about the Bible and what it says. For example: How's it physically possible for one to rise from the dead? Is it really God or is it all in my head? Why isn't God there to help me when I really need Him? Doesn't the Bible have Scripture saying that He will help? Sometimes the doubts are statements that electrocute my mind and belief, such as: "You're wasting your time." Or "You're believing a fantasy," and "It's only a part of your brain that makes you believe."

> …But it's not like I want to believe these doubts. Because when I think of them, something burns in my heart and mind. My depression begins to act up badly. Lately, I've had many anxiety attacks about it along with other stress. It's not helpful when atheists surround me in my school too. There really aren't many people I can ask for help. So, I'm asking you. What do I do? Because I'm scared to say I'm lost.

Can you sense her agony, emptiness, confusion, and split mind? Of course, I responded, but unfortunately, I never heard back. And many times, I've wondered how Jane turned out. What's obvious is that by the time Jane pressed send, her doubts all but appeared to be applying the final touch of full-fledged apostasy. I don't know about you, but if you've ever found yourself wandering through the agonizing land of doubt, then you know how hard it can be to find your way out. Sadly, there are many other teens out there suffocated by doubt who don't know where to turn.

If there is one thing that is true about doubt, it's this: Empathy goes a long way when *helping people through doubt.* As Jude reminds us, "Have mercy on those who doubt" (Jude 22 ESV). When we bypass the heart, we'll fail to connect. When we bypass the head, we'll fail to correct. We need a head-and-heart approach to helping doubters. That said, there's no one-size-fits-all approach to helping doubters. That's because everyone is different, which means we need to listen carefully to people's doubts so we can tailor the best approach to each person we seek to help.

Eight Practical Ways to Help Doubters Through Doubt

In the remainder of this chapter, we'll do just that. By listening more closely to Jane's email, we'll consider a customized approach by unpacking eight practical ways to help doubters through doubt, after which I'll end the chapter by giving three concluding thoughts for those currently journeying through a season of doubt.

First, if someone reaches out to you for help, validate the courage it took to ask for help.

Jane did the right thing. She reached out for help. As she said, "There really aren't many people I can ask for help. So, I'm asking you." And I'm glad she did. Regrettably, sometimes people don't know where to turn when they're battling doubt. More regrettably, some Christians have been taught to never doubt. But *think* about that. Unexpressed doubt is still doubt, right? Therefore, isn't it better to have expressed doubt that can at least be addressed than for someone to suffer from unexpressed doubt? It's hard to address what's unexpressed. And unexpressed doubt doesn't go away just because the doubter remains silent. That said, when a doubter expresses their doubt to us, we can consider it a tremendous honor that they are willing to be vulnerable enough to entrust us with his or her pain. I'm thankful Jane turned to me for help. While I don't know if my reply ever did, I do recognize that she was courageous to reach out, and I wanted her to know that.

Second, realize that Christians aren't immune to doubt.

Jane admitted, "I've been a Christian for many years." Perhaps her confusion was tethered to the idea discussed above that Christians aren't supposed to doubt. I don't know. But I do know this: Doubt doesn't discriminate. Doubt isn't a Christian problem. It's a human problem. And in the absence of certainty, the question remains: Which worldview best closes the doubt gap? To walk away from Christianity is to walk into another worldview that is all too ready to greet you with a new set of doubts. As I've often said, if Adam and Eve could doubt in Paradise, how much more are we susceptible to doubt living in Paradise Lost? Doubt is no stranger to the characters in the Bible. Scripture is replete with doubters, from Adam and Eve, to Abraham, the psalmists, Habakkuk, Zechariah, John the Baptist, Thomas, and many others.

Third, don't underestimate the angst doubters feel by not sensing God's presence.

You can sense Jane's bewilderment: "I've always had God inside of me keeping me comforted." But where did that go? That sense of *with-ness* she once knew hung over her like a fleeting memory. That's because her life had been disrupted by doubt. Doubt does that. It unsettles us. And that's no way to live. Without resolve, doubts eventually lead to what Jane described as a "crisis of belief." Hence, the reason her comfort was all but a memory. It's hard to feel comfort during a crisis, but it's also hard not to end up in a crisis if we always expect comfort.

When doubt settles in, comfort turns to discomfort. Peace turns to panic. Calm turns to chaos. Clarity turns to confusion. We go from sensing God's presence to wondering if He's present at all. And that's all part of the agony for the doubter. We can't underestimate the existential pain the doubter experiences. The person who walks away from Christianity without first feeling flayed through the process of doubt is a person who never had an intimate relationship with Christ to begin with. You won't find the true Christian celebrating their doubts. No, they will loathe them. And like Jane, they will long for God's comforting presence once again.

Fourth, identify the type of doubt inflicting the doubter.

Jane had a growing list of doubts. As you will recall, she had questions about the resurrection, existence of God, unanswered prayers, and the Scriptures.

I appreciated her list of questions because it helped me decipher the type of doubt she struggled with the most. When it comes to doubt, there are different types. There are *moral doubts*, where what God's Word says about a moral issue is now under debate. There are *emotional doubts*, where someone struggles to reconcile why God allows suffering. There are *spiritual doubts*, when that ancient serpent, the devil, seeks to dismantle faith as he whispers, "*Has* God said?" There are *volitional doubts*, when one doubts God's plan for their life. And there are also *intellectual doubts*, when one's doubts can turn suspicious and cynical of truly ever finding resolution.

While there's nothing wrong with a little skepticism, we want the right kind. When our skepticism causes us to be suspicious of truth, then we should be skeptical of our skepticism. For Jane, it's clear. The type of doubt that she was primarily suffering from was *intellectual doubt*. And you can see why. For she said, "It's not helpful when atheists surround me in school." Perhaps they even instigated some of her doubts, which were also emotionally depleting her.

If you're helping someone through doubt, or personally twisted up by doubt yourself, let me encourage you to write your doubts down on paper by creating a mind map. This can be a helpful exercise, allowing you to hone in on the type of doubt most in need of attention. To do this, begin by writing down the five types of doubt mentioned above (i.e., moral, emotional, spiritual, volitional, and intellectual) and circling each of them. Pick one type to start with, and list the statements or questions that reflect your doubts within that category of doubt, circling them and connecting them back to the primary category. Follow that same process for the remaining four types of doubt. Once you're finished, you'll have a mind map, featuring a clear and unique picture of the types of doubt that are pestering you the most. From there, rank your doubts from 1-5, with 1 being the weakest felt and five being the strongest. Following this exercise, develop a plan with someone else to begin seeking answers to these doubts, starting with the most important ones first.

Fifth, discern the difference between authentic doubt and antagonistic doubt.

Some people doubt simply to doubt. Perhaps they possess a superiority complex that enjoys sitting in intellectual judgment over Scripture. Others hate their doubts. They aren't looking for doubts, but rather, doubts find them. Somewhere along the way they find themselves bumping into questions that they struggle to reconcile, which, in turn, develop into doubts. Antagonistic doubters celebrate their doubts to move beyond their faith, whereas authentic doubters confront their doubts to resolve them. When we think about Jane, it's evident that her doubts weren't antagonistic, but rather, she authentically desired resolution. The problem was that her doubts were metastasizing and overwhelming her to the point of despair. What she needed were some solid answers to help assuage her doubts. Fortunately, the questions she had aren't hard to answer. And yet, unfortunately, she didn't know where to find the answers.

Sixth, understand the toll doubt can take on one's mental health.

As Jane so aptly put it, "It's not like I want to believe these doubts. Because when I think of them, something burns in my heart and mind. My depression begins to act up badly. Lately, I've had many anxiety attacks about it along with other stress." Can you sense the toll her doubts were taking on her? It's obvious she didn't love her doubts; she loathed them. These doubts hijacked her peace. As she said, her heart and mind *burned* torturously when she thought of them, and the catastrophic result was that, unaddressed, her doubts sunk her into a hard-core depression, anxiety attacks, and other various forms of stress. There's no other way to put it—this young lady was living in torment.

When it comes to doubt, there is a certain personality type that can receive an extra barrage of jabs in the ring of battling doubt. I'm referring to the *obsessive analyzer*. Typically, this person has OCD tendencies that attach to the doubter and are brutal to ward off. While some people are analytical, they can unlock from their thoughts. And while others might be obsessive, it doesn't necessarily show up in the form of existential doubts. The doubter with this personality makeup may want to talk with a counseling expert about whether to seek out therapy to treat any underlying issue of OCD that contributes to their doubt.

Here's the issue: Often the obsessive analyzer demands certainty. But demanding certainty is a fool's errand. Why demand something we can never obtain? If there is one thing we can all be certain of, it's that no one can be certain about all the details of *anything*. I'll show you what I mean, but first, I need you to grab a cup. Are you ready? Alright, I am going to ask you a series of questions. How many total ounces have been consumed from this cup in its lifetime? How many people have used it? How many different types of fluids have been poured into it? How many dust particles are on it now? Or have been throughout its existence? What was the cup before it was a cup? Okay, I trust you get my point. And it's this: If we can't be certain about some of the ins and outs of a simple cup, what makes us think we can demand certainty of God? What we are after is reasonable evidence. And Christianity *certainly* provides that. Pun intended. Confidence, not certainty, is what we are looking for, and confidence is strengthened by considering the evidence on offer.

Seventh, be ready to point doubters to a solid Christian community.

As we saw above, Jane was surrounded by atheists, which was wearing on her. She admitted, "It's not helpful when atheists surround me." It's not that Christians are supposed to live quarantined from the world, but they should establish and maintain relationships with a solid group of believers who they can share their doubts with when others challenge their faith. Sadly, this type of community is hard to come by in many churches. And bouncing one's doubts off the wrong person may turn out to be a demoralizing experience, especially if the person ridicules or shames the believer for having doubts. A better posture is empathetic listening while validating the pain the doubter is experiencing. If you don't know what to say, no problem—just be a friend who walks alongside the person who is in doubt.

Make no mistake. Some doubt is so severe that it will require qualified experts to walk with people through the complexities of their doubt. That's why pastors must foster a process in their local bodies to help doubters, while also leaning on some key, solid leaders who are apologetically equipped and relationally tactful, to help doubters navigate their way out of the labyrinth of doubt.

Eighth, help the doubter to refuse to throw in the towel.

The last part of Jane's email was jarring; she wrote, *"I'm scared to say I'm lost."* Perhaps the reason I was so touched by Jane's email is because I could relate to her affliction all too well. I can attest that my doubts brought me to the breaking point, landing me a seat in counseling, along with a prescription in hand for antidepressants. Suicidal ideation was no stranger, but in the end, neither was God. Fortunately, He saw me through.

When I reflect on that season all these years later, I stand amazed at God's faithfulness to guide me home again. And today, I can honestly say that I am no longer afflicted by doubts, nor do I panic when a doubt comes my way. Even more, I can now see the value that having these doubts produced in my life by giving me greater empathy for doubters, while also allowing me to write two books birthed out of my despair in order to help others. These books are *Doubting Toward Faith* and *Does Christianity Still Make Sense?* While I couldn't give Jane a hard timeline for her doubts, I could assure her that if she persevered by refusing to throw in the towel, God would eventually bring her out the other side—*stronger.*

Concluding Thoughts for the Journey

Having spent a considerable amount of this chapter unpacking Jane's email and showing what a customized approach might look like to help a doubter through their doubt, I'd like to end the chapter by offering three concluding thoughts for those journeying through a season of doubt.

1. Embrace a Big-Box Christianity

Some people want to be as conservative as they can be about their conservativism, but I seek to be as liberal as I can be about my conservativism, without slipping into heresy. When we are as conservative as we can be about our conservativism, we inevitably alienate true believers. But when we are as liberal as we can be about our conservativism, we don't isolate ourselves from others who truly believe. Embracing a big-box Christianity means welcoming people to the table of fellowship who hold alternative perspectives that aren't deal breakers to *mere* Christianity.

2. Don't Commit to Theological Positions too Quickly

Committing to theological positions prematurely sets us up for a future crisis of faith that will occur the moment we encounter views that challenge the positions we previously embraced. Instead, take some time to understand the various viewpoints before committing to one. That way, you'll have a greater confidence about your theological commitments. This takes time. So enjoy learning and don't try to conquer your studies simply to finish them. Be transformed by the process. And, remember, theological development is a journey, not a checklist.

3. Keep Your Eyes on the Big Picture

As you journey through the various theological landscapes, keep your eyes on the big picture of Christianity. And it's this: We're to love God, love people, and celebrate the gospel. That's living in the *Great Commandment* (Matthew 22:37-39) and the *Great Commission* (Matthew 28:18-20).

During a season of doubt, we often complicate the simple gospel. It's freeing to remember that the early church was busting at the seams, and they were doing so without a New Testament that was written down. Sure, they had apostolic oversight, but they weren't bogged down with 2,000 years of church history to wade through. It's a lot. So take a deep breath, embrace a little mystery, recall past special moments when you've encountered God, and keep your eyes on the big picture, my friend.

He's got you!

Bobby Conway is the lead pastor of Image Church in Charlotte, North Carolina. He is the host of the YouTube channel *Christianity Still Makes Sense*, and he cohosts the nationwide call-in radio program *Pastor's Perspective*. He is also the author of several books, including *Doubting Toward Faith* and *Does Christianity Still Make Sense?*

TAKING THE OTHER PERSPECTIVE

Tim Muehlhoff

You finally sat down to talk with a family member or coworker who you knew held different beliefs than you. You suspected there would be a clash of opinions but weren't prepared for the deep divisions that arose. Your view of politics, social issues, and God couldn't be further apart. The longer the conversation went, the more emotions crept to the surface and the volume of your speech rose. Now that the conversation is over, how should you proceed? You ask yourself the question, *What now?*

The answer will depend on what type of communication you choose to adopt. A *transmission* view of communication has the imparting of information as its goal; while a *ritual* view seeks to establish points of commonality with others. If you adopt a transmission view, then the next conversation will entail attempting to share new or perhaps more persuasive facts with your family member or friend. The problem is that while you are speaking, the other person is already thinking of facts that counter your view. Competing websites, experts, blogs, or news sources seem to cancel each other out. In the end, a type of informational stalemate emerges. Why talk about an issue if you can't even agree on the facts?

Conversely, a ritual view of communication starts in a different place and asks the questions: Even in the midst of our disagreements, how are we similar? and What common bonds can be formed? This view predates the transmission view and is linked to terms such as *shared experiences, association, fellowship, commonality, participation*, and most importantly, *cultivating bonds* with others.

In today's world of competing facts, I suggest that we adopt a ritual view *before* moving to sharing facts with others. In no way am I attempting to diminish the importance of imparting information or sending messages. After all, the New Testament is replete with examples of the importance of sharing the gospel message, Christian doctrine, and apologetical proofs. We need to be ready to impart, or transmit, the Christian perspective about a host of pressing issues, such as racial tensions, confusion over sexuality and gender, shifting definitions of marriage, maintaining God's provision in a world full of suffering, and so on. The transmission of biblical convictions will always be paramount to the Christian witness. However, in today's often hostile communication climate, this view runs into two pressing problems.

First, those interested in apologetics can become so full of facts and seemingly ironclad arguments for God it makes them poor conversationalists. While listening to others, it's easy for them to be distracted by the facts they are itching to transmit. For many, the goal is to simply present compelling arguments and win the informal debate.

Second, the more we learn about a phenomenon called *myside bias*—where people find counterarguments threatening and dismiss them out of hand—we need to create an environment in which people are willing to acknowledge biases and consider an alternative perspective. Like the creation of fine jewelry "is a word spoken at the proper time" (Proverbs 25:11 NASB). Today's apologist must deeply consider the delicate relationship between presenting facts and establishing points of contact. After serving as the codirector of the Winsome Conviction Project—designed to reintroduce empathy and perspective-taking into our disagreements—it's my assertion that we must *first* cultivate points of connection (ritual) before we challenge a person's point of view (transmission).

Forming Bonds Through Perspective-Taking

At the heart of the ritual view is the idea of *perspective-taking*, which requires that we temporarily set aside our own views to see an issue through the eyes of others on both an emotional and intellectual level. In other words, we don't merely try to learn what a person thinks, but also, how they feel. What emotions surface when we adopt the view of our coworker, classmate, or family member? Today, taking the view of others is not only discouraged, but often, silenced by our own in-group. *Why should we take the view of a person we are convinced is utterly wrong?*

Yet as we read the Scriptures, we see the theme of perspective-taking present in both the Old and New Testaments. For example, in the Old Testament, it is seen in Hosea's marrying of a soon-to-be adulteress—all to understand Israel's unfaithfulness (Hosea 1–3), in the writer of Ecclesiastes' invitation to imagine a world without God (Ecclesiastes 2:25), and in the Song of Solomon, where the narrative shifts perspectives between the young man, the young woman, and outside observers throughout.

Perspective-taking emerges in the New Testament as well. The writer of Hebrews encourages readers to remember believers in prison "as if you were there yourself" and to feel their discomfort "as if you felt their pain in your own bodies" (13:3). The prodigal son narrative allows us to do some perspective-taking with a father who faced his son's disrespectful actions and attempt to return (Luke 15:11-32). Even Jesus' incarnation can be seen as divine perspective-taking, leading the Scriptures to boldly assert that our high priest is not only aware of the human predicament but sympathizes with us (Hebrews 4:15). The word *sympathize* "points to a knowledge that has in it a feeling for the other person by reason of a common experience with that person." Thus, "our Lord's appreciation of our infirmities is an experiential one."[1]

Perspective-Taking in Action

"I don't care what power you pray to, just pray. Whatever version of God works, go for it. In the end, kindness towards others is all that really matters. God is not going send you to hell for getting particulars wrong." Nathan's comment took me by surprise.[2] Over the past year, we had gotten to know each other while working on different projects, and I brought up the topic of God as one conversation was winding down. He responded that he also believed in God and offered his modern take on religion—God is more a personal preference and let's not get bogged down with specifics. Whatever works for you is fine.

Nathan is not alone in his view of religion. A popular consulting voice on religion today is the Dalai Lama. In a lecture series given to Christians and Muslims, he states, "For certain people a Christian method is much more effective than others. Muslims find their own approach to better suit their lives." The mistake we often make, he asserts, is to think one religion is somehow superior to another. "So we cannot say, 'this religion is good, that religion is not good.' That we cannot say. On an individual basis, however, we can say that a particular religion is best for us."[3] His conclusion is that a person should choose a religion that most adequately addresses their particular struggles. For some, they'll find their needs met in Islam; for others, Christianity will do.

I had told Nathan I wanted to continue our conversation, and he eagerly agreed. I now had a decision to make. Do I go into our next conversation adopting a transmission view and offering a critique of his and the Dalai Lama's views? What each are espousing is a form of religious pluralism that asserts the unity of religious communities is more important than attempting to show which religion more closely lines up with reality. As a Christian communicator who regularly speaks evangelistically on college campuses, the topic of religious pluralism often comes up, prompting me to think deeply about its implications. In our follow-up conversation, I could have offered a critique that showed, in my opinion, the glaring weakness of such a view.[4] Yet might that have put Nathan in a defensive position? Would it be better to first surface the many factors—emotional and intellectual—that gave rise to his view? And, once surfaced, engage in perspective-taking to *feel* the weight of his take on religion? What follows is how I structured our follow-up conversation, appealing to a ritual view of communication.[5]

Follow-Up Conversation

"Tell me more." Through years of sharing Christ with others, I have found this simple phrase to be invaluable. "Curiosity—real, deep curiosity about what others are experiencing—goes a long way in important relationships," assert researchers with the Harvard Study of Adult Development. "It opens up avenues of conversation and knowledge that we never knew were there."[6] As I listened to Nathan, here were some of the areas I tried to take note of as his story unfolded.

Family. From birth on, we are handed specific definitions, rituals, themes, and values. While we may eventually abandon or alter these values, they are the starting point for each of us. Much is learned by asking about the family in which a person was raised. Nathan grew up in a very strict religious family that demanded he follow the rules of the church. Any deviation would result in not only parental discipline, but punishment from God. Nathan told me, "You live life always watching over your shoulder for the divine foot to fall."

Community. No family lives in isolation. Rather, a family encounters people who may support or challenge family views, norms, and convictions. While Nathan's church was uncompromising in its dogma and call for allegiance, he continually came into contact with people who held to different beliefs. Some of the kindest people he met were those outside the Christian tradition, including Muslims, Hindus, and Buddhists. Nathan shared, "They were such good people. So kind, and friendly." Yet his church leaders would surely view such groups as people forsaking the truth. Nathan resolved this tension by coming to believe that God is more concerned with kindness than what holy book you read or place of worship you attended. He reasoned, "How could God not accept such accepting people?" The more he interacted with different lifestyles and religions, the more his view of God crystalized: "I want nothing to do with a God who cares more about what religious book you read or church you attend than being kind."

Narrative injury. Philosopher Patrick Stokes identifies narrative injury as sudden or unplanned moments that "completely knock a life off of its trajectory." During this time, "we do not simply lose parts of ourselves" but most importantly, "we lose the capacity to make sense of the parts that remain."[7] For me, this is the most important category to consider when listening to a person share about their journey.

Nathan's narrative injury surfaced in one powerful sentence: "I lived my entire childhood in fear of hell." In adolescence, he understandably started to be attracted to girls. And with that attraction came what his parents called "sinful thoughts of desire." If these thoughts were not suppressed, God would surely send him to hell. Nathan shared, "As a young man, how could you not have these thoughts?" Nights were spent tossing and turning in bed trying to force them out! It was futile. At the time, Nathan's conclusion was, "I was going to hell." Or was he? His fate was sealed *only* if he thought of God as his church did. What if God cared more about love and peace than lustful thoughts? He then told me, "As an adult, I refuse to live in the fear of hell. No longer. I'm done!" When I asked if he'd made peace with Jesus, he responded in the affirmative, "Jesus was a messenger of peace, love, and kindness. He loved everyone. And, when I accept those around me, I'm most like Jesus."

When I left our conversation, I was conflicted. As he spoke, part of me was tempted to jump in to correct Nathan's views of God, judgment, and most importantly, Jesus. Yet I had asked him to tell me his story. To challenge it too early could possibly create a climate of defensive communication. One of the biggest mistakes I see myself and other apologists make is to think listening merely means getting the facts straight. I've come to believe that listening must also entail feeling what a person feels. In short, empathizing with them. Isn't that what the writer of Hebrews is advocating? Not just praying for people, but imagining you are in their situation (Hebrews 13:3).

After the Conversation

One practice I've adopted is that after a conversation is over, I write down what made an impression. What touched me? I try to write down quotes—often paraphrases—of what a person said that stood out. Professor, playwright, and actress Anna Deavere Smith calls these impressions "poetic moments," when a person's passion, hurt, anger, or conviction surfaces.[8]

Two impressions stood out from my discussion with Nathan. First, "I lived my entire childhood in fear of hell. I'm done!" Second, "I want nothing to do with a God who cares more about what religious book you read or church you attend than being kind." Once these were identified, I input them into my cell phone. And in the weeks that followed, I would look at them periodically. I asked myself, *What if this was my perspective?*

First, instead of God being a benevolent Father, what would it look like if He was an ever-present taskmaster who is constantly in judgment mode and threatens young boys with everlasting torment? The great existentialist philosopher Jean Paul Sartre once compared the God of the Bible to a cosmic voyeur who was always watching and judging.[9] To him, the thought was both unsettling and repugnant. While God's presence for me produces comfort—knowing my heavenly Father encloses me behind and before (Psalm 139)—for Nathan and Sartre, the divine gaze is terrifying. Does that perspective produce in me a desire to debate or to empathize?

Second, Nathan's other point showed a glimmer of hope. *What if God cared more about kindness than to what religion you belonged? Certainly, God would never send kind people to hell.* When engaging in perspective-taking with these thoughts, I had to be disciplined not to immediately rebut Nathan's view of divine judgment, or to think of times when Jesus did judge—sometimes passionately so (Matthew 21:12-13; 23:1-12; John 8:1-11). No, my goal was to temporarily adopt his view—seeing Jesus as a person of peace who rewarded anyone who sought the same. This view of Jesus took notice of Nathan's kindness and rewarded him. It took me weeks of regularly adopting Nathan's view in order to understand and empathize with it.

What Difference Does Perspective-Taking Make?

Taking Nathan's perspective helped foster a sense of identification. Kenneth Burke, one of the most quoted communication scholars of the last 100 years, argued that division is our natural bent as social creatures—we belong to different communities, look at opposing news feeds, grow up with differing family narratives, use different jargon, and so on. The result is that we quickly identify people as being outsiders, or other. The goal of a communicator, he asserts, is to break that separation by surfacing similarities or common experiences. "You persuade a man only insofar as you can talk his language by speech, gesture, tonality, order, image, attitude, idea, identifying your ways with his."[10]

Temporarily adopting Nathan's perspective quickly revealed God as a harsh taskmaster who demanded full obedience; even if unreasonable. As I lived in his story, the Spirit brought to mind a time before my conversion when I shared a similar view. I grew up in a non-Christian home in which God was seldom mentioned. However, my grandparents were devout believers and strategically gave my brothers and me a Bible as one of our Christmas presents. One day, after coming home from junior high, on a whim I decided to give the Bible a try. I randomly opened to the following: "If your hand—even your stronger hand—causes you to sin, cut it off and throw it away. It is better for you to lose one part of your body than for your whole body to be thrown into hell" (Matthew 5:30). *What?!* God wants me to cut off my hand because I don't measure up to His rules? I was mortified. I felt a sickening pit in my stomach as I read that such harshness equally applied to my eyes (verse 29). I closed the Bible and didn't pick one up again until I converted to Christianity years later. For a period of my life, my view of God mirrored that of Nathan's—God as a distant judge, utterly lacking compassion. It was a powerful moment of identification when I shared that story with Nathan. The distance between us seemed to shrink. It was no longer as great a chasm.[11]

With perspective-taking and identification come clarity. Living in Nathan's narrative showed me the nature of our disagreement: How do we each define kindness? For Nathan, Jesus' kindness focuses on our good intentions and doesn't exclude. While I understand divine kindness as presenting mankind with the truth and giving us the freedom to choose. The Scriptures assert that God's kindness was most apparent in the coming of Jesus (Titus 3:4-7). God's kindness is a mix of mercy and judgment. Coming to know that Nathan's and my disagreement was definitional was invaluable, and it is important as we move forward in future conversations.

Communication Through Connection

As new apologists seeking to open lines of communication with people holding different—and often antagonistic—views, we must seek to foster areas of identification. We are not that different, you and I—we have the same desires, experiences, questions, and emotions. Granted, it will take much effort and careful thought to surface points of similarity in today's argument culture, but it can be done. We can find intersections of connection with one another.

Songwriter Jack Michael Antonoff sought to explore what unites us in times of deep division. His answer: Everyone has lost a parent, child, or loved one at some time in their life.[12] Learning of a person's losses, hardships, or struggles is only the first part. Adopting their perspective helps us to feel their story, which, in turn, fosters empathy, understanding, and identification. Hopefully, all of this results in our speaking God's truth *in* love.

Tim Muehlhoff is a professor of communication at Biola University. He is a codirector of Biola's Winsome Conviction Project and cohost of the *Winsome Conviction* podcast. He is also the author of many books, including *I Beg to Differ* and *Eyes to See*. And he is the coauthor of many other books, including *End the Stalemate* and *Winsome Persuasion*.

PART 3:
NEW
CHALLENGES

INTRODUCTION
TO PART 3

ritical theory. Race. Gender identity. Mental health. Deconstruction. These are some of the thorniest issues today that Christians *must* address. Quite amazingly, when I first compiled *Apologetics for a New Generation* (2009), race was the only issue on this list that seemed pressing enough to cover. The others weren't even on my radar! Quite obviously, times have changed. And times will continue to change more rapidly than ever.

And yet, the gospel remains the same. God remains the same. Scripture is still true. Remember, the key in addressing these new challenges is to take the *timeless* principles of Scripture and apply them in a *timely* way. While some of these challenges are new, our task is not.

Since the beginning of the church, Christians have been responding to fresh challenges that arise in their generation. Discussing some of these issues might make us uncomfortable, and we might wish that we didn't have to deal with them. Yet it is vital to remember two truths. First, God has appointed you to live in this time (Acts 17:26). Second, God has equipped you with everything you need to do His will today (Hebrews 13:20-21).

You are going to enjoy each one of these chapters. They are fresh, unique, and timely. After reading them, and hopefully discussing these topics with a friend, classmate, or colleague, you will feel more equipped and confident to engage the toughest issues of our day with grace and truth. Let's go!

Sean McDowell

URBAN APOLOGETICS—
TWO TENSIONS

Christopher W. Brooks

rban apologetics has become an established and growing discipline with many dynamic, intelligent, and insightful voices. Men and women like Eric Mason, Lisa Fields, Vince Bantu, Jerome Gay, and Anthony Bradley are but a few who have added much-needed content to this critical body of knowledge. For a more comprehensive treatment on urban apologetics consider reading and engaging with the books, videos, and curriculum produced by these thought leaders. It is important to note that the vibrancy of apologetics in the urban context is found not only in its practitioners, but also in the communities which it attempts to reach with the gospel. The diversity of culture and spiritual expression has created an ever-expanding need for Christians to think deeply about how we can best present the claims of Christ in a manner that is both biblically faithful and relevant to the listener.

Those of us who desire to evangelize the unreached and unchurched in urban America must begin by recognizing that it is as equally dangerous for us to answer a question wrongly as it is for us to answer the wrong question. That is to say, we must actively listen if we hope to accurately answer the deep-heart questions of those whom we hope to win to Christ. Furthermore, it is crucial that we see both the people and the history behind each question that is asked. As men and women seek to navigate the fallenness of the world around us and to have a worldview that is coherent, practical, and virtuous, we must respect the complexities that shape this quest. Our answers to the deep-heart questions must be both evidentially true and ethically faithful—as a new generation is asking two foundational questions: Can God be trusted? and Is God morally good?

Looking back over another apologetics book I contributed to, *A New Kind of Apologist*,[1] it is refreshing to see that a significant majority of the content is just as relevant today as it was when the book was originally released. However, since that time, there have been several key worldview shifts that have led to the need to revisit prior assumptions and to tackle the present ethos of our evangelistic moment. The two most demonstrable shifts have been in the areas of anthropology and Christology.

In this chapter, we will explore the ways in which many who live in urban communities have changed in their view and redress of racial and ethnic inequities. We will also examine the Christological polarization that has led to a transformation in how urban apologists should communicate the mission and ministry of Jesus.

The Anthropological Tension

Over the years, many have found the early church tension between Jews and Gentiles to be analogous, in many ways, to the current challenges the church faces surrounding race and ethnicity. The question asked by the first generation of Christ-followers was, Can Gentiles be saved? The church was initially comprised of Jewish believers in Christ. It was not until Peter went to the house of Cornelius to preach the gospel in Acts 10 that we see the Bible record the conversion of Gentiles to Christ. But not even this miraculous moment alone was enough to settle the matter in the minds of early believers. In Acts 15, the apostle Paul, who had ministered among the non-Jewish peoples of the world, felt it necessary to go to Jerusalem to meet with the other Jewish leaders of the church to ensure that his ministry had not been in vain (verses 1-35; Galatians 2:2). Although, there is no specific verse that shows the early church had come to a place of clear closure over this tension, it is evident from Paul's roll call of colaborers in Christ in Romans 16 that, eventually, the church came to accept Gentiles as joint heirs with them in Christ.

Interestingly, a question faced by the church today, in particular because of the aftermath of the holocaust, is, Can Jews be saved and become members of the body of Christ? Ministries like Jews for Jesus, founded in 1970 by Moishe Rosen, began to address this very concern. Can a person become a Christian while maintaining their Jewishness? Some are still suspicious about this possibility, which is evidenced by the low number of Jewish believers in Christ. According to a Pew Research study, in the US, Messianic Jews "make up only 8 percent of people who are categorized in the report as people of Jewish affinity."[2] What an interesting turn of events and significant change in perspective the church underwent from the first century to the period following World War II.

In similar fashion, the church in America, dating back to the earliest days of the colonial settlements, questioned if blacks could be redeemed. While some slave masters encouraged the sharing of the gospel with their slaves, emphasizing biblical passages like Ephesians 6:5, which commands slaves to obey their masters. Many others within the church held to such a poor anthropology that they argued that blacks were outside of redemption and did not even possess souls. This convenient anthropological heresy was adopted according to Morf Morford to justify the brutality of slavery: "Any atrocity or exploitation, it seems, is allowable, if objects are without souls."[3] So again, the question posed in the church in America during its formational period was, Can blacks be redeemed?

But just as the Jew/Gentile question of salvation took an unexpected reversal over time, so has the issue of white/black redemption. Contemporary authors like Willie James Jennings[4] and J. Kameron Carter have raised more than a doubt on whether whites are beyond redemption.[5] They would argue that the corrupting and insidious nature of "whiteness," combined with the enormous list of social benefits that those who possess it accumulate, makes it as difficult to enter heaven as Jesus said wealth does for those who are rich.

This line of thinking, promoted by Jennings and Carter, has become broadly pervasive and mainstream—now reaching the point where to be white, in the minds of many, is antithetical to the gospel. The urban apologist must be aware of the presence of this racial construct and determine how they will address this ethnocentric understanding of salvation in light of the reconciling nature of the gospel.

If we see the gospel as binding to our conscience and actions, then we must also apply to our contemporary discourse on race the same text that declares:

> Christ himself has brought peace to us. He united Jews and Gentiles
> into one people when, in his own body on the cross, he broke down
> the wall of hostility that separated us (Ephesians 2:14).

Since 2016, there has been a marked shift in the way communities of color respond to the issue of racism. Prior to this period, in American politics most would have stated the goal of dealing with racism was to strive for a country that simply is not racist. However, as rhetoric became more contentious in our politics, the demand for a more militant approach arose. The result being that the new expectation for those who desire not to be labeled as racist is to become antiracist. While this may seem to be simply a linguistic shift, in reality, it represents far more. While not being racist is a personal and private choice to behave in an unbiased way toward others, antiracism, according to the National Museum of African American History and Culture, includes fighting against structural racism.[6] The goal of not being racist is focused on the individual, whereas the goal of antiracism is primarily focused on institutional deconstruction.

So how does the urban apologist navigate these shifts? Sociologist George Yancey offers a very helpful answer to this question. His book *Beyond Racial Gridlock: Embracing Mutual Responsibility* provides an effective framework for our current cultural moment. Yancey's primary thesis is summed up in these words:

> Both the structuralist and the individualist definitions ignore the
> spiritual dimensions of racism. They are secular definitions. Neither
> definition speaks to the nature of humanity or to spiritual forces
> that transcend individuals and society. Christians should not be

limited to thinking only about the spiritual dimensions of racism, but racism must ultimately be defined as a result of our human sin nature. The sin nature of both majority and minority group members leads to racial conflict and tensions. We cannot end racism until we confront our own sin nature.[7]

Yancey strongly warns us to avoid any attempts of trying to solve racism with solely secular tools. If racism is, in fact, a spiritual problem of the soul, then the response must first address this malfunction spiritually. This does not mean that we should ignore the practical damage that proceeds from both individualistic and structural racism. What it does mean is that these very real societal effects are symptoms of a deeper-rooted sickness—namely, the rejection of the teachings, and ultimately, the person and lordship of Christ. Therefore, a proper and uniquely Christian response would be to call men and women to repentance and to embrace the way of Christ wholeheartedly, rather than to the adoption of a secular anthropological perspective.

Consistent in all New Testament teachings on sin, the starting point of transformation is to fully admit and acknowledge that the problem resides within us. While it is easy to either ignore the problem ("colorblindness") or to fully blame others ("antiracism"), in his book *Beyond Racial Division*, Yancey begins his proposal for a way forward by stating,

> I am going to offer a solution to the racial problems before us. But no matter how good my approach, I must also recognize that I am a part of the problem...I...have a problem with racism.[8]

This is truly a humble approach. Yancey goes on to explain that Christians need to harness the power of mutual accountability in our dealings on race if we are to see true progress.

Mutual accountability includes "collaborative conversations" where "everyone is allowed to participate, and everyone's ideas are taken seriously. Everyone has a say in the final outcome."[9] These types of conversations neither ignore the problem nor simply place the brunt of the blame at the feet of others. Rather, they force us to ask ourselves the question: *How can I work with others to find solutions that will contribute to the well-being of everyone?*

Yancey's analysis is both instructive and helpful. He realizes that the reconciliation called for in Ephesians 2, bought with the blood of Jesus, stands upon the two pillars of repentance and forgiveness. Mutual accountability calls for us to continually assess if we are in a position that rightly demands our repentance, or if we are obligated, in Christ, to offer forgiveness to those who have fallen short of God's standard, just as we have. To be sure, this pathway is hard, but it aligns most faithfully with the gospel and provides the best hope for true unity in Christ among God's people.

The task of the urban apologist is to persuade others to reject the easier and detrimental ways forward of either (1) blaming all evil on the "sin of whiteness" or (2) demanding that people of color pretend that racial inequities do not exist and expect them to adopt a form of Anglo-conformity that strips them of their uniqueness, which reflects the glory of God. Both pathways are dead ends because they deny our individual agency and fall short of the beauty of biblical anthropology. Again, hope lies in mutual accountability as we, together, strive to create solutions that honor God and affirm the dignity of others.

The Christological Tension

Two of the most influential leaders of the twentieth century were evangelist Billy Graham and civil rights leader Martin Luther King, Jr. Their ministries unfolded during roughly the same time period; Graham's extended longer due to Dr. King's assassination. The impact of their messages were felt throughout our country and even reached nations around the world. One cannot tell of the history of the Christian faith without mentioning the way that their lives shaped the generations that would follow.

Here, I want to explore some repercussions that are reflected in the American church as a result of these two figures. While there have been many biographies written on the nuances of their ministries that are worthy of our attention, my hope here is to plainly provide an analysis of their preaching that seeks to contrast their differing presentations of Christ. My argument is that Graham presents us with a Christ who has come to save our souls from the marring effects of sin and enables us to have a relationship with God with the promise of eternity in heaven. Conversely, Dr. King declared

Christ to be the one who restores the *imago Dei* in the lives of those who have been marred by oppression and that Jesus offers us dignity and salvation from the forces of evil present in our world. For Graham, the primary ministry of Christ is eternal salvation; for King, the primary ministry of Christ is our current liberation.

While orthodox theology demands that we not make a choice between these two images of Jesus, American Christianity has existed in the tension of what seem to be opposing versions of the ministry of Christ. Evangelicals have broadly chosen the pathway of centering the gospel on eternal salvation. The influence of, especially, dispensationalism has produced books and movies with an intense focus on the rapture, such as with the Left Behind series. This spurred an evangelistic fervor that has led to the conversion of many.

Mainline, Pentecostal, and historically black denominations, such as National Baptist and the Church of God in Christ, have left more room for social liberation with an emphasis on justice. The civil rights movement of the 1960s was birthed in the basements and sanctuaries of the church. Since then, new generations of justice movements have also found the church as an indispensable and necessary ally. The church continues to be the gathering place for dialogue on matters of social transformation in the post-Mike Brown and George Floyd era. This has also contributed to the growth of the body of Christ.

Regretfully, the tension between these two Christological visions has been exploited by pundits and politicians in a way that continues to cause significant misconceptions. Social media has proven to exacerbate this problem by having an isolating effect on society—driving us deeper into our silos. It is within these platforms and echo chambers that we experience the amplifications of our stereotypes of one another and the supporting confirmation bias that allows us to feel as though our perceptions of each other are completely accurate. Over time, these stereotypes dangerously become the caricature of the groups that we seek to define, leaving no room for nuance.

This phenomenon has led to many false assumptions. For example, some have erroneously believed that evangelicals do not actively engage in social justice work. When, in fact, it has been evangelicals who have taken a leading role in fighting successfully to protect the pre-born and overturn

Roe v. Wade—arguably the greatest justice reform movement of the past generation. On the other hand, denominations more closely associated with social liberation are assumed to take little interest in evangelism. However, Pentecostalism has arguably been one of the greatest driving forces behind global missions over the past 25 years. Groups like YWAM (Youth with a Mission) have trained up a whole new generation of missionaries. Pentecostal denominations have also led the way in church-planting efforts that are occurring in nations all over the world. It is important that we recognize misconceptions like these if we are to effectively engage urban communities.

So how should these diverse realities impact the ministry of urban apologists? First and foremost, it should shape our evangelistic presentation of Christ. We should reject any notions to somehow bifurcate the ministry and mission of Jesus into salvation-versus-social justice categories. It is possible, as well as biblically faithful, for us to engage in both. While the priority must always be on calling individuals into a personal relationship with Christ and repentance from their dead works, we must never forget that the Bible teaches us that "faith without works is dead" (James 2:26 NASB) and that, without love, our faith has no value or effect on the world around us (1 Corinthians 13:1-3). Jesus preached the message of "repent and believe" (Mark 1:15 ESV), yet He also went about doing good (Acts 10:38). On the basis of Scripture, it is our obligation to proclaim a holistic picture of Christ that will, in turn, produce both salvation and social engagement.

Second, the urban apologist must recognize that we live during an age of mass deception and misinformation. If there is a silver lining to this reality, it is the fact that, by now, most individuals accept that our society is gripped by fake news. However, it remains that very few feel they are personally susceptible to the impacts of living in a post-truth culture. All of this should deepen our commitment to veracity. Fact-checking and going to original sources for our information is essential. Not only as an apologetic skill, but more importantly, as a matter of the soul. We should be known for our honesty and not adopting the win-at-all-costs ethic of culture.

Finally, urban apologists must understand that the men and women we are trying to reach for Christ have been deeply shaped by a political narrative about the world. It is unfortunate that the lens through which people often view themselves and society is that of a polarized, scorched-earth partisanship. The pressure to choose a political camp is enormous. Once selected, our partisan allegiances determine our priorities. Broadly speaking, for the Right, it is assumed that all that matters is the preservation of traditional institutions and hierarchies. Broadly speaking, for the Left, the assumed priorities are the deconstruction of historical structures and the policies that protect them. The urban apologist does not have the luxury to assume. Rather, they must ask deep, insightful, and probing questions that will reveal the actual worldview of the person they hope to win for Christ.

>> >> >>

The shifts discussed in this chapter, if understood, represent opportunities for Christians to demonstrate for a new generation the credible message of Christ. The urban landscape has been, and continues to be, an exciting ministry context. The potential for revival and community transformation is enormous. While no single chapter can provide a comprehensive exploration of how to effectively engage in urban apologetics, it is the hope of this volume to spur on greater awareness and serious scholarship for those who desire to become practitioners, in anticipation that the years ahead will produce a renewed faith in the gospel—until all have heard, until Christ's return.

Christopher W. Brooks is the senior pastor of Woodside Bible Church in the greater Detroit-metro area of Michigan. He is also the host of the national radio show *Equipped with Chris Brooks*, and he is the author of *Kingdom Dreaming* and *Urban Apologetics*.

HOMOSEXUALITY: TRUTH AND GRACE

Alan Shlemon

Since the beginning of the gay-rights movement, the church has struggled to reach people who identify as lesbian, gay, or bisexual (LGB). Our formula has been problematic. Condemn their behavior, blast them with a Bible verse, and then try to win them over with a cliché. "God hates the sin, but loves the sinner," we tell them. The only word they hear, though, is *hates*.

It's not surprising our efforts have limited effect. Armed with Bible verses for bullets, we're locked and loaded, ready to fire at the first chance to condemn homosexuality. But there's no grace in a gunshot. Instead of offering hope and healing, we cause more damage to our relationships.

The problem is that Christians were caught flat-footed. It wasn't due to a lack of direction from Scripture. Rather, our apologetic was shallow and our manner shrill. Our clumsy response sent many people who experienced same-sex attraction into the arms of "gay-affirming churches" who showed them the love and acceptance they expected from us.

Now we face a challenge on two fronts: from the world *without* and the wolves *within*. The world's ways have always been—and will continue to be—at odds with biblical sexual ethics. That's why there's always been—and will continue to be—a relentless assault on Christians to recant our theological convictions on homosexuality.

The challenge has become more acute because of the wolves. False teachers, working within the walls of the church, have deployed new tactics to undermine orthodoxy. They have capitalized on our mistakes. We have failed to get grounded in biblical truth and fumbled our relationships with friends and family who identify as LGB.

The approach we take today must follow Jesus' footsteps. John describes our Savior as "full of grace and truth" (John 1:14 ESV). Jesus never compromised the truth and always engaged others with grace. We should do the same: know the truth and navigate with grace.

Know the Truth

It's essential to start with biblical truth. That's our foundation, and it must not be compromised. You can't have a complete strategy without knowing God's view on sexuality.

The Bible, though, isn't just a book of dos and don'ts. While it contains commands and restrictions, it also paints a positive picture of what sex and marriage should look like. Therefore, if you want to present the Bible's position on homosexuality, you should start at the beginning.

After creating the heavens and the earth, God made humanity as "male and female" (Genesis 1:27) and outlined the blueprint for sex and marriage. The Bible says, "A man shall leave his father and his mother, and be joined to his wife; and they shall become one flesh" (Genesis 2:24 NASB). It's worth noting that *only* a man and a woman (not two men or two women) are described in Scripture as being able to create a one-flesh union. God "blessed them; and God said to them, 'Be fruitful and multiply'" (Genesis 1:28 NASB).

Some people object by claiming this Old Testament teaching isn't relevant for New Testament believers. Surprisingly, it's often Christians who raise this concern. It turns out, though, this blueprint for sex and marriage is not merely an Old Testament teaching. Jesus endorses this view in the New Testament when he quotes those exact two passages in Genesis:

Have you not read that He who created them from the beginning made them male and female, and said, "For this reason a man shall leave his father and his mother and be joined to his wife, and the two shall become one flesh"? So they are no longer two, but one flesh. Therefore, what God has joined together, no person is to separate (Matthew 19:4-6 NASB; see also Mark 10:6-9).

Jesus cites the Genesis account of creation because He believes it's still binding. His view on sex and marriage can be summarized as one man, with one woman, becoming one flesh, for one lifetime.

Notice that Jesus' teaching on sex and marriage *alone* disqualifies homosexual sex as an option. Even if there wasn't a single passage in Scripture that referred to homosexuality, it would still be evident that homosexual sex is sin because that behavior deviates from the Bible's blueprint on what sex and marriage are. Scripture, however, also contains verses that explicitly prohibit homosexual sex.

Both the Old and New Testaments teach homosexual behavior is sin. Although numerous verses affirm this, five commonly known passages are Leviticus 18:22; 20:13; Romans 1:26-27; 1 Corinthians 6:9-11; and 1 Timothy 1:8-11.

Of those five passages, Romans 1:26-27 is the most defensible and the clearest articulation on this topic. Therefore, it's wise to turn here first if you need to explain what Scripture says about homosexuality. Here is what Paul writes:

> For this reason God gave them over to degrading passions; for their women exchanged the natural function for that which is unnatural, and in the same way also the men abandoned the natural function of the woman and burned in their desire toward one another, men with men committing indecent acts and receiving in their own persons the due penalty of their error (NASB1995).

The word "function" is translated from the Greek word *chresis*, which, according to a Greek-English lexicon of the New Testament, means "use, function, especially of sexual intercourse."[1] Paul, then, is making a design argument. Men are designed to sexually function with women. Women are designed to sexually function with men. The men in this passage *abandoned the natural sexual function of the woman* and engaged in a "men with men" act that Paul describes as "unnatural" and "indecent."

There are three reasons this passage in Romans is an excellent starting point for explaining the Bible's teaching on this subject. First, it condemns both male and female homosexual sex. Other passages can imply that lesbian sexual behavior is sin, but they require an additional argument to make that clear. The Romans passage, however, says it explicitly.

Second, the epistle of Romans was written during the new covenant of Christ, which is the covenant that governs Christian behavior today. Citing Leviticus 18:22 or 20:13 will also get you muddled in a debate about whether, or how, the Mosaic law is relevant for New Testament believers.

Third, the Romans passage describes the behavior that is in question. Even though the word "homosexual" doesn't appear in the passage, Paul describes the behavior that is prohibited: the behavior when a man abandons the natural sexual function of a woman and has sex with another man.

It's worth noting that the context of this passage—a creation narrative—strengthens this interpretation. Paul explains how the evidence of God's handiwork in creation is so obvious that mankind is without excuse for not believing there's a God who made what we see (Romans 1:20). Some people, however, reject the obvious evidence of God's hand in creation and worship the creation rather than the Creator (Romans 1:25). These rebellious people reject the truth of God. It is within the context of rebellious people who exchange the truth of God for a lie that men exchange the natural sexual function and design of a woman for a man.

It is essential for believers to know what the Bible teaches about sex, marriage, and homosexuality. However, God's Word can be twisted by mankind for self-serving purposes. Believers, therefore, need to inoculate themselves to the false ideas that undoubtedly will threaten their church.

Wolves Within

One way that wolves within the church attempt to compromise Scripture's teaching is by advancing pro-gay theology. Their approach is cunning.

They claim the Bible *does* condemn homosexuality, but only abusive, coercive, or exploitive forms of homosexual sex. For example, they say the Bible condemns homosexual gang rape (e.g., Sodom and Gomorrah), master-slave sodomy, and pederasty (men who have sex with boys). These are obvious acts of sin because they are *abusive* forms of homosexual sex.

That's not the kind of homosexuality expressed by LGB men and women today. Rather, they have loving, consensual relationships that aren't abusive, coercive, or exploitive. Therefore, according to pro-gay theology advocates, the biblical prohibitions do *not* apply to modern expressions of homosexuality.

Notice the claim: There are two kinds of homosexual behavior—the abusive kind that's prohibited and the nonabusive kind that's permitted. The problem with that distinction is that it's foreign to Scripture. The Bible doesn't condemn *some kinds* of homosexual acts. It simply condemns homosexual acts in and of themselves.

In fact, here's a helpful strategy. You can undermine pro-gay theology if you can show a single Bible passage condemns *any type of homosexual sex* (and not just abusive forms). It turns out that at least five passages satisfy that requirement (Leviticus 18:22; 20:13; Romans 1:26-27; 1 Corinthians 6:9; 1 Timothy 1:10).

For example, note the straightforward language of Leviticus 18:22: "You shall not lie with a male as one lies with a female; it is an abomination" (NASB1995). The text says nothing about abusive or exploitive homosexual sex. It simply says if you're a man, you can't lie with another man as you would lie with a woman. Nothing about the verse indicates the prohibition is limited only to abusive homosexual sex. Not even the surrounding verses contain a qualification. The verse directly before forbids sacrificing your children to Molech, and the verse directly after prohibits bestiality. Therefore, nothing even in the context suggests Leviticus 18:22 is limited to abusive homosexual sex. There is also no exception made for loving, consensual relationships. The verse simply prohibits homosexual sex—the behavior—regardless of the intent or circumstances.

Leviticus 20:13, an almost identical verse, contains a clause that indicates the homosexual behavior is consensual: "If there is a man who lies with a male as those who lie with a woman, both of them have committed a detestable act; they shall surely be put to death. Their bloodguiltiness is upon them" (NASB1995). Notice that both participants are punished, which indicates this is a consensual act, not a coercive one. Had Leviticus been referring to homosexual gang rape, master-slave sodomy, or some other coercive act, only one man would need to be punished. In Deuteronomy 22:25-26, for example, if a man rapes a woman, then the aggressor alone is put to death. His forcing himself on a woman *is* coercive, which is why only he is punished. In the case of homosexual sex in Leviticus 20:13, both men are punished because it's a consensual act.

My point is not that homosexual sex is a sin today because it's forbidden in the Mosaic law. Rather, it's to show that reinterpretive efforts of Scripture fail. Besides, recall that the prohibition of homosexual sex continues under the new covenant of Christ as evident in Jesus' teaching and in the three epistles all mentioned above.

As described earlier, Romans 1 condemns homosexual sex. The passage's formulation also prohibits a pro-gay interpretation for several reasons. First, the plain reading of the passage describes the sinful behavior: "men abandoned the natural function of the woman" (verse 27 NASB1995). Paul is not concerned with the *circumstances* of the sexual act (whether it's abusive), but rather, that the men abandoned the sexual *function* that a woman provides (and vice versa [verse 26]). Second, the passage indicates the behavior was consensual. Notice they burned in their desire "toward one another" and it was "men with men" who committed indecent acts (verse 27 NASB1995). Third, lesbianism in the first century was not abusive, but consensual.[2] That's further evidence the passage is not talking about exploitive or coercive behavior.

Pro-gay theology advocates also reinterpret 1 Corinthians 6:9-11 and 1 Timothy 1:8-11. Both passages contain vice lists, where Paul identifies various kinds of sinners. One Greek word in those passages, *arsenokoites*, is translated as "homosexuals" (NASB), "men who have sex with men" (NIV, CSB), "practice homosexuality" (ESV, NLT, HCSB), or "sodomites" (NRSV). Pro-gay theology advocates claim that word wrongly insinuates that homosexual sex is sin. Instead, they suggest it mostly likely condemns *exploitive* homosexual sex.

The problem with such an interpretation is twofold. First, neither the word nor the context provides any evidence that Paul is condemning exploitive homosexual sex. Adding a qualifier (e.g., "exploitive") is pure invention. Second, *arsenokoites* is a word Paul created by combining two Greek words, *arsen*, meaning "male," and *koite*, meaning "lying." *Arsenokoites* literally means "men who lie with a male." The component Greek words that make up *arsenokoites* appear together in two Greek Old Testament (Septuagint) verses:

> *kai meta **arsenos** ou koimethese **koiten** gynaikos bdelygma*
>
> *kai os an koimethe meta **arsenos** **koiten** gynaikos bdelygma...*

These verses are Leviticus 18:22 and 20:13—two passages in the Mosaic law that condemn homosexual behavior. In other words, Paul invented a Greek word that literally means "men who lie with a male," and the two component words that he used to create this new word are found together in the only two verses in the Mosaic law that prohibit homosexual sex. Because the two Levitical passages condemn any type of homosexual sex, scholars and commentaries also interpret 1 Corinthians 6:9-11 and 1 Timothy 1:8-11 as condemning homosexual sex proper, and not limiting the scope to exploitive homosexual sex.

Remember, you need only one verse that categorically condemns any type of homosexual sex to undermine pro-gay theology. Five verses have been mentioned here. What the Bible prohibits, then, is a behavior—homosexual sex—regardless of what motivates a person to engage in that behavior or the circumstances of it. Therefore, people who engage in same-sex sexual activity today fall under the jurisdiction of the passages that condemn homosexual sex.

Navigate with Grace

Knowing what Scripture says and how to respond to pro-gay theology is foundational. It will help you discern truth from error as you interact with people. You will also need to learn how to navigate your conversations and relationships with friends and family who identify as LGB. The following ten principles will help you do that with grace. The first five are relevant in a church context, and the remaining five are relevant in any situation.

First, welcome people who identify as LGB to church. By "welcome" I don't just mean we should let them in the door. Instead, make them *feel* welcome. In other words, be glad they came, show them the best seat in the house, introduce them to the pastor, and invite them to the next church-wide event. After all, don't we want them to experience Christian love? Don't we want them to hear the gospel being preached from the pulpit? How will they experience these things if they're not made to feel welcome when they arrive?

Second, church leadership is off limits to anyone engaged in ongoing, unrepentant sin. Just because someone attends weekend services doesn't mean we allow them to influence the church body. Notice, though, that is not a rule only for LGB people. It applies to anyone. If there's a pastor, elder, deacon, worship leader, or Sunday school teacher who engages in ongoing, unrepentant sin, they should also be restricted from a leadership role.

Third, treat *faithful* Christians who *struggle* with same-sex attraction as any other believer. I'm referring to a genuine believer who is attracted to the same sex but does not satisfy those desires either in thought or in behavior. Rather, they reject those desires because they want to live in obedience to God's commands. They die to self and live for Christ. A believer like that should be treated the same way as any other believer because they *are* just like any other believer.

Every Christian experiences many desires, some of which would be sinful if satisfied. A mature believer rejects those sinful desires. They try not to satisfy them in thought or in behavior. Again, they die to self and live for Christ. A faithful Christian who experiences same-sex attraction is in the same boat as any other Christian. One of their struggles just happens to be with a different sinful desire than a faithful Christian who doesn't experience same-sex attraction. Therefore, they should be afforded the same privileges and leadership opportunities as any church member.

Fourth, don't make jokes about homosexuality. I know this seems like obvious advice, but I still hear Christians make jokes about men and women who identify as LGB. This is degrading behavior that mocks valuable image bearers of God. Furthermore, it alienates believers who experience same-sex attraction. If they hear Christians joke about their sinful temptations, they won't want to reveal that they need help living God-honoring lives in regard to their same-sex desires. Believers who struggle with same-sex attraction need our prayer, support, and accountability. Mocking their sin signals you want nothing to do with them. That's not how the church should function. Instead, we should create a different kind of culture.

Fifth, cultivate a loving and healthy environment at church for people who wrestle with same-sex attraction. They should feel the freedom to share the sin they struggle with—like any believer might—without fear they will be mocked or marginalized. Ask yourself, then: *What can I do? What new policies can the leadership adopt? What church ministries can help to create a biblically sound and healthy culture at church?*

It is also important to respond in a gracious and tender way if someone divulges to you their personal struggle with homosexuality. For example, thank them for being vulnerable. Invite them to share their story with you. Reassure them that you love and care for them. Someone who comes to you for help is going to need a loving person who can support them and pour into their life as they navigate their struggle. If you're not willing to be that person, you should help them find someone who can.

Again, these five principles are primarily relevant in church contexts. The following five are more relevant in any setting.

First, make a priority of your relationship with a friend or family member who identifies as LGB. There's no command in Scripture to sever ties with someone simply because of their sexual sin.[3] As Paul wrote to the Corinthian believers, if we had to end our relationships with sexually immoral people, "you would have to leave this world" (1 Corinthians 5:10 NIV). Instead, we should lean into our relationships with them because relationships function like a bridge by which we can talk about truth (especially biblical truth), show compassion, and share the gospel.

Second, avoid the cliché, "God hates the sin, but loves the sinner." Though this sounds compassionate and biblically consistent, LGB people only hear one word: *hates*. In their mind, being gay is who they are, not just what they do. That's why they think to themselves, *If God hates the sin, then God hates me. My Christian friend? They probably hate me too.* This cliché ends up having the opposite effect you intend.

If you want them to believe that God loves them despite their sin, then don't *say* something. Rather, *do* something. Treat them with love. Since you're claiming God loves them, you can show that by how *you* treat them. After all, being an ambassador for Christ (2 Corinthians 5:20) means how you treat others will impact how they perceive God. If you treat them with love, they'll infer God loves them too.

Third, don't fall for the false dichotomy of how to respond to a person who claims to be LGB. Secular culture and even many misled Christians suggest that you either rebuke and reject an LGB person or support and celebrate everything they do. Both options are mistaken. The first way wrongly characterizes faithful Christians as bigots who blast their LGB friends with the Bible, call them reprobate, and essentially kick them out of their life. The second way wrongly characterizes the biblical approach as total affirmation of the individual's decisions to satisfy homosexual desires.

Those aren't the only two options, though. The third way upholds the relationship but doesn't compromise Scripture's teaching on sexuality. Yes, you love them. Yes, you lean into your relationship with them. Yes, you treat them with kindness. However, that's not all. In addition, you uphold biblical standards of sexuality. Don't mislead them into thinking the Bible permits them to satisfy homosexual desires in thought or deed. In other words, lean into your relationship with them *but* don't compromise what Scripture teaches in the process. That's not easy and, in fact, it makes life messy. No one promised it would be easy, however.

Fourth, make a long-term difference, not a short-term statement. Many Christians resort to clichés that have a short-term goal: to declare their position on homosexuality. We say, "Homosexuality is sin" or something similar. Don't get me wrong. There's a place for telling people the truth. But resorting to short-term statements presumes that changing their behavior is the ultimate goal. While convincing them to change sinful or unhealthy behavior is good, it can risk short-circuiting a long-term relationship. Therefore, if you have a friend or family member who identifies as LGB, think long-term. Ask yourself what you can do to nurture a healthy relationship so you can have a lasting impact on their life.

For example, I met a couple who had a lesbian daughter named Kaitlyn (not her real name). Their daughter lived at a recovery home for homosexuals who struggled with substance abuse. Although Kaitlyn disagreed with her parents' stance against homosexual sex, she still knew they loved and cared for her. That's because Kaitlyn would visit and stay at her parents' home on many weekends. She didn't come alone, though. Other LGB residents at the recovery home would stay the weekend at her parents' house as well. Why? They all craved the selfless love Kaitlyn's parents showed each of them. In fact, they felt like part of the family and became such regular and welcome visitors, they often called Kaitlyn's parents "Mom" and "Dad." On Thanksgiving, the parents invited several of the LGB men and women over. Together, they found common cause on that holiday to give thanks for what they have. More importantly, the parents fostered vital relationships between themselves, their lesbian daughter, and many of the LGB residents of the group home. Also, the parents were able to invite those in their home to church on many weekends and expose them to the gospel message.

Kaitlyn's parents had ample opportunity to proclaim homosexuality a sin, remind Kaitlyn and her friends that "God hates the sin, but loves the sinner," or a make a myriad of similar short-term statements that would likely impede their long-term impact. Like Jesus with Zacchaeus, they fostered a relationship and were able to introduce others to God's message of reconciliation. They were uncompromising in their moral position, but relentless in their love for their daughter and the LGB community. They upheld the truth and showed grace.

Fifth, make the gospel the central issue. After all, isn't that what ultimately matters? Even if you were able to convince someone to stop satisfying homosexual desires, would that save them? No; their eternal destiny would still be in jeopardy. Merely stopping sin can't save anyone. Every person—including an LGB person—is guilty of crimes they've committed against God and desperately needs a pardon. That's why, if you have a chance to share your convictions, tell them the gospel. The only way they can be pardoned is through Jesus' work on the cross.

Keep in mind that our hope for our LGB friends and family is not heterosexuality, but holiness. We're not trying to make them "straight," but instead, point them straight to Jesus. Every time I've seen a man or woman abandon a life of satisfying same-sex desires, it was because they first put their trust in Jesus. Then the Holy Spirit came into their life and transformed them from the inside out. That's the kind of change we ought to hope for. Only Jesus can do that.

Alan Shlemon is an author and speaker for Stand to Reason, where he trains Christians to share their convictions in a persuasive yet gracious manner.

DEFENDING FEMININITY: WHY JESUS IS GOOD NEWS FOR WOMEN

Jonalyn Grace Fincher

When I ask teenage girls and adult women what they like about being women, some rattle off stereotypical things, like makeup, buying shoes, or chivalry, but the most common response is, "I don't know what I like about being a woman."

Women inside and outside the church remain unconvinced femininity is a good thing.[1] It's time apologists realized this female confusion is worth everyone's attention. Jesus came to renew every aspect of our humanity, including our gender.[2] And in the end, gender isn't merely a woman's issue. Men are affected by women's struggles (not to mention how men are also confused about what makes them masculine, unique, and valuable).

I want to defend women's value because I follow Jesus and He valued women. Jesus wanted women to live as fully feminine, fully human, and fully free. When I got married, I realized that I had elevated one view of femininity above all others. I was surprised that my husband wanted more than my cooking skills, my home-decorating expertise, and my nurturing abilities. I expected to start a family soon, but he wanted me to finish my seminary degree and partner alongside him on the road, speaking from the same pulpits, writing in the same field. He showed me that many viable and biblical options are available for women.

My husband encouraged and propelled me into a five-year study of femininity. Along the way, I've unearthed pagan ideas of femininity (and masculinity) in Bible studies, marriage conferences, men's and women's ministries, and my own prayer life. These pagan ideas, such as assuming that men and women come from different planets, or that only women are emotional or relational, or that God is male, are part of the reason women are confused about their value. If femininity only meant fashion, makeup, or cooking, we would have no problem. But these superficial earmarks of femininity are not the issue; women are actually floundering about why God would value their womanhood. This question cuts into the heart of every woman's identity, feeding a host of symptoms we'd all like to help resolve: eating addiction, cutting, image obsession, premature sexualization of the female body, and pornography addiction.

Apologists can help women with our hard questions: Is there only one biblical role for women? What does Jesus really have to say about women? How does Jesus compare with other religious founders in His treatment of women?

Jesus Is a Friend of Women

Apologetics for the value of women has been done for hundreds of years. It can boast a distinguished, well-documented history, with books like Thomas Webster's *Woman: Man's Equal*—a hot topic on the eve of America granting suffrage to women. Penned in 1873, the introduction opens with these words: "Christianity is the special friend of woman...This elevation is the natural outgrowth of the example and teaching of Jesus of Nazareth."[3]

Though the argument is more than 100 years old, it's worth renewing today. How do other religions—or better, how do religious founders—compare in their treatment of women? How do Islam's Muhammad, Buddhism's Gautama Siddhartha, Mormonism's Joseph Smith, and the Jehovah's Witnesses' C.T. Russell measure up next to Jesus of Nazareth? How fully did these founders bestow dignity on the women in their lives?

Muhammad, Founder of Islam

Muhammad (AD 570–632) could claim marital faithfulness to his first wife, Khadija, a wealthy woman 15 years his senior. But soon after her death, Muhammad married a woman each year, women of different faiths, often widows, some for family status, others for political statements, most for beauty. One of these women, Aisha, married Muhammad when she was seven but was permitted to wait until she turned nine before consummating their union. She brought her toys with her when she joined Muhammad at his home.[4]

Muhammad did act to protect females and prohibited the practice of infanticide upon baby girls. But his words about women were not always consistent:

- Regarding wayward wives: "Those whose disobedience you suspect, admonish them and send them to separate beds and beat them."

- Regarding sexual conduct: "Wives are fields to seed as you please."

- Regarding women's supposed lack of self-control: "[Wives] are prisoners with you [husbands], having no control of their person."

- Women are a distraction from prayer: "Prayers are annulled if a dog, donkey, or a woman pass in front."

- Hell is full of wives "who were ungrateful to their husbands, whose menstruation interferes with their religious duties and whose intelligence is deficient."

- "Women are the snares of the devil...Put women in an inferior position since God has done so."[5]

When I compare Muhammad to Jesus, whose female financial backers never felt the need to marry Him (Mark 15:40-41), I'm amazed at the differences. Jesus protected women and widows, not through polygamy, but through individual miracles (Mark 5:25-34), teaching (Mark 12:38-40), interpretation of the law's meaning (Matthew 19:3-9; Mark 14:6-9), and noticing them even when they were marginalized (Mark 12:41-44).

Siddhartha Gautama, Founder of Buddhism

Siddhartha Gautama, later known as the Buddha, was a prince born near India in 563 BC. His spiritual quest led him to do two drastic things. At age 29, he awoke among his harem and realized that his concubines no longer lured him with their beauty; instead, they reminded him of a heap of corpses.[6] He left them, made one final trip to look at his wife of 12 years, Yasodhara, and their newborn son, and then abandoned everyone (harem, wife, and son) to find enlightenment. The religiously tolerant Karen Armstrong's biography of Buddha shows us that Siddhartha wasn't delighted to be a father. "He had felt no pleasure when the child was born," naming the baby boy "Rahula," or fetter. He believed the child would shackle him to a way of life he hated.[7]

Some would say that Jesus commanded us to do the same (Luke 9:57-62), but a close reading of Jesus' words reveals that He never commanded a man to leave his wife or endorsed such behavior. According to Jesus' words, a man and wife are "no longer two, but one flesh. Therefore what God has joined together, let no one separate" (Matthew 19:6 NRSV). He made no exception for spiritual quests.

Joseph Smith, Founder of Mormonism

In 1843, Joseph Smith betrayed his wife, Emma, by secretly marrying 12 women, two already married to other men. One wife, Lucy Walker, wrote an autobiographical sketch and revealed how this practice horrified her.

Joseph and Emma had agreed to care for the motherless Lucy and her brothers while their father went on mission. Lucy served as Emma's maid while going to school. When she was 15, Joseph Smith invited her to live in his home, explaining, "I have a message for you. I have been commanded of God to take another wife, and you are the woman."[8] Smith's pressure, ultimatums, and claims of a heavenly vision convinced Lucy to wed him.

Lucy's testimony is not an anomaly. In the words of Columbia's renowned historian Richard Lyman Bushman, Lucy's example is "the standard autobiography for the celestial marriage narratives in Utah."[9] Wives were separated from their husbands and friends. They were disgraced if they conceived. Most of Smith's wives were teenagers who admitted that Smith's spiritual pressure induced them to marry him.

Smith's spiritual coercion and polygamy were defended as biblical because the Bible cites several instances of polygamy. But God never commands or endorses polygamy. He does the exact opposite, commanding that the king of Israel "must not take many wives, or his heart will be led astray" (Deuteronomy 17:17 NIV). Joseph Smith records God saying just the opposite: "Abraham received concubines, and they bore him children; and it was accounted unto him for righteousness." God commands Emma to cleave to her husband and accept Smith's additional wives.[10] However, Jesus consistently supports monogamy. He explains that faithfulness to one spouse was God's original intentions for men and women from the beginning (see Matthew 19:4-9).

Charles Taze Russell, Founder of Jehovah's Witnesses

Charles Taze Russell (1852–1916) married Maria Frances Ackley with an agreement that their union was a marriage of celibacy for the sake of partnering in their ministry. But within a decade, Maria did not find this situation agreeable.

In their divorce proceedings, Maria testified to witnessing a sexual relationship between her husband and their foster child, Rose Ball, a teenager at the time who worked as Russell's correspondence secretary. According to Maria's testimony, Russell regularly molested Rose in 1894.[11]

Even in the socially conservative culture of late nineteenth-century America, the courts judged Russell's behavior toward his wife as "insulting," "domineering," and "improper" so as to make her life intolerable. They ruled in favor of Maria and required Russell to pay alimony.

Russell did not pay, attempting to transfer his wealth to the Watchtower Bible and Tract Society. Friends covered his bills while he fled out of state. He appealed the alimony case twice over the course of five years, eventually losing. In the end, his alimony was increased.

Russell's failure to reconcile with his wife stands in stark contrast to Jesus' relationship with women of all walks of life. He wasn't wary of the Samaritan woman at the well or of the woman caught in adultery (John 4:1-42; 8:3-11). Jesus never hindered women from inheriting all He could offer them, and He allowed women to change His mind (Mark 7:24-30).

Jesus of Nazareth, Founder of Christianity

Jesus had multiple opportunities to take advantage of women. Women longed to touch Him, to serve Him, to spread their perfume on His feet, and to support Him with their money. Many men would have taken advantage of this type of female adoration. In ancient times, a weakness for females was overlooked as one of the particular rights of spiritual, powerful, or wealthy men. But throughout His friendships with women, Jesus refused to isolate Himself from women or to indulge in romantic rendezvous. Women were not wicked distractions to Him, but neither were they His lovers. Instead of practicing lewdness or asceticism, Jesus guided women along the road with Him. To Martha he said, "I am the resurrection and the life...Do you believe this?" (John 11:25-26). Jesus trusted women, treating them as if they offered more to the world than their seductive charms. He permitted Mary to stay near Him and learn along with the disciples (Luke 10:38-42). He directed Mary Magdalene to preach the good news: "Go to my brothers and tell them, 'I am ascending to my Father and your Father, to my God and your God'" (John 20:17 NET). He commended the woman who anointed His feet: "Your faith has saved you; go in peace" (Luke 7:50).

Jesus reminded the Jewish religious experts of God's original design for females: "Haven't you read...that at the beginning the Creator 'made them male and female'?" (Matthew 19:4 NIV). He is referencing the creation story: "God created mankind in his own image, in the image of God he created them; male and female he created them" (Genesis 1:27 NIV).

Given the first four men and their treatment and teaching of women, whom would you invite to spend a day with a woman you cared about? Which religious founder would you trust with your mother, your sister, or your wife?

Blaming Women?

Though Jesus valued females, many women have never heard or learned this side of Jesus.[12] A teenage girl might survey the Christian landscape and surmise that being a woman qualifies her to go to teas or women's Bible studies but excludes her from several places of service and leadership. It doesn't take much to connect the dots and figure out what some churches believe men and women ought to be doing. And if this girl happens to be one of the many who do not like handicrafts, she will wonder if her femininity is some sort of liability.

A woman who is not married (through celibacy or divorce or widowhood) may find that she has no voice in her local church. Some groups even teach that young men are the key to adding members to the church, taking the stance that by engaging young men and the heads of households, the women and children will naturally follow.

If this woman digs around, she will eventually learn about "the feminization of the church."[13] At its best, this topic addresses the church's failure to attract, empower, and deploy a balanced number of men and women, and men's failure to carry their share of the load. But this phrase alone might lead her to believe that too much of her sex is influencing the church. In her confusion and discouragement with her own femininity, she might protest. Perhaps a well-meaning older friend will tell her to have a gentle and quiet spirit. But being gentle is difficult for her when her femininity seems so confusing and even is viewed as a stumbling block for men.

Blaming women for the church's problems and humanity's problems is an ancient maneuver. Church fathers did it as early as 200 years after Jesus' resurrection, telling women to dress more modestly because "You are the devil's gateway...you are the first deserter of the divine law...On account of your desert—that is, death—even the Son of God had to die."[14]

When women become the scapegoat, I can't help but hear echoes of Adam's excuse in Eden: "The woman you put here with me—she gave me some fruit" (Genesis 3:12 NIV). Yet God created woman not to tempt or distract Adam, but to help him. In Scripture, strong men are never threatened by strong women. Quite the contrary—strong women sharpen and strengthen strong men (see Naomi and Ruth's suggestion of marriage to Boaz in Ruth 3:9, Lydia's hospitality to Paul and his companions in Acts 16:14-15, and Priscilla and Aquila's instruction to Apollos in Acts 18:24-28). Women may be made to feel as if their influence in the church were a problem, but Jesus would never make a woman feel that way. Apologist Dorothy L. Sayers explains Jesus' love for women well.

> Perhaps it is no wonder that women were first at the Cradle and
> last at the Cross. They had never known a man like this Man...A

prophet and teacher who never…flattered or coaxed or patronized; who never made jokes about them…who took their questions and arguments seriously; who never mapped out their sphere for them, never urged them to be feminine or jeered at them for being female.[15]

If some women cannot see Jesus because of our church strategy or culture, we need to change. Female humans are not any more fallen than male humans, but sometimes by our very church practice we communicate that women are somehow dangerous.

As Dan Kimball points out in his book *They Like Jesus but Not the Church*, many people believe that the church is dominated by males and oppresses females. Though I have been blessed with very encouraging Christian men in my life who have wanted my input, my mind, and my presence in church activities, I can see why churches can appear oppressive to females. I have witnessed leaders dismissing female opinions because they come from "women's libbers." Jesus knew that women and men reflect the wholeness of God. Both male and female must be visible, active, and influential in His church.[16]

All in the Family

Many intelligent women silence their questions because they are afraid of being called feminists. Most of these women do not have an agenda; they are honestly confused and hungry for answers. Our Scriptures include passages where women seem to be punished by God to experience pain in childbirth (Genesis 3:16), judged to be ruled by men (Genesis 3:16), relegated as weaker (1 Peter 3:7), commanded to be silent (1 Corinthians 14:34), disallowed to teach (1 Timothy 2:11-15), and instructed to call their husbands "Lord" (1 Peter 3:6), so we can cultivate understanding with those who are bewildered. Their questions are actually apologetic issues.[17]

We tell others about Christianity and Jesus by the way we treat these confused brothers and sisters. Are we willing to present our arguments for women's place in the church with equity and gentleness? Can we share many meanings to the word "head" (Greek *kephale*), the cultural background of 1 Timothy 2, and the examples of biblical female leaders? Do we know about the Christians who allowed women to lead men, including the seventeenth-century Quakers, the nineteenth-century Fundamentalist Feminists, and today's Christians for Biblical Equality?[18] If we believe that women should not preach or serve as elders (complementarians), can we argue for this beyond stating verses without context or claiming that we feel uncomfortable when a woman preaches? If we believe women should preach and serve as elders (egalitarians), can we face verses like 1 Timothy 2:11-15 and 1 Corinthians 14:34-35 without simply saying, "It's all cultural" or asserting, "It's only fair for women to be able to preach"?[19]

The truth of the matter is that there are many biblical views of what it means to be female, not just one. Biblically sound arguments can be found on both sides, for many complementarians and many egalitarians agree that the Bible is God's inspired, inerrant Word. This does not mean that God is confused about His ideas about women; it does mean that intelligent, God-fearing people do not agree. We can help those who come to us with questions when we cite another brother or sister's argument, even if we don't agree with it, as a possible biblically viable option. All these opinions are voiced in the same Christian family.

The way we talk about women's place in the home and church is an opportunity to model how Christians disagree. Let us be full of grace, truth, and humility.

Goddess Bless You?

Grian was raised in the church and attended Sunday school. As a teen, Grian taught vacation Bible school. In her Christian upbringing, Grian said her understanding of God was entirely male. She still believes that Christianity teaches that God is male.

In high school, Grian grew attracted to paganism because the goddess was more whole, more affirming to all people than the Christian's male God. The Wiccans and goddess worshippers that I have interviewed agree that the Christian God is distant, male, and unapproachable. One woman who converted from Wicca to Christianity explained to me, "The church does a very bad PR job when it comes to women. We do not generally espouse what Jesus taught. Many witches are former Christians who were never discipled beyond a rudimentary understanding of Christianity."

Jesus' resurrection reconnects women with dignity, simply by affirming the human body as good beyond the grave. But few Christians and even fewer Wiccans understand this. God is not ashamed to use female images to communicate His love; God cares for us like a mother (Isaiah 66:12-13); He tells Israel that He feels labor pains for them (Isaiah 42:14). Jesus even used the concept of being born again to illustrate how God is at work in the messy, intimate process of bearing us into spiritual life (John 3:3). All these examples are biblical, helpful pictures we must learn and present to those inside and outside the church. Christians, no less than Wiccans, need to know that God is not exclusively male.

Is God Male?

The ramifications of seeing God as an exclusively male deity deeply affect young girls and their walk with God. On occasion, I've asked groups of teen girls to draw pictures of God when they've done something good. Their sketches show Jesus with arms wide open, a smiling old man on a throne, or impressions of the Trinity like three happy faces in a cluster. Then I ask them to draw a picture of God when they've sinned. They illustrate God with dark black circles or male faces with furrowed brows. One girl drew Jesus pointing to His scars. Another drew the back of a tall, male figure.

Figures with feminine characteristics are very rare, especially when girls think of God's disapproval. God, it seems, is male when they are good and especially when they are bad. I've never seen them draw from biblical pictures like God weaning his child (Psalm 131) or longing to gather us like a hen gathering little chicks (Matthew 23:37).

For most teenage girls, God is angry and male when they've sinned. Perhaps because of their own father's neglect or abandonment, young girls often cannot picture a male God being close or approachable. They cannot fathom running to God when they've sinned.

If God is male, men will always share one more (rather significant) attribute with God than women will. If God is male, something about women's femininity is not suitable to be identified with God. These implications can destroy a young girl's security in her womanhood.

I am not about to say we should all call God "Mother" or that we should imagine God with breasts and be done with it. Overemphasizing God's use of female metaphors at the exclusion of the many male metaphors is not helpful or accurate. My point is that thinking of God in terms of sex leads to a dead end. God is spirit (John 4:24). God is not material; He does not have physical parts. God warned us about this in Deuteronomy 4:15-16:

> You saw no form of any kind the day the LORD spoke to you at Horeb out of the fire. Therefore watch yourselves very carefully, so that you do not become corrupt and make for yourselves an idol, an image of any shape, whether formed like a man or a woman (NIV).

Most language for God is metaphorical, but we must figure out where they touch reality. Every metaphor can be abused. "God is a rock" means that God is stable and strong, not that He is inert. "God is a vine" means God is the source of our life, not that He is green. When God says He is King or Judge, we learn many things about His courage and His ferocity for justice, but we know God is not male.[20] So when God says He is like a woman in labor or that Israel will be nursed (Isaiah 42:14; 66:13) we learn that God is a nurturing provider, but we know that God does not have breasts.

Today's New International Version: An Apologetic Issue

The title and metaphor for God the Father is a common stumbling block for men and women, especially if they've suffered abuse at the hand of their fathers. Renée Altson, an author and poet, explains why:

> My father raped me while reciting the Lord's prayer...
>
> My father prayed with me every night. He lay on top of me, touched my breasts, and prayed that I would be forgiven.
>
> "Father," he said.
>
> I cringed at the association.
>
> "Heavenly Father, make my daughter a better person."[21]

To go to her Baptist church and hear God addressed as Father left Alt-son feeling degraded and terrified. In Bible reading and sermons, she felt dismissed as a woman—the examples were always men and fathers. "I hadn't even noticed on any conscious level how the Bible itself had excluded me. It was such a part of my life, of my memorization, of everything I was," she writes.

Years later, a priest from an Episcopal church gave her a translation like Today's New International Version. "It was as if I was reading something that included me for the first time in my life." The simple words "brothers and sisters" instead of "brothers" brought belonging to her. She suddenly mattered.[22] Altson was stunned to realize that the God of the Bible did not share her father's view of women. God wanted her to feel safe and belong in His kingdom, which is what "Father" in Scripture is meant to communicate.

I think we need to pay attention to the power a TNIV Bible can have to communicate truth. We want to promote the translations that accurately include the marginalized as they are meant to be included in the original text. The TNIV, unlike gender-neutral Bibles like *The Inclusive Bible,* does not remove male pronouns like *he* or words like *King* to refer to God (contrary to much of the alarmist words on the street).[23] This means that the TNIV is a valuable tool and will offer a pivotal apologetic Bible to wounded women and men we long to reach out to and comfort.

What Does Jesus Do for Women?

Simone de Beauvoir, the brilliant French existentialist and pioneering philosopher in women's studies, was not a friend of Christianity. Still, she wrote, "It was Christianity, paradoxically, that was to proclaim, on a certain plane, the equality of man and woman…she is God's creature, redeemed by the Saviour, no less than is man: she takes her place beside the men."[24] Her words bring enemy attestation that Jesus was good news for women.

Jesus comes to restore all humans in the midst of our gender inferiority and gender confusion, a problem that has increased over the last 20 years. Jesus wants to end the battle between the sexes and show men and women how to make peace with their own God-given sexuality. He invites us all into His kingdom, where "there is neither male nor female; for you are all one in Christ Jesus" (Galatians 3:28 NASB). The world's division and explanation of the battle of the sexes, including things like Venus and Mars psychology, does not agree with God's story. In Scripture, we know that God made us both for the same planet, that He originally intended men and women to work together using our differences to serve one another.

I have found that Jesus, above any other religious founder, can make a real, life-changing difference to women today. He has work He wants to do in each of us. That's why I'm an apologist; I want to defend femininity the way Jesus did.

Jonalyn Grace Fincher is a philosopher and artist. Her first book *Ruby Slippers: How the Soul of a Woman Brings Her Home* explains the uniqueness of women. She and her husband home educate their boys and share a weekly podcast, *Back Porch with Dale and Jonalyn*. Find her at jonalynfincher.com.

AN INTERVIEW WITH
MICHAEL KRUGER

Sean: Is spiritual abuse an apologetics issue? If so, how?

Michael: Apologetics has a number of dimensions to it. Certainly, it involves intellectual questions. But it also involves moral questions. And anyone paying attention over the last few years knows that the primary objection to Christianity is ethical—it is that Christianity (and Christians) believe and behave in such ways that are morally objectionable.

Thus, if we are to effectively make the case for the Christian faith, we have to address the abuse issue in the church. We have to acknowledge the problem rather than minimize the problem. And we have to demonstrate that true Christianity is against abuse in all forms, and actually gives people the moral and ethical foundation for why abuse is fundamentally and objectively wrong. Simply put, addressing the issue of spiritual abuse *is* part of the apologetic enterprise.

Sean: How is spiritual abuse different from other kinds of abuse?

Michael: In years gone by, the church has begun to grow in its awareness of both sexual abuse and physical/domestic abuse. It took us a while to recognize the breadth and depth of these issues, and I am thankful to see some progress is being made. However, I think we still have some work to do in both areas.

But these types of abuse should be distinguished from spiritual abuse (although sexual abuse and spiritual abuse often go hand in hand). Spiritual abuse can be defined as abuse that takes place when a Christian leader wields his spiritual authority in such a way that he is harsh, domineering, heavy-handed, and authoritarian to those under his care.

In short, spiritual abuse is a violation of 1 Peter 5:3, which calls Christian leaders to shepherd their flocks "not domineering over those in your charge" (ESV). This explains why the term "spiritual" is used. This kind of abuse takes place when a person in spiritual authority abuses that authority and mistreats people under their care. And it is precisely this feature that makes spiritual abuse so damaging. It's one thing if your boss mistreats you at work. It's an entirely other thing if your *pastor* mistreats you at church.

Sean: How does spiritual abuse uniquely affect someone's faith? Do you think spiritual abuse is a significant reason why many people leave the church and sometimes the faith too?

Michael: We are just beginning to learn how deep and wide the effects of spiritual abuse can be. Due to the fact that it is perpetrated by one who represents God in some way, it can wreak havoc on someone's emotional, spiritual, and even physical life. Those who've experienced such abuse often experience fear, anger, shame, anxiety, and even depression. They also deal with loneliness and isolation because they are often driven out of the churches they love. It can also lead to health problems like insomnia, high blood pressure, tremors, and autoimmune disorders.

But the biggest problem is the spiritual damage that is done. People are suspicious of the church, they want to stay away from Christian activities, they lack trust in Christian leaders, and they begin to doubt the goodness and truth of Christianity. I don't think it is coincidence that we've seen an increased awareness of abuse in the last number of years along with an increase of people "deconverting" and leaving the faith.

Michael Kruger is the president and Samuel C. Patterson professor of New Testament and Early Christianity at Reformed Theological Seminary, Charlotte, NC. He is the author of many books, including the award-winning *Bully Pulpit*, *Surviving Religion 101*, and *Christianity at the Crossroads*.

WADING INTO THE ABORTION DEBATE: MAKING THE CONTROVERSIAL CIVIL

Stephanie Gray Connors

R ecently, while watching a film about World War II, my mind wandered to the subject of men on the battlefield. It has been reported that in the intensity of battle, when soldiers are injured, bombs are dropping overhead, and death seems to be knocking, grown men often cry out for one person in particular—their mothers.

That innate human response for she who carried us in her womb and gave birth to us is striking. It tells us about the first human relationship we ever knew. And how it was designed to be associated with comfort, nurture, consolation, and safety. It is this reality that makes abortion so horrifying—for it is a betrayal of a mother's divine calling to love her offspring, and instead, defines the mother's position to her child by disdain, danger, and destruction.

How do we effectively communicate this point to those unconvinced of the pro-life worldview, especially when they treat the preborn as inferior to the born and appeal to heart-wrenching circumstances a pregnant woman may face?

Strategies for Effective Communication

In general, when dialoguing with someone who has taken a position of supporting abortion, I suggest we take the following approaches:

1. Appeal to trusted authorities or examples to show how someone, or something, the person agrees with actually aligns with the pro-life perspective.

2. Ask questions to prompt deeper thought and discussion.

3. Make analogies to relatable things so that the person can easily visualize and understand a concept you're unpacking.

4. Undergird all your interactions with prayer, remembering that we are ministers who are wholly dependent on the Messiah.

With these four strategies in mind, let's now look at some specific examples of common challenges to the pro-life worldview.

Becoming "Mother"

We can ask both supporters of abortion rights and pro-life advocates, "What do civil societies expect of mothers?" Inevitably, people will respond that mothers are meant to care for their offspring and not to harm them. Hence, why there is universal outrage when child abuse cases are brought to light. Based on that answer, one who is pro-life can point out that a woman ought to maintain a pregnancy because doing so shows care for her preborn child, whereas the act of abortion is profoundly destructive, dismembering or in some other way destroying the body of the youngest of our kind.

When someone responds, "But it's not a child yet," we can then ask, "When does motherhood begin?" After all, someone becomes a biological mother when the next generation, bearing her DNA, comes into existence. We can appeal to the authority of science to point out that the moment that has been universally recognized is sperm-egg fusion. Consider the reproductive technology industry, which mimics in a lab what happens in a woman's body, reinforces this in its work of making sperm-egg fusion happen in order to generate off-spring for clients. In other words, the very title of "mother" acknowledges the existence of a child. Granted, at this moment of fertilization, the one-celled offspring still has much development to undergo, but so do newborns, tod-dlers, and even teenagers—the latter of which have brains that do not fully develop until they are in their twenties. The point is that *who* comes into exis-tence is someone new, and that someone is offspring of the female whose egg contributed to that new child's identity (and correspondingly, is offspring of the male whose sperm contributed to that new child's identity, thus com-pelling the now-father to live up to the responsibility of parenthood as well).

We can even look to entities like the United Nations, which, while they have embraced some troubling ideologies, have also maintained some good ones. Because many people, including supporters of abortion, view the UN as an authority, we can draw attention to the UN's *International Covenant on Civil and Political Rights* to help make the pro-life case. The covenant references countries where the death penalty occurs and states, "Sentence of death...shall not be carried out on pregnant women."[1] Regardless of one's opinion on the death penalty for the guilty, this article shows that everyone agrees we should never apply the death penalty to the innocent. So we can ask the question: What is the difference between a guilty pregnant woman and a guilty nonpreg-nant woman? Only inside the body of the former is there also an *innocent* child.

Does Consciousness Matter?

In a conversation on the topic of abortion, someone might say, "Early in pregnancy, when the vast majority of abortions occur, embryos aren't even con-scious." In responding, we can ask this question: "Why should one's current level of consciousness determine whether homicide is permissible?" Granted, a dead body is not conscious, and therefore, has no right to life; but such an individual lacks the right to life because *they lack life.* (In fact, one can-not even commit homicide on a corpse because there is no man [*homo*] left to kill [*cide*].) Such a human has ceased to exist. In contrast, the newly con-ceived human very much exists. (If they do not, no one would ever need to consider an abortion because there would be no human to terminate.) The preborn child is therefore alive and has the capacity to be conscious (just like a newborn has the capacity to talk), but due to their young age, early in pregnancy, they have yet to actualize or develop that capacity to its fullness.

If one's current level of consciousness is the determining factor for allowing homicide, it is not only the early embryo who would be in danger. So would newborns, those who are sleeping or comatose, or even people under anesthetic who, in these varied circumstances, are not conscious the way we who are reading this book are.

It is this topic that is perhaps one of the biggest sticking points for abortion supporters who wade deeply into the philosophical aspect of abortion discussions. They have a difficult time wrapping their minds (no pun intended) around the idea that a newly conceived human embryo can be equal to we who are born, since the early embryo does not yet manifest the complex brain structure and function that we generally associate with humans.

They may contend that if animals of other species don't get the protections we do, and those other species show more functional brains than human embryos, why should a human embryo get protections? In response, it is worth asking the following: "When a nonhuman species *does* get protections, are they applied only to the adults in that species, or for all within the species?" Unsurprisingly, it's the latter. If a species is endangered or exhibits higher-level qualities that we value, and we consequently protect that animal, it is *all* in the species that receive the protection, not only the adults. Even, and especially, the youngest of other species gets protected.

Similarly, in regard to human rights, the most fundamental is the right to life, and should be something that *all* within our species is granted (if we believe in equality), not just the adults among us. To deny preborn children protections because their brains aren't developed like ours is to be guilty of age discrimination, for it is only due to preborn humans' age that their brains haven't progressed to greater maturity.

Being a Dependent

Besides brain development, abortion supporters might use a preborn child's dependence on her mom's body as grounds to justify terminating a pregnancy. We can respond by asking them to consider the needs of an infant.

We can begin with feeding. A newborn child requires their caregiver's body, whether fed with breastmilk, in the case of the mother, or by the hands and arms of someone who will prepare formula and bottle-feed the baby. What if a caregiver decides they no longer wish to use their breasts, hands, or arms to meet the basic needs of an infant? What if they claim their right to bodily autonomy absolves them of responsibility for this child? What if they cease to hold, feed, clothe, change, and shelter the child? What if they abandon the newborn and the baby dies? Would we say that the caregiver would be at fault for neglect and homicide? Most definitely.

The reality is, to varying degrees, we who are the most mature must use our bodies to sustain the lives of those who are the least mature. Pregnancy is no different. If anything, pregnancy brings with it a *greater* responsibility for the most mature mother to care for the most immature child because *no one else is capable* of providing such primary sustenance. By way of analogy, consider this hypothetical scenario: If a baby falls into a pool and is drowning, and there are ten lifeguards and fifty other swimmers present to jump in and help, the involvement of everyone is not necessary (and, quite frankly, would complicate the rescue). If, however, a baby falls into a pool and is drowning, and only one lifeguard is present with no other person around, the duty of that lifeguard to rescue the child is heightened beyond compare. Likewise, because no one but a pregnant woman can care for her preborn child, far from being absolved from her maternal role, she is obligated to fulfill it.

That the child is *in* the woman's body does not give the mother grounds to harm her offspring, because (A) the child is *her offspring*—thus necessitating parental responsibility, and (B) the child is in the one and only place they should be at that stage of their development. For the person who touts a belief in bodily rights, we could remind them that preborn children have bodily rights too.

Facing the Hard Cases

Often, abortion supporters will bring up what are typically classified as "the hard cases" to justify abortion. Common examples are a preborn child with a disability or illness, pregnancy from rape, or circumstances when a pregnant woman's life is in danger. Here we certainly need to be sensitive in communicating truth and should acknowledge these situations can involve great trauma and suffering. We should remember the apostle Paul's words that "love is patient and kind" (1 Corinthians 13:4). We shouldn't be so focused on making a statement of truth that we plow through a conversation without listening. Instead, we should seek to understand where the other person is coming from and whether their question is grounded in a personal experience they or a loved one has faced. We must carefully balance affirming the difficulty of one's predicament, while being cautious not to grant license to commit immoral behavior. In love, we need to come alongside to help people see that homicide is not the ethical solution in such circumstances. In fact, when we remove abortion from being an option, it forces us to get creative about life-affirming alternatives.

If a child has a disability, we can ask: What improvements can we make to our society to better accommodate and communicate with such individuals? How can we be creative about using technology, for example, to help people be more mobile or more communicative? We can share stories of people with disabilities who have been properly loved and cared for, and have thrived. We can point out that if it would be wrong to kill such individuals for their disability now, it would also be wrong to have done so when they were younger (i.e., in the womb). If a child is so sick they will die shortly after birth, we can connect families to the caring support of a perinatal hospice organization, which affirms a dying baby's dignity by respecting the fullness of their life in and out of the womb, without hastening their death, even when that life will naturally be quite short.[2]

If a woman gets pregnant from rape, we need to consider this question: How will an abortion undo that horrific trauma? Obviously, it can't. Sadly, the mother will still have brutal and terrible memories. What cannot be avoided in this situation is that her baby will need to come out of her body one way or another. At that point the question is: Dead or alive? This is the time we must ask, How is it just to end the child's life when they are innocent, like the mom? The only guilty party is the man who raped the mother. We can share stories of people like Ryan Bomberger, who was conceived in rape and whose birth mom bravely placed him for adoption, or Lianna Rebolledo, who was raped at 12 years old and lovingly raised the daughter she conceived through that traumatic event.

When a woman's life is in danger in relation to her pregnancy, our society should ask, What treatments, medicines, and interventions can we pursue or develop that address her underlying condition without killing her child? and How can we employ modern technology, like incubators, to keep her child alive while responding to the mother's pathology? These are the types of questions we want to ask, instead of hastening toward actions that only answer the question, How quickly can we end this dilemma?—resulting in the taking of an innocent life. Analogously, in the same way we would not kill a born person for their organs in order to save other peoples' lives, we should not kill a preborn person to save the mother's life. We need to choose ethical alternatives.

A short chapter of many in one anthology does not permit me to go into the detail required to fully address all these hard cases, but my books and other writings address such points at greater length.[3] Here I will reiterate, when discussing "the hard cases" with others, love must lead the way in our conversations. Do not compromise truth, but speak with patience, compassion, and love.

What Inspiring People Teach Us

In 2017, I had a unique opportunity to present the pro-life message at the Google headquarters for the speaker series *Talks at Google*. One of the points I shared there was that in my work over the years, I have found it helpful to ask people this question: "Who inspires you?" At first glance, such a question seems off topic for the issue of abortion. And yet, there is an important connectedness. I have found that when people reflect on the types of individuals they find personally inspiring, the shared qualities of such a variety of people found in their responses are similar to the qualities necessary for a person who is carrying through with an unplanned pregnancy.

At the end of the day, embracing the pro-life message involves embracing a worldview that is not always easy to live out. It requires great courage and commitment to doing the right thing; it requires being others focused. By tapping into a person's natural attraction to people who have faced hard circumstances in other settings, and who have, nonetheless, been courageous, selfless, and committed to the morally correct path, we can show others how embracing the pro-life perspective aligns with the qualities they look up to in another person.

This brings to mind a man named Wesley Autrey. What would you do if, while waiting for a subway train to arrive, you noticed a man convulsing from seizures fall onto the tracks? To Wesley Autrey the answer was clear: Jump onto the tracks and help him. On January 2, 2007, that's what he did.[4] Except Autrey wasn't just helping a man in need. He was putting himself in danger. Because as the fallen man convulsed on the tracks, the lights of an oncoming train flashed before them.

Autrey couldn't get the man off the tracks in time. But rather than abandon him and save himself by scrambling back up to the platform, Autrey laid on top of him, protecting the young man's flailing body with his lanky frame. And then train cars came. Not just one, not two, but five—*five*—train cars rolled over the men before coming to a stop.

Miraculously, the men survived. Miraculously, they were unharmed. Miraculously, the center space between the tracks that they were squished into, with the bottom of the train hovering over them, was just enough clearing (around 21 inches) for them to be safe.[5]

Much has been said to describe Autrey's actions. Universally, people from all backgrounds are inspired by what he did. Undoubtedly, those who know the story of the Good Samaritan from Scripture (Luke 10:29-37) will see the connection between this selfless man from New York City and the compassionate man who cared for a half-dead stranger on the road to Jericho. Jesus' admonition for us at the end of the parable was, "Go, and do likewise" (verse 37).

We who know the love of a mother will also see a connection between those stories and a mother's daily service to her children. Although the specifics in each case are different, the overall witness is the same. It involves self-sacrifice. It involves willing another's good, and acting on it. It involves choosing the right path. In short, it involves love.

Humans are naturally attracted to the good, the true, and the beautiful. God designed us that way. So it is our job to illustrate that embracing the self-sacrificing love of a mother, which bears semblance with the actions of other inspiring people, is at the heart of the pro-life message.

Engaging in Spiritual Battle

Finally, we need to approach any encounters we have with a spirit of prayer. People are often profoundly passionate when discussing abortion because they are connected to an abortion decision (whether having had one themselves or having facilitated another's choice). Feelings of guilt and shame can cause people to put up their guard. We must remember: We should not position ourselves as being against any particular person we are speaking with, but instead, we are engaging in a spiritual battle of good versus evil: "We are not contending against flesh and blood, but against the principalities, against the powers, against the world rulers of this present darkness, against the spiritual hosts of wickedness in the heavenly places" (Ephesians 6:12 RSV).

God created man in His image. When God commanded us to "be fruitful and multiply" (Genesis 1:28), His design was that it would be fulfilled through pregnancy. When God became man through Jesus, He chose to enter the fullness of the human experience as a newly conceived embryo (by the power of the Holy Spirit [Matthew 1:20]). God clearly values preborn life, which means that attacks on such life come from "the powers" and "the spiritual hosts of wickedness" from Satan himself.

We need to be rooted in prayer so we will respond to others with the wisdom and power of our heavenly Father. He knows what people ultimately need to hear, and He will help us interact with others so that their "hearts of stone" be transformed to "hearts of flesh" (Ezekiel 36:26 ESV). Through calling on the Holy Spirit, we can partner with our good God to "do justice, and to love kindness, and to walk humbly" (Micah 6:8 ESV). Whether our prayers are that of John the Baptist, who declared, "He must increase, but I must decrease" (John 3:30 ESV), or that of Jesus' mother, who said, "My soul magnifies the Lord" (Luke 1:46 ESV), may the cry of our hearts in our encounters with others be like the cries of these souls who went before us, putting Christ first.

Stephanie Gray Connors is an active international speaker on the subjects of abortion, In Vitro fertilization, and assisted suicide. She is the author of several books, including *Love Unleashes Life: Abortion and the Art of Communicating Truth* and *My Body for You: A Pro-Life Message for a Post-Roe World.*

CRITIQUING CRITICAL THEORY

Neil Shenvi

I became a Christian as a graduate student at UC Berkeley, shortly before the terrorist attacks of September 11, 2001. The intellectual climate that surrounded me as a new believer was very different than the one surrounding most students today. The late 2000s and early 2010s were the zenith of the New Atheist movement. Richard Dawkins's *The God Delusion* was a runaway bestseller. Christopher Hitchens's *God Is Not Great* railed against all forms of theism. Sam Harris's *The End of Faith* urged people to throw off the chains of religion and embrace reason and science. Atheist blogs multiplied. Comment sections turned into battlefields.

In his fascinating essay "New Atheism: The Godlessness That Failed," atheist Scott Alexander offers us insight into the spirit of those days:

> In 2005, a college student made a webpage called The Church Of The Flying Spaghetti Monster. It was a joke based on the idea that there was no more scientific evidence for God or creationism than for belief in a flying spaghetti monster. The monster's website

received tens of millions of visitors, 60,000 emails ("about 95 percent" supportive), and was covered in *The New York Times*, *The Washington Post*, and *The Daily Telegraph*. Six publishing companies entered a bidding war for the rights to the spaghetti monster's "gospel", with the winner, Random House, offering an $80,000 advance. The book was published to massive fanfare, sold over 100,000 copies, and was translated into multiple languages. Putin's thugs broke up a pro-Flying-Spaghetti-Monster demonstration in Russia. At the time, this seemed perfectly normal.

Two decades later, the landscape looks almost completely different. The New Atheist movement is nearly defunct. Its former champions are bitterly divided. Its missionary zeal has dissipated. But what happened to it? Alexander answers, "I think it seamlessly merged into the modern social justice movement…We woke up one morning and the atheist bloggers had all quietly became social justice bloggers."[1]

The co-option of the New Atheist movement by the social justice movement mirrors a larger trend in our society. In 2019, NBC News ran an opinion piece entitled "Your Fancy New Brunch Place Is Probably Colonialist, and You're a Colonizer" with the subtitle "Gentrification is just the latest iteration of colonization. But now it comes with eggs Benedict and bottomless mimosas."[2] In 2020, the Smithsonian Institute posted a chart naming "Emphasis on Scientific Method," "Objective, rational linear thinking," and "Cause and effect relationships" as "Aspects and Assumptions of Whiteness and White Culture in the United States."[3] The official Black Lives Matter website announced that their organization "foster[s] a queer-affirming network" and wants to free themselves "from the tight grip of heteronormative thinking."[4] In her confirmation hearing, Supreme Court Justice Ketanji Brown Jackson was asked to define the word *woman* and replied, "I'm not a biologist."[5] Perspectives like these regarding race, class, gender, and sexuality are ubiquitous and unavoidable.

In this chapter, I'll argue that we are witnessing the emergence of a new worldview with its own anthropology (doctrine of man), hamartiology (doctrine of sin), and soteriology (doctrine of salvation). What atheist James

Lindsay called the "Postmodern Religion of Social Justice" has infected education, government, entertainment, and even the church.[6] Sharing the gospel with the next generation requires that we understand people's background assumptions, their epistemology (the way they attempt to know truth), and their overarching moral framework. Therefore, as Christian apologists, it's crucial for us to understand this new worldview and then to offer an assessment and critique rooted in Scripture.

Due to space limitations, I'll provide only a brief overview. However, at the end of the chapter, I will recommend several important primary sources. Interested readers should also consult my book *Critical Dilemma*, where my coauthor Dr. Pat Sawyer and I provide an accessible but heavily footnoted analysis of contemporary critical theory.

Origins

The ideas at the heart of the social justice movement grew out of an area of knowledge known as critical theory. The term *Critical Theory* was coined in 1937 by Max Horkheimer. Horkheimer was a leading member of the Frankfurt School, a group of sociologists and philosophers who worked in Germany and later in the US. These men sought to extend the theories of Karl Marx beyond economics. In particular, they wanted to know how relations of domination and oppression were produced not merely by economic arrangements but through mass media and the "culture industry."

Over the past 80 years, critical theory has grown from a particular school of social analysis into a broad category that encompasses critical race theory, queer theory, critical pedagogy, intersectional feminism, and postcolonial theory. It has interacted with, challenged, and incorporated the ideas of postmodernism, and it has deeply influenced more traditional disciplines like history, sociology, psychology, political science, and law. Notable theorists within the critical tradition include Max Horkheimer, Herbert Marcuse, Paulo Freire, Pierre Bourdieu, Michel Foucault, Jacques Derrida, Judith Butler, Derrick Bell, and Kimberlé Crenshaw. Dozens of lesser known, but still prominent, critical theorists have produced tens of millions of words of scholarship.

In short, critical theory is a vast, sprawling area of knowledge that can be difficult to define. Making matters even more complicated, scholars engaged in critical scholarship today do not always identify with the label *critical theory*. For example, a great deal of antiracist scholarship is deeply indebted to the critical tradition. Yet antiracist scholars will not necessarily identify the historical origin of their ideas. On the ground, activists may employ phrases like *white privilege* or *heteronormativity* or *systemic injustice* with little awareness of their ideological roots. Therefore, rather than focusing on particular authors or particular labels (e.g., *wokeness* or *cultural Marxism* or *intersectionality*), it's helpful to identify the ideas at the heart of contemporary critical theory. We can then analyze these ideas from a Christian perspective and better understand the viewpoint of those who have embraced them.

Ideas

Four ideas lie at the heart of contemporary critical theory: the social binary, hegemonic power, lived experience, and social justice.

First, the concept of the *social binary* maintains that society is divided into oppressor groups and oppressed groups along lines of race, class, gender, gender identity, sexuality, disability status, religion, and a host of other identity markers. For example, Whites, the rich, men, cisgendered people, heterosexuals, the able-bodied, and Christians are all oppressor groups (also known as "dominant groups" or "privileged groups"). In contrast, people of color, the poor, women, transgendered people, homosexuals, the disabled, and non-Christians are all oppressed groups (also known as "subordinate groups" or "minoritized groups").

Hegemonic power is a second concept that's central to contemporary critical theory's understanding of oppression. Traditionally, oppression referred to cruelty, tyranny, or sustained injustice. However, in the 1960s, critical theorists redefined oppression to refer to the subtle ways in which the ruling class, whether Whites or men or heterosexuals or Christians, imposes their values, norms, and expectations on the rest of culture to justify their own power and privilege. These dominant, hegemonic norms are so pervasive that they are taken for granted and are seen as natural, normal, objective, and even God-ordained. Thus, groups can be oppressed not only by cruel, unjust treatment but also by being positioned as "Other" via social norms.

If all people, whether they belong to oppressed or oppressor groups, are socialized into oppressive hegemonic norms, how are these norms recognized? The answer is found in the third central idea of contemporary critical theory: *lived experience*. Both oppressed people and oppressors take for granted the norms and values of white supremacy, patriarchy, capitalism, and heterosexism. However, oppressed people simultaneously experience racism, sexism, classism, and homophobia in their daily lives, allowing them to achieve a "critical" or "liberatory" consciousness. Colloquially, they can "get woke." They can see through the thinly veiled excuses and rationalizations that blind the rest of us to the reality of systemic oppression. As a consequence, those of us with privileged backgrounds should defer to people with oppressed backgrounds, just as a blind man would defer to the guidance of someone who can see.

Finally, the end goal of contemporary critical theory is *social justice*, defined as the elimination of the social binary. By dismantling the systems, structures, and hegemonic discourses that perpetuate the power of privileged groups, we can achieve a state of diversity, equity, and inclusion. Critical theories are never bare descriptions of the ways things are. They are also prescriptions for how institutions and individuals ought to behave to secure liberation and justice for groups deemed oppressed.

Far from being mere analytic tools, these ideas provide a coherent, comprehensive view of social reality. They speak to fundamental issues like identity (who we are), epistemology (how we know truth), and phenomenology (our day-to-day experience). They identify our fundamental problem as human beings (oppression) and the solution to that problem (activism). Consequently, contemporary critical theory functions as a worldview, one that a Christian apologist must recognize and address in any evangelistic encounter.

Identity Marker	Type of Oppression	Oppressor Group	Oppressed Group
Race	Racism	Whites	People of color
Class	Classism	The rich	The poor
Biological sex	Sexism	Men	Women
Sexuality	Heterosexism	Heterosexuals	Homosexuals

Identity Marker	Type of Oppression	Oppressor Group	Oppressed Group
Gender identity	Cisgenderism	Cisgender people	Transgender people
Physical/ mental ability	Ableism	The able-bodied	People with disabilities
Age	Ageism/Adultism	Adults	The elderly/ children
Religion	Religious oppression	Christians	Non-Christians
Colonial status	Colonialism	Colonizers	Indigenous people
Skin color	Colorism	Light-skinned people	Dark-skinned people

Table 1. A few of the oppressor/oppressed groups that constitute the social binary, according to contemporary critical theory. Reproduced by permission from Neil Shenvi and Pat Sawyer, *Critical Dilemma* (Eugene, OR: Harvest House, 2023), 96.

Analysis

Because of the pervasiveness of contemporary critical theory within our culture, its assumptions often go unnoticed. Our first job as apologists is to unearth these assumptions and then to subject them to the scrutiny of reason and the Bible. As we'll see, Christianity and contemporary critical theory conflict in many ways.

First, the very nature of contemporary critical theory as an all-encompassing worldview necessitates a conflict with an equally all-encompassing Christian worldview. Christianity and contemporary critical theory offer mutually exclusive answers to life's big questions. Either Christianity or contemporary critical theory will be the primary lens through which we view the world and will slowly capture more and more of our mental landscape, emotional life, and priorities.

Worldview Question	Christianity	Contemporary Critical Theory
Who am I?	A creature made in God's image	A member of various social groups locked in a struggle for dominance
What is the fundamental human problem?	Sin	Oppression
How can that problem be solved?	Redemption through Jesus	Activism and solidarity
What is my primary moral duty?	Glorifying God	Dismantling unjust systems and structures
How do I know the truth?	Revelation and reason	Lived experience
What is the end goal of history?	The new heaven and earth	Social justice

Table 2. Worldview questions answered by Christianity versus contemporary critical theory. Reproduced by permission from Neil Shenvi and Pat Sawyer, *Critical Dilemma* (Eugene, OR: Harvest House, 2023), 282.

Second, contemporary critical theory believes all the oppressions that produce the social binary are interlocking and must be dismantled simultaneously. For example, racism, sexism, heterosexism, and transphobia are all oppressions that must be opposed. Ibram Kendi writes candidly: "We cannot be antiracist if we are homophobic or transphobic...To be queer antiracist is to understand the privileges of my cisgender, of my masculinity, of my heterosexuality, of their intersections."[7] This position conflicts inescapably with a biblical sexual ethic.

Third, contemporary critical theory consistently analyzes hegemonic values and norms as arbitrary impositions of the ruling class. However, this assumption is incompatible with the Christian belief that God's moral law is good, true, and universally applicable to all people in all cultures. For example, the gender binary is not just an arbitrary convention devised by oppressive White, heterosexual males. Rather, it is God's universally good design for humanity. Critical theory's skepticism towards norms and values leads rapidly to the deconstruction of any doctrine that can be cast as regressive, oppressive, or outdated.

Fourth, contemporary critical theory depends on dividing people along lines of race, class, and gender. It requires us to view ourselves and others primarily as members of demographic groups locked in an internecine struggle for dominance. In contrast, Christianity insists that we're bound together by three great doctrines of human solidarity. All of us—young or old, male or female, rich or poor, Black or White or Hispanic or Asian—are created in God's image. All of us are sinners who deserve God's righteous judgment. And all of us need the salvation that is only found in Jesus Christ. The divisive nature of critical theory is particularly pernicious in the church, where all of us have been united as coheirs with Christ, members of God's household, and fellow recipients of God's grace.

Finally, from a Christian perspective, contemporary critical theory has a heretical hamartiology (doctrine of sin) and soteriology (doctrine of salvation). Contemporary critical theory teaches that our fundamental problem is external: Certain groups have culture power and are oppressing us. In contrast, Christianity teaches that our fundamental problem is internal: We have sinned and are separated from God. Similarly, critical theory believes that we can solve our problems ourselves. We can divest from and repent of our privilege. We can center marginalized voices. We can stop taking up space. We can do the work. We can be on the right side of history. Christianity says: You cannot save yourself. All your righteous deeds are filthy rags. You need to be rescued. For all these reasons and more, contemporary critical theory and Christianity are incompatible.

Engagement

Engagement with those who have been captivated by the ideas of contemporary critical theory should begin with sympathy for their concerns. Contemporary critical theory latches on to our good and righteous desire to protect the vulnerable. It appeals to people who have faced actual racism, sexism, or other forms of mistreatment. Christians should never downplay or dismiss these problems. White (or Black) nationalism, misogyny, anti-Semitism, and other forms of hatred do exist and are soul destroying. Critical theory is not wrong to oppose these evils and we dare not let our rejection of critical theory tempt us to soft-pedal them.

In a similar way, we must engage in honest reflection on our nation's horrific racial history and the continuing presence of racial discrimination today. Too many young Christians are raised with a hagiographic, rose-colored view of America's past; they don't encounter the realities of slavery or events like the Tulsa Race Massacre until college. As a result, the progressive scholars who first confront them with the many disturbing events in our nation's history are viewed less like fallible human beings and more like divine oracles. Christian students start asking themselves, *If my parents hid these facts from me, what else did they hide?* An honest, accurate treatment of history, that handles the United States neither as sinless nor as evil incarnate, will inoculate students against the notion that only critical theorists care about injustice.

Another major concern when addressing people who are attracted to critical theory is establishing the centrality of truth to the discussion. Few people today are thoroughgoing relativists. They recognize that the earth orbits the sun, that germs cause disease, and that 2 + 2 = 4. Moral relativism also seems to be on the decline, since contemporary critical theory takes it as axiomatic that justice is objectively good, and that injustice is objectively evil. However, critical theory runs into problems when objective, empirical truths conflict with its preferred narrative.

Queer theory's radical rejection of the gender binary (the division of humanity into male and female) is a case in point. Fifty years ago, the gender binary would have been as uncontroversial as heliocentrism. Yet today, transgender activists decry the notion of the gender binary as outdated and hurtful. They see it not as a fact of nature, but as patriarchal, heterosexist, and oppressive. Here we see critical theory's ambivalence toward objective truth. On the one hand, it takes a decidedly modernist perspective on the objective immorality of oppression. On the other hand, its commitment to lived experience leads it to problematize or outright reject truths that are deemed to be "harmful" or "oppressive."

In conversations, then, it's vital to assert the preeminence of truth. Point out that being "loving" and "compassionate" is necessary but not sufficient. A very loving, compassionate doctor can nonetheless kill his patient if he prescribes the wrong medicine. A very loving, compassionate captain can run his ship into an iceberg because he's trying to appease—rather than to guide—his passengers. In the same way, advocates of social justice must promote policies not because they are attractive, but because they are rooted in truth.

Finally, Christian apologists must recognize that the essence of critical theory's appeal is spiritual. According to the Bible, all human beings know that we are alienated from God because of our sin. We feel our guilt and shame and, like Adam and Eve, we attempt to cover our nakedness with garments of our own making. Contemporary critical theory is therefore a very effective spiritual anodyne. It replaces sin against God with the sin of privilege and then tells us we can expunge the guilt of our privilege with our good works, self-abasement, and social justice allyship. It lets us feel good about ourselves and makes us feel righteous (especially when compared to hateful bigots). Jesus vehemently rejected this posture as deeply offensive to God.

Therefore, Christians can't merely expose the poison at the heart of critical theory. We must also point people to the bread of life, Jesus, the only one who can truly satisfy our deep hunger for forgiveness and the one who came to call not the righteous, but sinners.

>> >> >>

Resources

A familiarity with primary and secondary sources will be extremely helpful for Christians engaging with critical theory. The following books are particularly useful.

Critical social justice:
Özlem Sensoy and Robin J. DiAngelo, *Is Everyone Really Equal?*, 2d ed. (New York: Teachers College Press, 2017).

Critical race theory:
Khiara M. Bridges, *Critical Race Theory: A Primer*, Concepts and Insights Series (St. Paul, MN: Foundation Press, 2019).

Queer theory:
Riki Wilchins, *Queer Theory, Gender Theory: An Instant Primer* (Bronx, NY: Magnus Books, 2004).

A critical, secular perspective on critical theory:
Helen Pluckrose and James A. Lindsay, *Cynical Theories*, 1st ed. (Durham, NC: Pitchstone Publishing, 2020).

A critical Christian perspective on critical theory:
Neil Shenvi and Pat Sawyer, *Critical Dilemma* (Eugene, OR: Harvest House Publishers, 2023).

Neil Shenvi has worked in theoretical physics as a postdoctoral associate at Yale and a research associate at Duke University. He homeschools and teaches at his children's homeschool co-op. His writing on apologetics has appeared in many journals, he is the author of *Why Believe: A Reasoned Approach to Christianity*, and he is the coauthor of *Critical Dilemma: The Rise of Critical Theories and Social Justice Ideology—Implications for the Church and Society*.

19

CHURCH OF INVISIBLE DISEASES: APOLOGETICS AND MENTAL HEALTH

Jeremiah J. Johnston

She calls it her "invisible disease." Why? Because mental illness is real. At 22 years of age, it is constantly holding her back, weighing her down, and obliterating her self-esteem. But the problem is that no one else can "see" this disease—which is so very real to both Lucy[1] and her family. Lucy's story is mirrored by so many people in our churches, who are struggling silently and wasting away on the inside. Lucy does not fit the stereotype of one who struggles with a mental illness. Lucy comes from a wonderful Christian home. Her parents and four siblings are committed followers of Jesus, active in their local church, and serve in their community. She is talented, educated, articulate, and from the outside, you would never guess she struggled with anything, which compiles the stigma and shame.

For Lucy, it all began after she was diagnosed with juvenile type 1 diabetes. A diagnosis that, for her, spiraled into years of extreme anxiety and depression culminating in a debilitating eating disorder. Lucy informed me eating disorders are the most fatal of all mental illnesses. She shared, "I never realized I was depressed. I never even thought of depression. Probably because no one ever talked about it." Lucy's mental pain caused her to feel as if she had no control over her body. She asked, "How could God curse me with this dysfunctional, disgusting body?"

Going to church only made things worse. When the congregation would stand to sing, Lucy was so embarrassed by her body she couldn't worship. She did not want anyone to see her. Lucy even refused to take communion; she was counting every single calorie. Her mental illness lied to her and caused her to believe she was a failure as a Christian.

Lucy made a key statement during our conversation: "No one ever talked to me about my mental illness. None of my teachers, my pastors, my youth group leaders, or my parents ever talked with me about it." Lucy's eating disorder (and the associated depression with anxiety) consumed her thoughts. She said, "They took everything from me." She pushed everyone away, lost connection with all her friends, broke up with her boyfriend, questioned her faith in God, and stopped working at a job she loved. The shame choked her prayers, "No matter how hard I prayed, I never got better. I was sick of praying about it."

An intervention by Lucy's parents and psychiatrist saved her life. Lucy was treated in an inpatient treatment center, which started her road to recovery and her healing from the inside out. She shared, "Once my brain was properly nourished, I realized that it was not my fault. My anxiety, depression, mental illness, and eating disorder did not make me a bad person nor a failure as a Christian. I had a medical condition and needed professional help! I can't help but wonder, if I had learned about depression, anxiety, and mental disorders growing up, maybe I would have seen red flags sooner and asked for help. But how could I seek help for a problem I didn't know I had?"

Stopping the silence was a key component to Lucy's healing equation. Lucy says, "Opening up and sharing about my mental illnesses has been such a huge part of my recovery. Silence and hiding my depression, anxiety, and eating disorder gave these illnesses so much power over me. I am no longer a slave to my eating disorder." With God's strength and a supportive care team, Lucy has experienced the golden word in mental health treatment—*freedom*.

The Most Important Question of Our Time

Most apologists and Christian media today observe a surge in questions about mental pain, mental illness, and suicide in the context of Christian life. The real problem we face is that many non-Christians perceive Christianity as an answer to yesterday's questions, believing it offers nothing relevant to today's pressing issues. To address this, we must use the tactic exemplified by C.S. Lewis. That of being a "faith translator" to the masses: "My task was therefore simply that of a *translator*—one turning Christian doctrine, or what he believed to be such, into the vernacular, into language that unscholarly people would attend to and could understand."[2]

As Christians, we need to stop the silence, stop the shame and exclusion; raise awareness and remove the stigma surrounding mental illness, which is widespread and affects many followers of Jesus. No one is unaffected by mental illness. If you have not personally struggled with mental illness, chances are that your friend, spouse, child, coworker, or neighbor has. The ministry of Jesus focused on removing barriers to belief and restoring people who were suffering. The church needs to follow His example. Yet a LifeWay Research survey found that 66 percent of pastors rarely or never address the subject of mental illness from their pulpits, and the same survey revealed that the majority of churchgoers wish their pastors would talk about it.[3]

Many stigmatize the mentally ill as people in hospital gowns committed deep inside a psych ward. But that is a very inaccurate depiction of someone with a mental illness. Would it surprise you to learn that people with mental illnesses worship at your church and probably attend your Bible-study group with you?

It is very sad that we say so little about mental illness in the church. We act as if it does not exist. Rarely do we hear sermons or read Bible-study material on this topic. It has left some Christian leaders in a quandary because of how prevalent mental illness is. One article summarized the findings of the LifeWay Research study and further added that "Nearly 1 in 4 pastors (23 percent) acknowledge they have 'personally struggled with mental illness,' and half of those pastors said the illness had been diagnosed, according to the poll."[4]

Research indicates that individuals experiencing psychological distress are more likely to seek help from clergy (such as pastors, priests, or rabbis) before turning to any other professional group, including mental health experts.[5] As I have elsewhere written, "The church is central in the healing equation for the multitudes who are seeking peace and joy but struggling with anxiety. There is a great opportunity for Christian leaders and the global church to minister to the afflicted."[6] To show how Christianity holds the answers to today's questions, we have to improve our understanding and discipleship strategies by including mental pain and the various mental illnesses in our apologetics framework.

Historian Will Durant pointed out the educational value of shock: "Nothing so educates us as a shock."[7] The church has been shocked (and educated) in recent times by the suicides of not only Christians who listened in the pews, but of prominent pastors and leaders as well. Invisible illnesses of the brain have the power to isolate you, kill you, shorten your lifespan, and cause you to cease to be a productive member of society. According to the American Foundation for Suicide Prevention, "Suicide claims more lives than war, murder, and natural disasters combined."[8] Mental illness is not a choice, but the good news is that it is treatable. The Bible says we were born into sin (Romans 5:12). We are prone to do wrong. Character is not natural, but sin is. We inherit a curse from Adam that manifests itself in the human body in many ways. The body grows old; strength dissipates; and eventually, our immune systems cannot fight off diseases. Our cell structure breaks down, and eventually, we expire. In strange ways that not even the best mental-health professionals can fully explain, many people experience mental illness.

Studies indicate that in some cases, mental illness is biological and perhaps even generational. In other instances, severe psychological trauma triggered by harrowing, unexpected, and extremely difficult circumstances in life have induced mental illness. And of course, in the backdrop of all illness is daily spiritual war (see Ephesians 6:10-18) being waged by the devil (see John 8:44) and his myriad of demons working to cause Christians to fail. Therefore, we must be discerning enough to determine whether the errant or odd behavior in a person is sin or something induced by a mental illness. Thank God for the growing number of trained, licensed, board-certified specialists in the mental-health vocation who are Christians and understand these competing factors.

Mental Health America of Wisconsin identifies, "More years of life are lost to suicide than to any other single cause except heart disease and cancer."[9] I've noticed in ministry, though, that if we are not careful, we can develop a detached view of these grim statistics. Mother Teresa is known for saying, "If I look at the mass, I will never act. If I look at the one, I will." We must remember, behind all the statistics are very personal stories of *one*, like Lucy. You probably have a "Lucy" in your classroom, church, youth group, or serving in your ministry right now.

This is a global issue. It is an individual issue. And I believe the issue is reflected in the most important question the church faces today: *How can I live in the peace of God?*[10]

The Peace Plan

The apostle Paul confessed, in 2 Corinthians 2:13, "I still had no peace of mind" (NIV) during an anxiety attack he experienced on the second missionary journey in the city of Troas (in modern-day Turkey). The time frame was AD 51–52. Paul was searching the city for his friend Titus and could not find him anywhere. Anxiety and catastrophic thinking set in. Troas became a trigger for Paul, and he immediately left, even though "a door was opened to me by the Lord" (verse 12 NKJV). You might be able to identify with Paul. Perhaps you've experienced a situation where God opened a great door for your life, but anxiety prohibited you from entering through it. The experience is a memory, which can trigger an emotional response.

Paul worried because he could not find Titus. But Acts 16 records that one of God's purposes in this was for him to meet a new friend named Luke (Acts 16:10). From that point on, the famous "we" passages are present in Acts with Luke accompanying Paul on his missionary travels.

What's more, Paul probably thought the door of ministry in Troas was forever closed. Yet again, God had other plans. Not only did God bring Paul (and Luke) back to minister in Troas during the third missionary journey (AD 57–58), but the Lord also used Paul to perform Paul's greatest miracle— raising Eutychus from the dead there (Acts 20:7-12).

A question we are left with is this: What happened in Paul's life in between his travels to Troas? He left Troas in anxiety and returned a few years later in the peace of God. And evidently, he "talked on and on" (verse 9 NIV) and left them "greatly comforted" (verse 12 NIV). How did Paul receive freedom from his anxiety?

Scripture corroborates scripture and the answer becomes clearer when we study the "peace of God plan" Paul developed in his walk with Christ. Paul shared his personal peace plan in the greatest anti-anxiety chapter in all the Bible— Philippians 4. Using six adjectives and two nouns, all anchored by one present-tense verb (*meditate*), Paul shared his plan to experiencing the peace of God:

> Whatever things are true, whatever things are noble, whatever things are just, whatever things are pure, whatever things are lovely, whatever things are of good report, if there is any virtue and if there is anything praiseworthy—meditate on these things (verse 8 NKJV).

The contrast is stark. Paul knew anxiety in Troas, even with a "great open door" from the Lord. But later, Paul knew peace, even within a prison cell in Rome while writing this epistle to the believers in Philippi under the agency of the Holy Spirit. We receive the promise of Philippians 4:6-7 when we— like Paul—develop the discipline of God's peace in our lives:

> Be anxious for nothing, but in everything by prayer and supplication, with thanksgiving, let your requests be made known to God; and the peace of God, which surpasses all understanding, will guard your hearts and minds through Christ Jesus (NKJV).

No one among the first-century followers of Jesus likely grasped God's *shalom* more profoundly than the apostle Paul. Before his encounter with the risen Jesus on the road to Damascus (Acts 9), Paul was far from peaceful. He aggressively persecuted Christians, even to the point of causing death. Following his conversion, he confessed to having tried to justify himself through strict adherence to the law of Moses. However, upon meeting Jesus, he began to truly comprehend the essence of peace.

If Paul needed a peace plan, we do too. In 2021, my wife inspired me to write my own "Peace Plan" and it has been shared thousands of times since via social media. The goal of my personal peace plan is not to achieve perfection, but to find freedom. When I orient my values and priorities around the peace of God as a discipline in my life, everything changes for the better. I begin to experience the moment-by-moment peace of God.

Jeremiah's Peace Plan
Practical Ways to Implement Shalom
by Managing Anxiety, Stress, and Uncertainties

1. Stop obsessively checking the news.

2. Check your sources and stop doom scrolling.

3. Don't contribute to the panic.

4. Stay social.

5. Isolation is the worst punishment for a human being.

6. Establish a daily schedule.

7. Leave the house.

8. Get out into nature.

9. Exercise.

10. Thank God more for what He's done instead of always worrying about what comes next.

11. Look at art more. We need more beauty in our life.

12. Have quiet time/prayer in any sleepless moments lying in bed.

13. Use Scripture Memory app to memorize Scripture.

14. When stress or anxiety fills my mind, I seek to replace it with key verses.

15. Say THANK YOU JESUS throughout the day.

16. There are things only God can control, and things He allows me to take part in controlling. I try and discern which are which and only work to resolve the things He allows me to help control.

17. A true sabbath each week to be able to rest and do what feeds my soul—specifically, resting my mind from thinking about sermon prep or leading organization.

18. Say no more often.

19. Do not make decisions when you are tired or discouraged.

20. Prioritize your physical health: eat nutritiously, be physically active, and get adequate sleep and rest.

But what is biblical peace and how do we find it? Is biblical peace a truce, an absence of conflict, or something more? What did Jesus mean when He referenced the *shalom* of God?

Biblical Peace Surpasses All Understanding

Although the word *peace* (Hebrew *shalom*; Greek *eirene*)—along with its variations—appears around 614 times in the Scriptures and was a constant theme in Jesus' teachings, it is a neglected topic today. As a result, God's peace has been elusive to many followers of Jesus, which is why so many are stressed and not managing anxiety in healthy ways.

The Scriptures tell us, "There is no peace for the wicked" (Isaiah 48:22). And again, "'There is no peace for the wicked,' says my God" (57:21). Anything that costs you your peace is too expensive. But how do we *find* peace? How do we *recognize* peace? How do we *know* peace?

Truth is the first step. For Jesus said, "I am the way, and the truth, and the life. No one comes to the Father except through me" (John 14:6 ESV). The Bible guides us into unending peace with God through a person—the God-Man.

After the name *Jesus* itself, there is no finer word or concept than *shalom* (peace). Shalom originates from God. And it epitomizes the gospel and the active relationship God initiates, pursues, and perfects within each of us as His followers. Shalom is eschatological, for it looks forward through the eyes of faith to the resurrected and re-created cosmos, where everything and everyone will live in peace. Shalom is both holistic and active. (Active in the sense that it invites us to flourish.) Here, *peace* can only mean that sense of wholeness and completion that the Hebrew word *shalom* (from the verb *shalēm,* "to be complete, sound") often conveys.

One of the most overlooked aspects of balanced Christian living and teaching is the concept of unleashing the shalom of God into our lives. The first Christians were Jews; therefore, even in the world of the New Testament, when the early church used the word peace, they used it with an Old Testament understanding of shalom.

The Discipline of Peace

The content of our thinking directly effects our peace and happiness. We must continually ask ourselves, *Am I trusting what I know is true about my life through Christ, or am I focusing on my problems and adversity I am facing to the extent that I have factored God out of my situation?* God's holy Word says we have been "granted...His precious and magnificent promises" (2 Peter 1:4 NASB). What does God want us to do? We must continuously trust Him. With God there are no hopeless situations, and that is why we can be assured of His peace that passes all understanding. His peace will guard our hearts and our minds through Christ Jesus.

As followers of Jesus, we have to *cultivate* peace and happiness. Mental, physical, emotional, and spiritual health is a never-ending exercise. And the peace of God is unleashed when we are disciplined thinkers. Learn from everyone and in every situation, but don't allow others to think for you. Own your faith. Think through your faith. Live your faith as a discipline.

Matthew 9:35-36 is a key passage in ministry to fellow believers struggling with invisible illnesses. Notice two important points in this passage. First, Jesus healed every disease and sickness. Jesus has the power to heal all kinds of infirmities—physical, psychological, emotional, and spiritual. Second, don't miss what caused Jesus to heal these people: His compassion for them. Our ministry to "harassed and helpless" people (verse 36)—and those words certainly describe many people with mental illnesses—begins with compassionate hearts. As Christians, as Jesus' hands and feet on earth, we have the responsibility and privilege to help people who are dealing with sin in their lives. At the same time, we cannot assume that sin is the problem. We must understand that there are differences among spiritual struggles, weaknesses, and mental illness. So we also have the opportunity to bring comfort and encouragement in people's weaknesses and to care for them in their mental illnesses. Be aware of what you have the knowledge and ability to do and when it is time to refer a person to a trained professional for help. Most important, allow God to change your heart to be more like Christ's in His compassion and care for harassed, helpless people. His grace can shine through you into the lives of people with mental illness.

Four Healing Practices

I would like to share with you four practices that the body of Christ can use to foster loving and understanding communities that support those struggling in the area of mental wellness.

1. Admit That Every Family Struggles

We're all broken. We're all messed up. In the church, we need to change our perception of mental illness and the ways we approach it. How can we come together to help, rather than looking at people struggling with a mental disorder as a problem? We need to reach out to one another and begin honest conversations.

2. Love Instead of Judge, Condemn, and Misunderstand

One of the funny observations I made very early in my ministry is that Christians don't gossip, they share prayer requests (joke). One of the reasons we do not discuss mental problems in the church is the fear of people gossiping and ostracizing us. We have lost our first love. John 13:35, "By this all people will know that you are my disciples, if you have love for one another."

3. Build Support Groups in the Church

Mental illness does not separate people from the love of God, so it shouldn't separate them from the church. Establish and maintain support groups in your local church that minister to every age level. If you look at the studies, one of the boldest myths is that children are not affected by mental illness in the home. Did you know mental illness among adolescents and young adults is increasing?[11] We need to educate ourselves.

I learned from my conversation with Lucy that one of the most helpful things for her in recovery was being surrounded by positive, supportive people who discussed the mental illness and didn't ignore its existence. Having a community is a major part of the treatment process. We can encourage those with mental disorders in their efforts to establish appropriate boundaries and practice coping mechanisms. And we can help identify mental health professionals with a biblical worldview who can help people determine whether counseling is appropriate for them. I personally know committed Christians who regularly have Christian counseling and therapy.

4. Encourage the Mentally Ill in Our Church Communities to Serve!

Many people struggling with a mental illness are extremely witty, well-humored, and highly intelligent. It is often overlooked that some of history's most influential Christians have had lifelong struggles with depression, thoughts of suicide, and mental illness.

When my wife and I lived in Oxford during my doctoral residency, at the encouragement of my friend Mike, we traveled about an hour outside of Oxford (near Milton Keynes) to the little town known as Olney. This town is understatedly remarkable because it was there that John Newton, while preparing a Bible study for New Year's Day 1773, wrote perhaps the most famous song of all time, "Amazing Grace." This song was published a few years later in the now-famous *Olney Hymns*. But many are not aware that the hymnbook had a coauthor, John Newton's dear friend William Cowper (pronounced "Coo-per"), who wrote nearly 70 of the 300 or so hymns in the collection.

You've no doubt sung some of Cowper's hymns without realizing it, like "There Is a Fountain Filled with Blood." Or another beloved Cowper hymn is "O For a Closer Walk with God." Aside from being John Newton's best friend, William Cowper is remembered as one of the great poets of the eighteenth century. Benjamin Franklin cherished Cowper's book of poems. A window in the grand Westminster Abbey honors William Cowper.

Yet Cowper struggled with paralyzing depression his entire life. He attempted suicide numerous times. His depression was chronic, and before meeting John Newton, Cowper spent years at St. Albans Insane Asylum before relocating to Olney. The local pastor was John Newton; thus Newton and Cowper became friends. Even though he was afflicted with so much mental illness, he wrote beautifully comforting lines of poetry. You've probably quoted Cowper without realizing it: "God moves in a mysterious way, His wonders to perform; He plants His footsteps in the sea, and rides upon the storm."

Mental illness touches us all. We can learn from the example of John Newton who rescued his friend by simply being there, supporting him, loving him in his mental illness, and ultimately, putting him to work on hymns.

As we close this chapter, where do you find yourself in these stories? Perhaps you are a John Newton, and you have a friend or family member you need to minister to with your own "ministry of presence." Our churches are filled with William Cowpers—gifted individuals who struggle with mental illness. Let's commit to God that "invisible diseases" in the church will be invisible no longer.

Jeremiah J. Johnston is a New Testament scholar and the president of the Christian Thinkers Society. He also serves as a Bible teacher, radio host, and pastor of apologetics and cultural engagement at Prestonwood Baptist Church. He is the author of several books, including *Unleashing Peace* and *Body of Proof.*

ENGAGING THE TRANSGENDER DEBATE

Katy Faust

My husband and I have been doing ministry for nearly 30 years. We both agree that the four years he served as a junior-high pastor in Colorado were some of the best. I want to share with you a key lesson we learned from that time: Establish a strong relationship with youth *now* to be able to speak into their lives beyond junior high. Some of those former youth we served now have kids of their own in junior high, and still write to us for advice.

One of those students was a girl I'll refer to as Ann.[1] During her time in our ministry, she attended every Sunday school class, special event, and retreat. After my family and I moved to Washington State, Ann and I lost touch. We reconnected shortly after she graduated from college, where she had taken a deep dive into gender theory. She crossed the dais to receive her diploma as a trans man.

Ann and I got together several times. Over one dim sum lunch, she explained that gender "is not a binary, it's something you perform." I had never heard such a thing. I didn't say much. I was still processing how the adorable, curly-haired girl I had known years ago had become the faux-hawk presenting man who was sipping jasmine tea across the table.

In the last 10 years, the number of Americans who identify as transgender has exploded. One young adult in 20 now claims to be nonbinary or transgender.[2] This data is particularly alarming considering that, when I was picking at my xia jiao with Ann back in 2013, *The New York Times* hadn't even printed the word *nonbinary* yet. That's how rapidly the trans phenomenon has swept the nation, especially America's youth. When I was growing up in the 80s and 90s, I knew no transgender people. When I could find a ride across town to the roller rink, I saw a few men dressed as women gliding around the skating floor, but that was it.

Today, however, everyone knows someone who identifies as something other than a "cis" male or female—*cis* being terminology for a person whose gender identity aligns with their biological sex. We have reached a time when being uninformed about topics, such as the difference between gender dysphoria and autogynephilia (both defined below) isn't an option that we have, especially as Christians who seek to speak effectively and compassionately into our current cultural moment.

Talk the Talk

Much has been written about the gender-bending (or gender-obliterating) phenomenon that is overtaking our culture, institutions, children, and even our churches.[3] (For example, the practice of identifying one's pronouns when introducing themselves in public discourse: "I'm Pastor Glenn, he/him.") While this book is primarily about the *how* of cultural engagement, it's worth spilling a bit of ink covering some of the basic terms that are important when discussing transgenderism.

- *Gender identity*—one's "innermost concept" of self as male, female, a blend of both, or neither.

- *Transgender*—a person whose "sex assigned at birth" does not align with their gender identity.

- *Gender dysphoria*—a person who experiences distress over their mind-body disconnect.

- *Early, late, and rapid onset*—psychologists identify three manifestations of gender dysphoria:

  » *Early onset* is extremely rare and is observed as early as 2 to 4 years old, when the child—usually a boy—*insistently*, *consistently*, and *persistently* reports feelings of being the opposite sex.

  » *Late onset* is also rare and diagnosed primarily in adult men with transvestite fetishes (sexually aroused by cross dressing) or who experience autogynephilia (sexually aroused by the thought of himself as a woman). When a 30-something man starts wearing dresses and demanding access to female bathrooms, locker rooms, and spas, there's a good chance one of the two above fetishes are at play.

  » *Rapid onset* is the primary explanation for today's explosion of trans-identifying youth and what researcher Lisa Littman deemed "rapid-onset gender dysphoria."[4] These are adolescents with no previous gender dysphoria or early gender confusion. Also, overwhelmingly, they are girls. A decade ago, there were more gender-dysphoric boys by a two-to-one margin. Today, girls are more likely to identify as trans by a factor of nearly three to one.[5]

Why the flip in rapid-onset gender dysphoria? The answer is *social contagion*. Girls have always been more susceptible to trending behaviors (whether in fashion, or anorexia, or cutting, etc.) because they are more sensitive to peer and online influences. Littman observed that girls with high social media use and who have one or more trans peers were more likely to identify as transgender themselves.[6] Simply put, girls do things in groups, whether it's going to the bathroom together, or "transitioning" together.

When experiencing gender dysphoria, these kids will be encouraged to "transition" by the prevailing culture in a four-phase process I call the Activist Treatment Plan:

1. *Social transition.* The child adopts a new name, pronouns, and hair and dress styles that align with opposite-sex stereotypes. For girls,

APOLOGETICS FOR AN EVER-CHANGING CULTURE

social transition often involves chest binding with the accompanying risk of "damage to their chest, ribs, lungs, posture, nerves, and skin."[7] Some boys may "tuck and tape," which can lead to "urinary tract infections, problems with urine flow and twisting or inflammation in the testicles."[8] Parents are often pressured into a child's social transition by counselors or activists asking, "Would you rather have a dead daughter or a living son?" But the best available data reveals that children who follow the Activist Treatment Plan have higher rates of depression and suicide than those allowed to develop normally.[9]

2. *Puberty blockers*. Puberty is a necessary part of human maturation and a sign of *health*. It is the second-most rapid phase of physical development during which children gain 50 percent of their adult body weight, become capable of reproduction, and experience critical brain development. But the second step of the Activist Treatment Plan "blocks" puberty via off-label hormones, such as Lupron, that are also used to chemically castrate sex offenders. While puberty blockers halt the development of "undesirable" secondary sex characteristics such as an Adam's apple, breasts, and facial hair, they also "block" critical growth of the lungs, bones, and brain. Far from simply being a "pause" on development, children on puberty blockers are at increased risk of cognitive impairment, osteoporosis, heart attacks, and strokes.[10] And it is not yet known whether they will ever recover from the developmental loss experienced while their puberty was "paused." In essence, puberty blockers induce a state of sickness in a child's otherwise healthy body.

3. *Cross-sex hormones*. Once puberty is "blocked," opposite-sex hormones are recommended to chemically masculinize or feminize a child's features. Women who take testosterone increase their muscle mass, grow masculine-located body hair, and develop a deeper voice. Men on estrogen develop more feminized facial features, softer skin, and breast-like tissue. Hormone supplements, even those aligned with our natal sex, are no joke. One recent study found

a 15 percent increase in depression and psychiatric visits for girls taking oral contraceptives.[11] Men on high doses of estrogen have a higher risk of diabetes, strokes, blood clots, and cancers.[12] Their sexual function is impaired,[13] and their testicles may shrink up to 50 percent.[14] Girls on testosterone raise their levels 10 times above normal.[15] In addition to correlations between testosterone levels and mood disorders,[16] concerns of atrophy is listed as a primary cause for them seeking a hysterectomy.[17]

The combination of steps 2 and 3 often renders a child infertile. If they persist in presenting as the opposite sex, patients must take hormones all their life. Likewise, if they desist, they may take hormones all their life as their hormone-producing organs may have been destroyed or removed. Phase 3 turns children into lifelong customers of Big Pharma.

4. The final stage of the Activist Treatment Plan is gender "affirmation" surgery. Girls will amputate fully functioning breasts and/or strip their forearm of tissue to create a never-functional phallus. For boys, the penis will be spliced and inverted in an attempt to create a faux vagina. Some patients, like trans-child icon Jazz Jennings, will have "bottom surgery" complications due to a puberty-blocked "micropenis," which leaves insufficient tissue for vaginal construction. Instead, material from the stomach or anus will be harvested to create what the body will regard as a permanent wound, requiring daily dilation. One 18-year-old in the Netherlands died after his "vaginal reconstruction." Step 4 of the Activist Treatment Plan is literally the amputation and disfigurement of the patient's sex organs. A more accurate label would be gender "mutilation" surgery.

It is important to recognize that transgender supporters typically believe they are helping kids. They see the distress of gender confusion and believe "transition" will offer some relief. But regardless of their good intentions, kids are being objectively harmed. And that's because they have a faulty worldview.

Agree to Disagree?

In no way can Christians endorse, or regard as neutral, any of these four steps. Every phase of the Activist Treatment Plan harms children. Even seemingly benign "social transition" encourages children to seek a fantasy that, despite surgeries and lifelong injections, their body can never deliver. The majority of children who socially transition will continue along the Activist Treatment Plan, with two-thirds altering their bodies with hormones or surgery.[18] In contrast, "80–95 percent of children with gender dysphoria accepted their biological sex by late adolescence" if "watchful waiting" rather than "treatment" was pursued.[19] We cannot affirm in any way that children are "born in the wrong body," else we participate in their lifelong harm.

This is one reason why I do not use preferred pronouns. I realize some well-meaning Christians disagree, but I cannot go along with the cultural narrative. Here's why. First, the very idea of "stating your pronouns" is a tacit assent to the idea that a mind-body disconnect is not only possible, but could be normal and healthy. When it comes to kids, using preferred pronouns pushes them further along the Activist Treatment Plan, which aims at bodily harm.

Refusing to use preferred pronouns requires moral courage as some people view pronoun decliners as Nazi-adjacent. Further, you may reason, *How much does a two- or three-letter word matter if it makes someone feel better?* But as my husband and I have raised our kids in Seattle, and thus navigated parenting through nearly every imaginable cultural flashpoint, we have found that there has been one bright line that has helped us remain *in*, but not *of* the world. That line is *don't lie.*

Unlike names that are more subjective, like going by our middle name, or using a professional or nickname, pronouns speak to an objective reality. So if a trans friend changes her name from Iris to Ian, I may use it. But pronouns are different. They speak to an objective reality. *He* and *she* indicate something undeniably true about a person's design. Using incorrect pronouns, or simply playing the pronoun game, is specifically telling a lie about a person's body, and God's creation in general. As for me and my household, that is a no-go. Even if you feel you can't speak truthfully about someone's transgender identity, it's better to be silent than utter a falsehood. Aleksandr Solzhenitsyn famously said, "Let the lie come into the world, let it even triumph. But not through me."[20]

When asked whether or not the issue of transgenderism is something on which Christians can disagree, Rosaria Butterfield (former lesbian turned pastor's wife and sexual orthodoxy apologist) responds with an emphatic no! Adopting a sexual minority identity conflicts with the "creation ordinance [of] Genesis 1:27," of male and female which she says is "not an application of personhood but a definition of personhood." She rightly posits that "homosexuality and transgenderism are an attack against the image of God."[21] The Activist Treatment Plan makes clear it's a physical, not just a metaphorical, attack.

In the Mosaic law, even "presenting" as the opposite sex through cross-dressing is an "abomination to the LORD" (Deuteronomy 22:5 ESV). From prohibitions regarding the mixing of fabrics or crops, God seems to love the purity and distinctions of the categories of His creation, of which male and female are the pinnacle. I won't pretend to understand all Paul is communicating about hair and head coverings in 1 Corinthians 11, but it's clear that an accurate presentation of our maleness and femaleness somehow reflects Trinitarian headship and a kind of human glory that matters to God, and angelic observers as well. We are not only to embrace our bodies, but use our clothing, hair, and adornments to reveal our gendered distinctiveness.

Speak Truth with Courage

We cannot allow a hollow understanding of compassion or tolerance to encourage anyone to embrace an identity that will damage their mind and body. The reality is that God's design and recognition of male and female distinctiveness is not only *true*, but also *good*—for individuals, as well as society—and we cannot keep that truth to ourselves. But bridging the gap between knowing the truth and having the courage to speak the truth can feel like an insurmountable chasm.

Approaching conversations with loved ones who identify as LGBTQ can strike fear into the heart of a Christian. I know; I'm one of those Christians. I spent much of my childhood splitting time between the home of my father and the home of my mother and her female partner. I love them both and gravitate toward conversations with members of the LGBTQ community, even before they get a chance to share their pronouns. Furthermore, I don't like confrontation, especially with those I am trying to win for Christ. I wager many of you feel the same.

The fear of alienating those who identify as gay or trans has prompted some Christians to be silent, or worse, to bend God's truth in the name of love, unity, or maintaining relationships. Maintaining relationships *is* important but must never be of ultimate importance. When unity becomes a god, truth is always the casualty. As Luther noted, "Peace when possible; truth at all costs."

The need to prioritize truth over relationships is challenging, especially when the LGBTQ-identifying person is a member of our family. In our almost 30 years of ministry, we've observed that, other than someone being entangled in personal sexual sin, having an LGBTQ family member is the leading cause of compromise for Christians. The powerful influence our friends and family exert over our doctrine can be seen in Deuteronomy 13, where Israel was prescribed to take extreme action against "your very own brother, or your son or daughter, or the wife you love, or your closest friend" who might "entice" you away from truth and toward worshipping other gods (verses 6-11 NIV). We must ensure that we are *influencing*, rather than *being influenced by*, those walking outside God's established standards for mankind. So the question is not a matter of *whether* to speak truth, but rather, *when* and *how* to speak truth.

Cornerstone and Stumbling Block

Christ was filled with grace *and* truth, and God expects us to go and do likewise. But what does speaking truth, or at minimum, not lying, look like in real life? Here, I recommend what I call the "1 Peter 2 Principle," derived from 1 Peter 2:7-8:

> The honor is for you who believe, but for those who do not believe,
> "The stone that the builders rejected has become the cornerstone,"
> and "A stone of stumbling, and a rock of offense." They stumble
> because they disobey the word, as they were destined to do.

What do we learn about Christ and His truth from these verses? Whether we accept or reject Him, His nature and truth are a rock. Jesus is either the cornerstone around which we build our lives, or a block over which we will stumble. Either way, His truth claims are hard, unbending, and immovable.

From these verses, we can identify two important practices to apply to our conversations with our transgender friends.

1. **Say No to Play-Doh.** Sometimes we watch our friends stumble over the truths that our bodies are distinctly male or female, that in God's creation there is no genderless in-between, and that He insists that our minds be *transformed*, rather than our bodies *conformed*. Some (indeed, entire denominations) attempt to alleviate our LGBTQ friends of this doctrinal discomfort through recasting the stumbling block by using softer statements like "You can be gay and Christian," or "If God's pronouns are they/them, yours can be too," or "It's what happens in your heart, not your body, that matters to God."

   When using a "more-compassionate-than-Jesus" mentality, we remake the rock of Christ into Play-Doh so there's no sting when our LGBTQ neighbor catches their foot on the block. They will not be alerted to the truth. Sure, an elastic, moldable material is certainly less likely to injure, but neither is it a firm foundation that you can build a house upon. "Upgrading" God's truth in the name of love, compassion, or maintaining relationships not only robs your friend of a rare source of gender sanity but it may also indicate that you yourself are not building your life upon a firm doctrinal foundation. It is better to believe God's Word and speak it, than imperil yourself or your hearer (1 Timothy 4:16).

2. **Avoid Creating Trip Hazards.** Another error is littering the path of our transgender neighbor with unnecessary tripping hazards. How many stumbling blocks does Peter list in 1 Peter 2:7-8? Exactly *one.* That stumbling block is Christ, not you. We must take care not to scatter hazards or become an additional stumbling block to someone's understanding of God's truth by failing to demonstrate God's love for them.

I've done this by failing to not just reciprocate, but initiate relationship. I've caused difficulty by communicating online or over text rather than in person. I've charged forward with truth telling without first demonstrating love through sacrifice. Romans 12:18 tells us, "So far as it depends on you, live peaceably with all." So far as it depends on us requires that our lives flex rather than God's truth. Refusal to bend in nondoctrinal matters in order to love our neighbor can add unnecessary stumbling blocks to their path.

Pray for Wisdom

Let me conclude with a hypothetical scenario. Your friend's daughter Addi is now "Andy." Her parents expect you and your children to refer to her using he/him pronouns. You don't want to encourage Addi down a path of physical and psychological harm, neither will you lie to your children about Addi's body. And you don't want to lose contact with this family that you love. You can live out the 1 Peter 2 principle by saying, "We love you and Addi. But we would never want her to believe that she needs to surgically or chemically alter her body to be her 'true self.' Do you have any suggestions about how we can remain in relationship with you and Addi without using he/him pronouns?"

When you are facing the difficult conversations, such as, "Here is why I can't use those pronouns," "These are the reasons I won't be attending your wedding," or "Here is what I am concerned about if you start testosterone treatment," you may experience the same fears that I do. In those moments, I pray this prayer:

> Lord, I know You want me to speak Your truth. Please tee up the conversation. Let them literally beg me to tell them this information. And when You throw the door open, I will walk through it and kindly, but clearly, say what is true.

So far, God is batting 1.000 in answering that prayer for me. And it helps me to know that I'm not alone during those difficult conversations. And I can state, with confidence, neither are you.

Katy Faust is the founder and president of Them Before Us. She writes, speaks, and testifies widely on why marriage and family are matters of justice for children. She is the coauthor of *Them Before Us: Why We Need a Global Children's Rights Movement* and *Raising Conservative Kids in a Woke City*. She is also the editor of the book *Pro-Child Politics*.

AN INTERVIEW WITH
JOHN MARRIOTT

Sean: Why have you chosen to study the issues of deconstruction and deconversion in such depth?

John: My deep dive into studying deconversion resulted from discovering that an individual who was a deeply committed believer, and who had personally ministered to me during a painful period in my life, renounced his faith. I still remember when he said he was happier and more content as an atheist than he ever was as a Christian. Over the last ten years of researching deconversion, I have become convinced that it's one of the biggest, if not *the* biggest issue facing the church today. I study deconversion because I want to help the church understand why it happens so we can help believers avoid it.

Sean: What does the data show about the number of young people questioning and leaving the faith?

John: The data is frightening. For example, the Pew Research Center reports that for every one person who converts to Christianity, four deconvert from it.[1] Pew also claims that nearly one-third of Christians leave the faith by the time they are thirty years old.[2] Perhaps most troubling are the findings of the Pinetops Foundation, which claim that between 2020 and 2050, 35 million young people will leave the faith.[3] If projections are correct, within one generation there will be more people who identify as religiously unaffiliated than as Christians in the United States.[4]

Sean: There is a lot of disagreement about how to define *deconstruction*. Can you provide some definitions as to how it is used and how you distinguish it from deconversion?

John: If you ask five people what *deconstruction* means, you'll get six answers! Some use it to describe the process of tearing down their faith after they concluded it wasn't true. Others use it to describe the process of putting all their religious beliefs on the table and questioning if any of them are true. For others, deconstruction is not so much directed at the truthfulness of the Christian faith but the essence of it. In these cases, the individual isn't asking *if* Jesus is the way, but rather they want to know what the way of Jesus is supposed to look like. Deconversion differs from deconstruction in that deconstruction is a process of rethinking what one believes, whereas deconversion is the rejection of one's faith. All deconversions result from a process of deconstruction. But not all deconstructions end in deconversion. In fact, some result with a healthier, more biblical faith.

Sean: What are some helpful (and unhelpful) things people can do to guide their kids, or friends, who are going through a season of deconstruction?

John: First, don't panic. It's not easy, but try to keep calm when a loved one expresses their doubts. Second, express gratitude. When a person opens up to you, it's because they trust you with that information. Third, listen carefully. Doing so will allow you to both demonstrate your love for them and discern what the root of their faith crisis might be. Fourth, express your love for them. Loving them is crucial for two reasons. First, Jesus calls us to love everyone regardless of whether they agree with us or not. Second, it's the one thing that will keep the door open to future conversations. Finally, pray. Remember, James tells us that the passionate prayer of a righteous person can produce incredible results.

Sean: Any final words of advice for apologists on how to best approach the phenomenon of deconstruction?

John: Keep in mind that although an individual who is deconstructing might point to intellectual reasons as the catalyst for their faith crisis, the real culprit may lie elsewhere. No doubt intellectual reasons play a role, but maybe not the one we assume. Deconstruction is driven by values, emotions, desires, and cultural factors as much as it is the intellect. Those in the throes of deconstruction may point to intellectual reasons for why they are wrestling with their faith. However, in many cases, the intellect may only be justifying a decision already made by a person's values, emotions, and desires.

John Marriott is a faculty affiliate at Harvard University's Human Flourishing Program, part-time professor at Talbot School of Theology, and a former pastor. He is the author of five books on deconversion, including, *Going...Going...Gone!* and *The Anatomy of Deconversion*. He is also the coauthor of *Set Adrift: Deconstructing What You Believe Without Sinking Your Faith*.

JESUS FOR AN EVER-CHANGING CULTURE

Jason Carlson

Once, on a flight from Minneapolis to Seattle, I had an amazing encounter with a young businessman named Matt. It all began when I noticed the book he pulled out of his messenger bag, a popular work from a well-known influencer in the New Age movement. Curious about his reading selection, I turned to Matt and said, "Excuse me, but I happened to notice the book you're reading. If you don't mind me asking, what's it all about?" Well, this was the opening to a nearly three-hour conversation during which Matt shared with me his long journey in pursuit of truth and his interest in the world's philosophies and religions. You can imagine my excitement.

Bridges for the Gospel

As a pastor and apologist, I regularly encourage people to look for "bridges" for sharing the gospel. A *bridge* is simply a ready-made opportunity that lends itself toward a spiritual conversation in which believers can tell others about Jesus. These bridges can be found in subjects like current events, popular movies and songs, or even a person's situation in life. As I often tell people, these bridges are all around us, all the time. We just need to have eyes to see them and the boldness and faith to use them when they present themselves.

So here I was, sitting next to a young man who had just acknowledged his personal quest for spiritual truth. Talk about a bridge for sharing the gospel! I quickly said a silent prayer and then began to share my own spiritual journey with Matt. For the remainder of our flight, we had a truly engaging conversation. Matt was hungry for answers, and I thoroughly enjoyed his openness and obvious grasp of many of the religious and philosophical concepts we talked about.

Why Christ?

During the course of our discussion, Matt asked me a very interesting question: "Jason, tell me something, when you boil it all down, why are you a Christian?" As I quickly reviewed the numerous reasons I could share for why I've placed my trust in Jesus, suddenly one word came to mind—*resurrection*. Without hesitation I said, "Matt, I'm a Christian for a number of reasons, but there's one that stands above all the others. I'm a follower of Jesus because He is a living Savior. Jesus was God in human flesh, and He is the Savior of the world; and He proved this by conquering death and rising from the grave."

My response definitely piqued Matt's curiosity, and he replied, "You don't really believe that, do you?" And with this question I began sharing the exciting case for the resurrection of Jesus Christ.

The Fundamental Issue

I began by pulling my Bible from my backpack and reading from 1 Corinthians 15:12-20:

> If it is preached that Christ has been raised from the dead, how can some of you say that there is no resurrection of the dead? If there is no resurrection of the dead, then not even Christ has been raised. And if Christ has not been raised, our preaching is useless and so is your faith. More than that, we are then found to be false witnesses about God, for we have testified about God that he raised Christ from the dead. But he did not raise him if in fact the dead are not raised. For if the dead are not raised, then

Christ has not been raised either. And if Christ has not been raised, your faith is futile; you are still in your sins. Then those also who have fallen asleep in Christ are lost. If only for this life we have hope in Christ, we are of all people most to be pitied. But Christ has indeed been raised from the dead, the firstfruits of those who have fallen asleep (NIV).

After reading this passage, I said, "Matt, the entire Christian faith rests on the claim that Jesus Christ was physically resurrected from the grave. Even the earliest followers of Jesus recognized this. As the apostle Paul says, if Jesus didn't rise from the grave, our faith is 'useless' and 'futile.' You see, if the resurrection didn't happen, Jesus was just another guy crucified by the Romans on a cross; and if that's the case, there is no forgiveness for sins or any hope for eternal life. If the resurrection didn't happen, the Christian's faith is futile. Christianity stands or falls on the historical reality of the resurrection of Jesus Christ."

Before I could go any further, Matt jumped in and asked, "So what's the evidence?" At this point, I was getting really excited. I love talking about the evidence for the resurrection of Jesus Christ. And I believe that a persuasive case can be made for the historic Christian claim that Jesus physically rose from the grave, conquering sin and death.

A Compelling Case

Over my years of ministry, I've found it extremely helpful to be prepared with simple, ready-made presentations for some of the common issues and questions that arise when engaged in apologetic conversations. One of these is a case for the resurrection of Jesus based on the acronym T.E.S.T. In response to Matt's question, I encouraged him to T.E.S.T. the claim of the resurrection, and we discussed the following points of evidence:

T—Tomb

E—Eyewitnesses

S—Spread

T—Transformation

Using this simple memory device, I began to share with Matt some of what I believe to be the most persuasive arguments for the historical credibility of the resurrection of Jesus Christ. We talked about the evidence for the empty tomb, that three days after His execution and burial Jesus' tomb was found open and His body was no longer there. Jews, Romans, and Christians all agreed on this fact. I highlighted the eyewitness testimonies to the risen Jesus, and how Scripture reveals that more than 500 people saw and physically experienced the resurrected Christ. We talked about the incredible growth and spread of the early church in the hostile environment of first-century Israel—a climate religiously dominated by Judaism, which was vehemently opposed to other faiths, and politically subject to the Roman Empire that was wholly committed to the lordship of Caesar and maintaining the empire's fragile peace. I shared about the transformative experiences of those who claimed to have seen the risen Jesus, including the disciples, Jesus' halfbrother James, and the apostle Paul—once a zealous Jewish persecutor of the early Christian church. Matt seemed especially impressed when he found out that all of these people went to their deaths, all but one as martyrs, convinced of the fact and unwilling to deny that Jesus truly was the resurrected Messiah.

Before we knew it, our flight had landed in Seattle, and unfortunately, Matt and I were just getting warmed up! We'd had a wonderful conversation for more than two hours, and I could tell that Matt's heart was truly searching. I don't know where Matt is today in his spiritual journey, but I do trust that the Holy Spirit used the evidence I shared to move him toward a greater openness to Jesus as the risen Savior and Lord.

Apologetics and Theology

As we equip ourselves with compelling reasons to believe in the resurrection of Jesus Christ, and helpful resources for making our case, we must also be prepared to speak to the theological significance of the resurrection.

On one occasion, a young Christian woman named Amy came to me with some questions she'd been pondering as a result of a lecture in one of her college classes. Her class had been examining the Bible as literature, and her professor had challenged the integrity of the Bible's accounts of various historical events, including Jesus' resurrection. As this young collegian reflected on her faith and what she'd been hearing in class, she soon found herself wrestling with a significant question: What difference does it make if Jesus' resurrection was literally true or not? As Amy shared her thoughts with me over a cup of coffee, she added, "I mean, does it really matter? What if Jesus didn't rise from the dead? What if the story was just made up? Does that really change the power and significance of what Jesus taught and how He lived?"

How would you have answered Amy's questions? This experience was a powerful reminder to me that resurrection apologetics and theology often go hand in hand. As apologists, we need to be prepared to speak to both the historical evidence and the rich theological significance of the resurrection with the people in our day.

The Life-Transforming Power of the Resurrection

I know that there is life-transforming power in the truth of Jesus' resurrection, and as I visited with Amy, I desperately wanted her to see this too. I said, "Amy, the historical reality of Jesus' resurrection makes all the difference in the world!" And I went on to highlight the following points.

The Resurrection Proves the Deity and Lordship of Jesus Christ

Apart from His resurrection from the dead, Jesus was, at best, a great teacher of morality, but that's it. If Jesus did not rise from the grave, today He lies buried alongside all the other philosophers and religious teachers of antiquity. He is not the Son of God. He is not the Messiah. He is not the reigning and returning King.

However, the apostle Paul tells us, in Romans 1:4, that Jesus was "declared to be the Son of God with power according to the Spirit of holiness by his resurrection from the dead." I said to Amy, "Many people have claimed to be divine; many have claimed to know the way to salvation; but only one person who has claimed these things has verified them by rising from the grave!" It's because of Jesus' resurrection from the dead that we believe He truly is the eternal Son of God who is "the way, the truth, and the life" (John 14:6). And because He lives, we can confidently put our trust in Him as the Lord of our lives.

The Resurrection Guarantees Our Personal Salvation

"Do you believe you are saved? If so, why?" These were the questions I posed to Amy as I came to this second point in our conversation. As is common for many Christians, Amy said she believed she was saved because "Jesus died for my sins, and I've put my faith in Him." I replied, "So what? People put their faith in lots of things. Why do you think putting your faith in Jesus is so special?"

This question might sound harsh, but this is something we need to seriously challenge people to consider. Why do we put our faith in Jesus Christ? Why not Buddha? Reincarnation? Muhammad? Or even the Easter Bunny? The point people need to grasp is that our faith in Jesus means something only because Jesus is a risen Savior! The only reason we have any hope for salvation by faith in Jesus Christ is because Jesus not only died on a cross for our sins, but He also proved the efficacy of His death by conquering the grave.

In Romans 4:25, the apostle Paul reports that Jesus "was delivered over to death for our sins and was raised to life for our justification" (NIV). What does this mean? *Justification* is a word that brings to mind the image of standing in a courtroom, guilty in the eyes of the law. As you stand there awaiting your sentence, suddenly another person walks in and says, "I will serve her sentence in her place." And with that the judge reports that you are free to go, the penalty has been taken from you.

Isn't that amazing? Jesus died in our place, for our sins, but as the apostle Paul says, it is because Jesus was raised to life that we are justified, or pardoned, in the eyes of God. The apostle Peter affirms this, writing in 1 Peter 1:3, "Praise be to the God and Father of our Lord Jesus Christ! In his great mercy he has given us new birth into a living hope through the resurrection of Jesus Christ from the dead" (NIV).

Notice the significance that both Paul and Peter place on Jesus' resurrection from the dead, directly connecting the resurrection to our personal salvation. As I said earlier, many Christians are quick to point to Jesus' death on the cross, and their faith in Him, as the reason for their salvation. And yet, this is only half of the story. If we as apologists fail to emphasize the significance of the resurrection, we are missing the mark in giving people a biblically comprehensive understanding of our salvation in Christ.

The Resurrection Guarantees Our Future Resurrection and Eternal Life with God

In my opinion, this is the most exciting significance of the resurrection. As I shared this truth with Amy that day, I did so with the knowledge that she was grieving the loss of her godly grandfather, who had recently passed away. Knowing that Amy's heart was heavy, I said to her, "Can I show you two of the most exciting verses in the Bible?" And with that, I opened my Bible and read John 11:25-26: "Jesus said to her, 'I am the resurrection and the life; the one who believes in Me will live, even if he dies, and everyone who lives and believes in Me will never die'" (NASB).

After reading this passage, I said, "Amy, your grandfather put his trust in Jesus Christ as his Savior and Lord. And because of this, and because of Jesus' promise, your grandfather is alive today." As she thought about this, Amy's lips briefly curled into a smile, but then she asked somewhat somberly, "But how can that be?"

I replied, "Well, it gets more exciting!" I then turned to 2 Corinthians 5:1-2, and read, "We know that if the earthly tent we live in is destroyed, we have a building from God, an eternal house in heaven, not built by human hands. Meanwhile we groan, longing to be clothed instead with our heavenly dwelling" (NIV). I stopped and explained, "The Bible describes this physical body of ours as a temporary dwelling, or house, that our soul lives in. If you read 2 Corinthians 4, the apostle Paul calls the body an 'earthen vessel.' It's only temporary." I then turned to 2 Corinthians 5:8, and read, "We are confident, I say, and would prefer to be away from the body and at home with the Lord" (NIV).

"You see," I continued, "for the Christian, to be absent from this physical body is not something we should fear. Rather, when a believer passes away, their soul leaves their body, and they instantaneously go to be at home with the Lord. How do I know this? Because of what we just read a moment ago, where Jesus said, 'I am the resurrection and the life. If you believe in me, you shall never die.' And why won't believers, like your grandfather, ever die? Because when you accept Jesus as your personal Savior and Lord, He comes to live within you. And in living within you, Jesus empowers you with His Spirit and gives you His resurrection power."

I could tell that Amy was starting to see it now, the life-transforming power found in the resurrection of Jesus Christ. So I added, "Believe it or not, it gets even more exciting!" And I turned in my Bible to Philippians 1:21, where the apostle Paul says, "To me, to live is Christ and to die is gain." I then asked Amy, "Why would Paul say that 'to die is gain'?" And Amy, now with enthusiasm, declared, "Because for a believer, to be absent from the body is to be at home with the Lord." And then, as if to just make sure that I knew she got it, she added, "Because Jesus said, 'I am the resurrection and life. If you believe in me, you shall never die.'" Amy's spirit had visibly changed. Her doubts and sadness had been lifted and totally replaced by the truth of God's Word and our hope in Jesus, the risen Prince of Peace.

This is the Christian's great confidence: Because of Jesus' resurrection from the dead, we need not fear death. Jesus has defeated death. He is a risen Savior. And when a person puts their trust in Jesus Christ as Savior and Lord, they immediately receive Jesus' resurrection power and new life in Him. This is why the apostle Paul could so confidently declare that to be absent from the body is to be at home with the Lord. This is also why Paul could so boldly taunt death in 1 Corinthians 15:55, where he says, "Where, O death, is your victory? Where, O death, is your sting?" (NIV).

The Shadow of Death

A close family friend, my father's mentor and teacher, was the late Dr. Walter Martin. He was a pioneer in the field of Christian apologetics, specializing in the area of non-Christian cults. His book *The Kingdom of the Cults* is still considered a classic to this day. Martin's mentor and teacher was the late great theologian Dr. Donald Grey Barnhouse, and Dr. Martin used to share a powerful story from Barnhouse's life.

Dr. Barnhouse's wife had passed away, and he and his young daughter were driving together to her funeral service. As they drove, Dr. Barnhouse attempted to explain to his daughter what death was. In sharing with her, he quoted from Psalm 23, and then began trying to describe what King David meant when he said, "Even though I walk through the valley of the shadow of death, I will fear no evil."

Have you ever wondered what that verse means? Why does David speak of "the valley of the shadow of death"?

Dr. Barnhouse was trying to explain this to his daughter when their car pulled up to a stoplight. It was a bright and sunny day, and while they were waiting, suddenly a large truck pulled up next to them. The truck blocked the sun and cast a huge shadow over their car. Inspired, Dr. Barnhouse asked his daughter, "Tell me something: Would you rather be hit by the truck or the shadow of the truck?" His daughter replied, "Well, I'd rather be hit by the shadow of the truck." Dr. Barnhouse then declared, "That's exactly what David means when he says, 'Though I walk through the valley of the shadow of death, I will fear no evil.'"

Jesus Christ took the hit of death for us when He died on the cross of Calvary. He then conquered death by rising from the grave. Followers of Jesus, therefore, do not face death. We face only the shadow of death, not death itself. As we saw earlier, for the Christian, to be absent from the body is to be immediately at home with the Lord. And as Paul says, "To me, to live is Christ and to die is gain" (Philippians 1:21 NIV). For those who trust in Jesus Christ, death is only a shadow. It has lost its sting! And because of Jesus' resurrection, believers can be confident that we too will rise again to new life. The grave held no power over Jesus Christ, and it holds no power over those who've put their trust in Him. Praise the Lord!

The Gospel for an Ever-Changing Culture

The historical reality of Jesus' death and resurrection has been the cornerstone of the Christian faith for more than 2,000 years. Countless millions have found peace with God and abundant life in Him because He is a risen Savior. This is why the message of Jesus is known as the gospel, the "good news." The historical reality of Jesus' life, death, and especially His resurrection is very good news. It's good news for a world that's desperately searching for something to believe in. It's good news for all who are hurting and without hope. And it's good news for everyone living in an ever-changing culture. What a privilege we have to be the bearers of this good news!

》 》 》

Quick Tips on Resurrection Apologetics

1. Raise to attention the unique nature of the biblical record and historical evidence for Jesus' physical resurrection from the grave. Encourage non-Christians to explore whether any comparable claim can be found outside of biblical Christianity.

2. Equip yourself to share a simple and clear presentation of the evidence for the resurrection of Jesus Christ. Memory devices like the T.E.S.T. acronym can be helpful.

3. Understand the theological significance of the resurrection and use that knowledge to build bridges for apologetic conversations. For example, all people think about what happens after death. Share your personal hope in a future resurrection and explain that your hope is rooted in biblical truth and affirmed by the evidence for Jesus' resurrection from dead.

Jason Carlson is the president of Christian Ministries International and the senior pastor of Lakes Free Church in Lindstrom, Minnesota.

NOTHING NEW UNDER THE SUN: ENGAGING NEW AGE

Melissa Dougherty

Without question, New Age is one of the most sinister deceptions of mankind. It's like a mutating virus that has been around since the dawn of mankind. Many people turn to New Age practices because they yearn for a sense of power. Others do so because they believe it will help them.

But what exactly is the New Age? Why are people attracted to it? And how can we reach those who hold to New Age beliefs? I personally know how alluring these types of beliefs can be. When I had my first child in 2010, I decided that I needed to dig deeper into understanding my own spiritual beliefs. In this process, I stumbled upon an internet forum where there was a discussion taking place about this thing called the "Serpent's Lie"—that we could be like God. I was embarrassed and stunned to discover that I had fallen for this. The Bible clearly taught the exact opposite. I did a ton of research and dove into studying the Bible. It didn't take long for me to discover that I wasn't the only Christian who had been taken by these teachings.

The New Age is mysterious, mystical, magical, and enticing. Many New Agers say that Bible-believing Christians are unintellectual, intolerant, and close-minded. If that is you, many New Agers consider you a Bible-thumper who is a judgmental, fundamentalist spiritual dinosaur. New Agers believe they stand on a higher spiritual and moral ground because their faith seems more loving, tolerant, and open-minded.

Many Christians don't know how to navigate or challenge New Age ideas once they are identified. While the church has done well addressing naturalistic challenges to the faith, it is under-equipped on how to deal with the type of New Age spirituality that is taking over the culture and is now seeping into churches. This chapter has two main goals: (1) to define and explain New Age beliefs, and (2) to offer practical strategies for reaching those involved with New Age.

Understanding New Age Beliefs and Practices

For many, the term *New Age* conjures up images and ideas relating to the hippie generation of the 1960s. But in reality, New Age is not a twentieth-century phenomenon. Its key ideas have been around a long time, like a virus that mutates with the culture. It is not unlike the *Fast and the Furious* movie series. It just won't go away! Just when you think the storyline has run its course, another movie is released. The series adapts with each generation to stay relevant.

Defining the New Age can feel like pinning down a cloud because there is a subjective element that varies with individuals. But for clarity and simplicity, here is a chart of common New Age practices and beliefs:

PRACTICES	BELIEFS
Meditation	Channeling/Psychics/Spirit Guides: The goal is to communicate with spirits or other entities who are said to guide and assist us.
Crystal Healing	Astrology/Starseeds: The belief that stars tell us information about our lives and it's possible to be a spirit from another planet sent here to bring spiritual light

PRACTICES	BELIEFS
Energy Work/Reiki	Numerology: A mystical interpretation of numbers. Aura: Every being has an energy field surrounding them.
Yoga	Crystal Energy
Astrology	Astral Travel: Detaching our spirits from our bodies and traveling in the astral realm
Vision Quests	Reincarnation: Souls are reborn in different bodies over time
Past Life Regression	Enlightenment/Inner Divinity/Spiritual Evolution of Humanity: Humanity is evolving spiritually and consciously
Labyrinth Walking	Universalism: All spiritual paths lead to the same divine source
Psychics	Oneness: All beings and the universe are interconnected
Tarot Reading	Higher Self: There's a divine, perfect self within everyone
Chakra Balancing	Karma: Actions have consequences that play out across lifetimes
Sound Healing	Sacred Geometry: Specific shapes have spiritual significance

This chart isn't exhaustive, but it lists some of the better-known ideas and teachings that New Agers embrace. The main takeaway is to understand the *goal* of the New Age: *Recognize that your inner divinity and that humanity should work together to obtain the goal of a spiritual utopia.* New Age practices are aimed at bringing you enlightenment. If enough individuals experience enlightenment, then we can have cosmic enlightenment. This movement teaches that we don't become divine but we already *are* divine, and we just need to awaken to this and tap into our existing power. The enlightenment that the New Age movement seeks to bring about is arrived at by leaving a state of self-ignorance and realizing that ultimately, the inner self is God.[1]

Again, remember, people experience New Age practices differently. What one New Ager accepts as truth, another might reject. In many ways, identifying the New Age is intended to be rather ambiguous. This is by design because it's a pick-and-choose belief system, not unlike a salad bar. You simply believe what you prefer and discard what doesn't jive with you. New Age is oftentimes more about preference than truth, which confuses many Christians.

At the heart of New Age is the regurgitated lie Satan told Adam and Eve in the garden: *You are God.* This is a stealthy deception that comes in many forms. It appeals to the heart and the mind. Thus, we must have a wise and discerning response.

Reaching Someone in the New Age

Here are six steps to reaching those involved in New Age. They all come from my past experience in New Age or from ministry to New Agers.

1. Pray and Don't Be Afraid

Many Christians might be afraid to approach a New Ager, as they see them as someone who is participating in what they would consider occultic beliefs. Remember, *New Agers need the gospel too!*

Please hear me: whether atheist or Satanist, everyone needs the gospel. The Great Commission is a command. There's no power New Agers have participated in that is stronger than what God can do in their life or the Holy Spirit living in us.

I once had a very devout Christian tell me that they would never allow anyone in the New Age around them because they didn't want their "bad ju-ju" to affect them negatively. I challenged the person and asked how a Christian would get a New Ager's "bad ju-ju" (whatever that meant) if the Christian were not participating in New Age beliefs and practices. When I asked the Christian how they felt about sharing the gospel with New Agers, the response was heartbreaking: "That's for someone else to do. I want no part of it."

This must not be our posture. The Christian was letting their fear get in the way of sharing the gospel with someone who desperately needed it. Understand, I'm *not* saying there aren't evil forces behind New Age occultic practices. There are. God forbids these practices for a reason. But this in no way should lead us to think these forces can somehow overpower the Holy Spirit inside of us.

Some Christians might be afraid to speak up at all because they don't want to start a fight or upset the other person. But here's what I say: When someone is opening the gates of hell to make a deal with the devil, thinking it's going to bring them peace, you should not stay quiet to "keep the peace." Be blameless, kind, and loving when speaking to them, and don't provoke or demean them. But whatever you do, you cannot be silent.

Courage often comes from prayer, a spiritual weapon you can use when it comes to reaching someone in the New Age. They're under immense spiritual oppression. Praying for them—or even *with* them if they allow it—can be quite powerful. I've seen God draw New Agers to Him over the years, and there were faithful Christians praying for them all along.

2. Ask Them What They Know About Jesus and the Bible

New Agers have spiritual yearnings, but most of them have a complete misconception of what Christianity is. Many believe in well-debunked beliefs, such as Constantine taking away books of the Bible at the Council of Nicaea, or even fringe topics such as aliens in the Bible, Jesus as an ascended Master, and so on. However, don't assume every New Ager believes the same things. When you're asking a New Ager about what they believe, you're gathering important intel. You're showing interest in what they believe, which shows that you care, and you're being polite by making sure you *understand* what they believe.

This also allows you to bring up questions to them about the Bible and Jesus, and perhaps gently challenge them and correct their misconceptions. It's not your job to play Holy Spirit and convert them. Your goal should be to get them to think about their beliefs enough that they are bothered—or as my friend Greg Koukl says, to put a stone in their shoe. This is a good strategy because it doesn't put them on the defense. Many New Agers appreciate spiritual conversations, and if you are friendly, kind, and interested in their position, you'd be surprised how many are receptive to talking. Because many New Agers view Christians as dimwitted and judgmental, being knowledgeable and approachable helps break down barriers and stereotypes.

3. Know Your Audience and Be Creative

One of the best ways to reach people in the New Age is by making connections that involve real life. For example, I love video games. I like the storylines, the art, and listening to podcasts as I mindlessly play the games. One time, I was challenging a friend about some of the ideas he had adopted that happened to originate from New Age thinking. Because of this, he was insistent that the Bible had been tampered with and books were missing. He started reading *The Aquarian Gospel of Jesus the Christ* by Levi H. Dowling, which is a channeled book claiming to be the real account of Jesus' life. His biggest hang-up was his claim that the Bible had been tampered with and changed. He reasoned that if the Bible was false, then it didn't matter what he believed. I wanted to challenge his premise. How exactly was the Bible tampered with?

Because we both loved video games, I brought up an example that would make sense to him. In the video game world, there is something called "modding" a game. "Mod" is short for "modifying," which is when a savvy gamer knows a bunch of fancy gamer computer stuff and can modify a game's files or add new ones to change or enhance the gameplay, graphics, sounds, characters, items, environments, or other aspects of the game. To do so, you must have the *original* game to adapt. Because doing this is fun, people sometimes change the whole design and purpose of a game. This was my connection point to the Bible.

We know what a game *should* look like. But how do we know this? Because there are millions of copies of an original game that many people have already seen, when we see a mod, we immediately know it's been "tampered" with. There was no PS5 or Nintendo in AD 40, so people had original manuscripts of the Bible that they copied. And copied. And copied. When a copy was tampered with—modified—people knew it immediately, and it was discarded.

If the Bible were a game, they would have to know what's been modded and what's original. Only then can they know whether they're playing a knockoff game and believing in a knockoff version of Christianity. This example made sense to him and took apologetics out of the realm of the abstract and made it personal and relatable.

When you interact with New Agers, get creative!

4. Understand New Age and Why People Are Attracted to It

If you care about reaching New Age people, do your homework. This will allow you to ask better questions. Use the chart above as a reference point, consider additional (reliable) resources, and ask questions to learn about their beliefs. For example, if they're into astrology, know what a birth chart is and maybe ask them questions about its accuracy. You can also tactfully bring up Bible passages in Deuteronomy chapters 4 and 18, where God commands us not to read the stars to know the future. Many New Agers don't even realize the Bible forbids this. (Some are even quite startled to know this.) Some might scoff and dismiss you or the Bible, but to bring this up opens the door for conversation.

It is also vital to know *why* people are attracted to New Age. Interestingly, according to my research and experience, many people embrace New Age not because they really believe it is true, but because *it personally helped them.* There's an emotional attachment to these beliefs that often goes deep. Imagine a mom who's just lost her young child. She's devastated with grief. A friend tells her to talk to a psychic medium so she can have closure. Desperate for relief, she decides to go. She is shocked and stunned by the personal information that the medium knows. She breaks down in tears upon knowing her child is safe and happy. Nobody will ever tell the mom that the medium was talking to a demon or that what she did was wrong. She *feels* much better—and concedes that even if the medium was lying, the medium's message brought her peace.

Please don't miss this point. The connection to New Age can run very deep. It is an emotional connection built on a lie, but the emotional connection is very real to them. While there are often intellectual barriers to faith, many times, the key barrier is emotional. Discovering the difference, by asking good questions and listening, can help you to navigate the conversation better.

5. Don't Blur the Lines

This might be obvious, but it is absolutely vital today: *Never adopt a syncretistic position when it comes to the New Age.* Unfortunately, some Christians have decided to *redeem* New Age ideas instead of rejecting them. These instances are subtle and appealing because there are certain beliefs and practices that sound Christian but are not. To adopt them is not only dangerous but highly spiritually irresponsible.

When we are trying to reach someone with differing beliefs, we must know the difference between contextualization and syncretism. We wouldn't advise any Christian to become a Muslim and practice the religion in order to reach Muslim people any more than we would spiritually interact with and accept occultic practices in order to reach people who are New Age. We should aim to reach New Agers in a way that they can understand the gospel, but we must not compromise biblical beliefs in the process.

6. Perspective

Most New Agers adopt certain beliefs because they want what most of us want: love and belonging. Many of them have been hurt by a church or other Christians. They want to be understood, respected, and cared for. They're searching for spiritual meaning and a spiritual position that allows them to be in control of their lives. Many of them are attracted to the New Age for autonomy. They've been hurt, and New Age beliefs allow them to not only have control and spiritual power, but to stop others from oppressing them. People don't go into the New Age to become your enemy. They go because they're looking for answers and they feel unfulfilled. They need Jesus. Being kind to them often breaks many barriers and misconceptions they may have about Christianity.

Like all people, New Agers long for spiritual fulfillment. But here's the key: *We have what they're really looking for.* The gospel and the church can fulfill their deepest needs. This will be a hurdle for you to overcome when you approach them, so keep this in mind: Many have emotional hang-ups and are sensitive to what they perceive as judgment or anything giving off negative energy. You might find this frustrating. Use discernment and wisdom to know when to engage, and try to remember 2 Timothy 2:23-26:

> Have nothing to do with foolish, ignorant controversies; you know that they breed quarrels. And the Lord's servant must not be quarrelsome but kind to everyone, able to teach, patiently enduring evil, correcting his opponents with gentleness. God may perhaps

grant them repentance leading to a knowledge of the truth, and they may come to their senses and escape from the snare of the devil, after being captured by him to do his will (ESV).

Nothing New

New Age is nothing new. It has much in common with Eastern religions, such as Hinduism and Buddhism, but ultimately, it goes back to the original lie in the garden: *You can be like God.* And yet New Agers are spiritual seekers. Although they don't realize it, Christians have what they need most. Christianity offers real power. Christianity offers life transformation. Christianity offers community. And Christianity offers truth. My prayer is that you will boldly engage the New Agers around you. Go for it!

Melissa Dougherty is a Christian apologist best known for her YouTube channel, with videos that primarily cover New Age and New Thought. Melissa currently holds degrees in Religious Studies, Liberal Arts, and Early Childhood Multicultural Education. She is currently working on an MA in Religious Studies from Southern Evangelical Seminary. Her work can be seen at https://www.melissadougherty.co/.

RECENTERING BIBLICAL AUTHORITY

Jonathan Morrow

What is the biggest issue facing the church today?

If you ask most people, you will probably hear answers like sexuality, gender ideology, justice, tribalism, critical theory, progressive Christianity, threats to religious liberty, cancel culture, consumerism, skepticism, and relativism—just to name a few. And they're not wrong. Those *are* significant issues. But they are not *the* issue. Underneath all those responses is the issue that I believe is the greatest challenge for the church today—*authority*.

As I teach and disciple high school, college, and graduate students year-round at Impact 360 Institute,[1] speak around the country, and study the next generation, I am more convinced than ever that the number one topic that must be addressed is biblical authority. For some, the Bible has drifted to the margins through neglect, and for others, it has been shoved aside by unrelenting attack. It is time to recenter biblical authority as we disciple a new generation. But before we can do that, we must first gain clarity about what the most pressing challenges are to biblical authority in the church today.

Resisting Authority Is "Normal"

If the broader culture has an authority problem, then it's not surprising that the church struggles with biblical authority. Many Christians have drifted far away from biblical authority. And it's not just happening in progressive Christian circles that champion deconstruction. Culture is simply what you come to see as normal without having to think about it. Good things can be seen as normal and bad things can be seen as normal. The problem is that challenging authority just seems *normal*. And it has become normal for people to see themselves as the highest authority in life. Unless you pause and reflect while actively renewing your mind (Romans 12:2), then this will be the predicable, inevitable outcome.

Ten Cultural Challenges That Undermine Biblical Authority

In this section, I will survey ten cultural challenges to biblical authority that show how today's worldviews have shaped perceptions of truth and reality. I will finish with a key principle for each issue that provides us a way forward in responding to these challenges. If we are to be effective in apologetics today, these challenges to biblical authority must be overcome.

1. Culture of corruption and abuse of power. Everywhere you look there are scandals, cover-ups, and abuses of power. Misconduct sells and the entertainment news cycle is aggressively buying its stories so that they can drive clicks to create controversy and sell ad space. Sadly, some high-profile Christian leaders and churches have been in the news for this reason as well. The result is that you see a general institutional distrust setting in—especially in younger generations. And if we're honest, it's not hard to see why some people are wary of authority.

> **Key Principle:** Ultimately, we should judge a religion by its founder, and not its imperfect followers. When we do this with Christianity, Jesus' life of integrity, teachings, and example set Him apart.

2. Loss of truth. We live in a world that says, "Follow your heart," "You do you," and "True for you, but not for me." The slogans and soundbites are everywhere. Sadly, the spiritual and moral fallout is all around us as well. No matter how well-intentioned and no matter how many Disney princesses sing about these ideas, reality does not work this way. As the end of the book of Judges put it, "all the people did whatever seemed right in their own eyes" (21:25). And if you have ever read that far into the Old Testament, trust me, that approach didn't end well back then, and it certainly doesn't work today. If there is no objective truth, then you lose any possibility of authority.

> **Key Principle:** Just because you believe something doesn't make it true. Reality makes things true or false. Sincerity is not enough. Truth is discovered, not created.

3. Crisis of knowledge. One of the unspoken assumptions of our age is that science alone gives us knowledge of reality. But if moral, spiritual, and historical truth cannot be known, then it becomes very difficult to navigate life. To be clear, the Bible assumes moral, spiritual, and historical knowledge. One of the more surprising shifts we observe today is that we see an increasing number of people growing skeptical even of scientific knowledge. (For example, consider the confusion playing out in the transgender revolution that says that men can get pregnant, biological men—who are, on average, bigger, stronger, and faster than women—can compete in women's sports without an unfair advantage, or a person can be born in the wrong body.) If something as evident as biological reality can't be known, that's a big problem. But as predicted by Friedrich Nietzsche, when you lose truth and knowledge, all that is left is power and tribalism. People take sides and form alliances (for example, the formation of the internally contradictory but ubiquitous LGBTQ+ acronym) to impose their worldview rather than try to persuade people of what's true and good.

> **Key Principle:** The Bible gives us knowledge revealed by our Creator concerning every area of life. Humans flourish when we live consistently with God's good design and His commands.

4. Expressive individualism. One of the most significant seismic shifts that has taken place over the last century is that from a *culture of authority* (external) to a *culture of authenticity* (internal). (See Charles Taylor's book *A Secular Age*.[2]) Out of this shift (with many ideas and intellectual dominoes that had to fall before it) comes "expressive individualism." Carl Trueman describes in great detail the historical context for and causes of how this mindset became such a powerful driving force today, but the essence of this view is that "human beings are defined by their individual psychological core and that the purpose of life is allowing that core [The Authentic Self], to find social expression in relationships. *Anything* that challenges it is deemed oppressive" (emphasis mine).[3] It's that last part that undermines *any* external authority.

If something like tradition, government, law, education, or the Bible limits that expression of who people feel they really are, then it is seen as oppressive and harmful. Likewise, if a person, like the church, society, parents, counselors, doctors, or God, limits that expression, then they are viewed as oppressive and harmful as well. The locus of authority has moved inward. Unfortunately, a spiritualized version of this has been absorbed by many in the church today.

> **Key Principle:** How you feel doesn't determine what's real. Good intentions don't necessarily lead to good outcomes and having a strong personal desire does not reshape reality. As wisdom reminds us, "There is a way that seems right to a man, but its end is the way to death" (Proverbs 14:12 ESV).

5. Digital distraction and hyper-personalization. This cultural factor operates in the background of all our lives. The unprecedented level of distraction we are experiencing coupled with the worldview shaping that is constantly occurring as we consume ever-increasing amounts of social media and entertainment each day does not position us well to look to an authority outside of our own desires.

To make matters worse, we have stopped thinking. With the hyper-personalization that occurs with everything tailored to our preferences and digital footprints, a new generation wonders why reality shouldn't conform to their preferences. Fueled by expressive individualism, people believe that issues like sexuality, gender, morality, and spirituality should be personalized to our preferences as well.

Key Principle: Even though marketing conforms to our desires and feelings, reality does not. There is a truth revealed by God outside of ourselves that we must conform to—objective truth. You can't have reality your way.

6. Misunderstanding freedom. Along the way, our broader culture, and many Christians, have adopted a flawed understanding of freedom. Our culture says that *freedom* is the ability to do whatever you want to do, whenever you want to do it, without constraint—as long as you don't hurt anyone. (This obviously overlooks the fact that you can hurt yourself with the misuse of freedom.) But that is not freedom; it's slavery. Freedom is more than just the satisfaction of our ever-changing and ever-increasing desires. Our culture's understanding of freedom and external authority are in serious tension.

Key Principle: If there is a God (and there is!) and He defines reality (and He does!), then true freedom means living according to God's good design and commands. Happiness and holiness are connected. As Paul puts it so well in Galatians 5:1, 13: "It is for freedom that Christ has set us free. Stand firm, then, and do not let yourselves be burdened again by a yoke of slavery...You, my brothers and sisters, were called to be free. But do not use your freedom to indulge the flesh; rather, serve one another humbly in love" (NIV).

7. "That's just *your* interpretation." When moral or spiritual conversations turn to the Bible, then things can get challenging. If you are not careful, you'll find your moral point of view dismissed with the popular slogan, "That's just *your* interpretation." But don't allow yourself to be brushed aside too easily. Learn to ask a follow-up question: "Are you saying you don't like my interpretation, or do you think my interpretation is false?" If the former, we can explain there are many things that are true in the Bible that you and I may not initially like, or that don't make us feel good, but that doesn't change the fact that they are true. But if they think it's false, then ask them *why* they think it's false. The bottom line is, if we allow this slogan to rule the day, a day in which only 4 percent of Gen Z holds to a biblical worldview[4] and biblical illiteracy is off the charts, then biblical authority in any meaningful sense is out the window.

> **Key Principle:** God has spoken authoritatively in the Bible. The meaning of a text is determined by the intent of the author and not the response of the reader. The words of Scripture carry the authority of God. Our job is to discover that meaning and obey.

8. Our sinful desire for autonomy. One of the clearest and least popular barriers to biblical authority is our—and humanity's as a whole—sinful desire for autonomy. Sin is not just brokenness, it's rebellion. We want to have the final word and claim God's authority for our own. If we're honest, sometimes we find ourselves echoing the words of the serpent in Genesis 3:1, *Did God really say?* God has spoken, and when we do this, we need to repent.

> **Key Principle:** People aren't basically good (Romans 3). The heart is desperately wicked; who can understand it? (Jeremiah 17:9). Rebellion against our Creator and King comes naturally. We need to humble ourselves and put *our* authority under *God's* authority (1 Peter 5:6).

9. Skepticism toward the Bible. Another barrier to biblical authority is that some people don't think the Bible can be trusted. They think it's unreliable and false, so they are not going to obey what it says. Perhaps they think the text was corrupted or changed over the centuries. Or possibly, that it records historical details with errors or that the canon does not contain the right books. Whatever the case may be, if people's genuine questions are not sufficiently answered, it will undermine a posture of willingness to obey God's Word as authoritative.

> **Key Principle:** There are good reasons the Bible can be trusted, and if someone is open minded, then they will find good responses to these objections. I address many of these questions in my book

Questioning the Bible: 11 Major Challenges to the Bible's Authority.[5] Apologetics is an important part of building confidence in biblical authority (1 Peter 3:15).

10. Fear of being canceled. Sometimes people are afraid to repeat out loud or online what God has said. People don't want to lose their friends, jobs, opportunities, or relationships with family members. However, there is a social cost to following Jesus. That's part of taking up our cross. As Jesus reminded us, we need to be as wise as serpents and as innocent as doves (Matthew 10:16). That takes discernment and courage. It also takes being a part of a community in which people stand together to say what needs to be said, in the context of loving as God has commanded us to love—in grace and truth.

> **Key Principle:** God and His Word will not be canceled. Though the grass withers and the flowers fade, the Word of God is eternal (1 Peter 1:24-25). In other words, God has the final word.

Now that we have briefly examined the factors that are converging to undermine biblical authority in the church today, we are better positioned to find a way forward.

A Disciple's View of Biblical Authority

One of my favorite passages about God's Word is found in 1 Thessalonians 2:13:

> We also constantly thank God that when you received the word of God which you heard from us, you accepted it *not as the word of men, but for what it really is, the word of God*, which also performs its work in you who believe" (NASB1995, emphasis added).

Make special note: not the word of men, but the word of God. I love that clarity! We need more of a Thessalonian-kind of response today. The Holy Spirit can clearly work when we take that posture and allow Him to change us to be more like Christ. At the end of the day, it comes down to this: *Does God know what He is talking about?*

I think John Stott captured the centrality of biblical authority to the Christian life when he wrote, "*Submission to Scripture* is part and parcel of our acknowledgment of the lordship of Jesus…[and] is fundamental to everyday Christian living, for without it Christian discipleship, Christian integrity, Christian freedom, and Christian witness are all seriously damaged, if not actually destroyed"[6] (emphasis added). We need a new generation of Christians who make disciples like Jesus did, while increasingly becoming transformed to take on the character of Jesus.

Biblical Authority Applied to Sexuality—a Clear Test Case

Today, when reading the headlines on the internet, one would think that the Bible is unclear when it comes to controversial topics being debated, both inside and outside of the church. However, the clarity of the passage below is instructive as we think about our own application of biblical authority. Read the following passage slowly and carefully, then answer these two questions: *Whose authority does Paul appeal to?* and *Who are you rejecting if you discard this teaching?*

> Finally then, brethren, we request and exhort you in the Lord Jesus, that as you received from us instruction as to how you ought to walk and please God (just as you actually do walk), that you excel still more. For you know what commandments we gave you *by the authority of the Lord Jesus.* For *this is the will of God,* your sanctification; that is, that you *abstain from sexual immorality*; that each of you know how to possess his own vessel in sanctification and honor, not in lustful passion, like the Gentiles who do not know God; and that no man transgress and defraud his brother in the matter because the Lord is the avenger in all these things, just as we also told you before and solemnly warned you. For God has not called us for the purpose of impurity, but in sanctification. *So, he who rejects this is not rejecting man but the God who gives His Holy Spirit to you* (1 Thessalonians 4:1-8 NASB1995, emphasis added).

The meaning of this passage could not be clearer. It may not be popular, but it is certainly not unclear. Ultimately, the controversy about sexuality today is not about sexuality itself—it's about authority.

A Transferable Framework for Clarifying Biblical Authority in a Confused Culture

With so much pressure to conform to the "patterns of this world" all around us, what does it look like to live out biblical authority as a disciple of Jesus? How do we recenter the Bible in our discipleship of others?

I have created a simple, four-word "biblical authority grid" to help us reliably and repeatedly discern what a proper response to biblical authority looks like. You can practice using this grid and use it to teach others to do the same. Teaching in grids—I call them the "Grids for Growth"—helps clarify the most important questions and concepts to be addressed, and then prompts the ability to act on them. And most importantly, these grids are easily shareable as we disciple others.[7]

All you need to start is a blank sheet of paper and something to write with. Draw a horizontal line across the middle of the paper and bisect it in the center with a vertical line to create four quadrants. Then you will write down four words, one in each quadrant, and later, your thoughts prompted by each of the four words.

The first word is *Bible*. The goal here is to clarify what the biblical text actually says. What is the Holy Spirit-inspired principle or truth in its context? The reader is after the intended meaning of the author. Write your thoughts and ideas down. Once we have clarity here, we can go to the next step.

The second word is *Culture*. What does our culture see "as normal" about this topic, issue, or question? Write these things down. This tilts imagination and action in a certain direction and could make obedience either harder or easier. For example, if all the cultural momentum is going in one direction and clear biblical teaching is going in a different direction, then I need to be aware of these trajectories.

The third word is *Me*. Is there any resistance in your heart to embracing this biblical principle or truth? If so, why? Write this down. It is likely, given we live in a fallen world and our heart is affected by sin, that you will face tension between what you wrote in the Bible and Culture squares. To move toward biblical authority, you must be aware of this internal obstacle to obedience.

The final word is *Response*. What would it look like for me to obey and encourage this biblical truth? How do I make this actionable? What is my first step and what are the next steps? Write these down. Be clear and act.

Applying this to our controversial issue above—sexuality—we see that the *Bible* clearly teaches that we are to avoid and run away from sexual immorality. Our *culture* sees sexual freedom (i.e., no boundaries) in behavior and identity as good and normal. I may experience a tension in *me* between what I have absorbed from culture through a thousand little nudges in entertainment and social media scrolling. My desires might even have been aimed at things outside God's good design and commands. Armed with the awareness from reflecting on the first three words, I am now to a point of *response* to God's Word. What would it look like for me to obey and encourage this biblical truth? In my choices, when do I need to say yes or no? How can I help others have the courage to obey, and not wilt in the face of cultural pressure?

Biblical Authority Grid

BIBLE	CULTURE
What does the Biblical text actually say? (Principle / Truth)	What does our culture see "as normal" about this topic / issue / question?
ME	RESPONSE
Is there any resistance in my heart to embracing this Biblical principle / truth? If so, why?	What would it look like for me to obey and encourage this Biblical truth?

© Jonathan Morrow

The heart of the issue of biblical authority ultimately comes down to two questions:

1. What does the Bible say?

2. Will I obey? (*Even if I don't want to, at least at first.*)

It's not always easy, but it's also not complicated. Keep it simple. Just ask yourself: *What does the Bible say?* and *Will I obey?* Will you allow your thoughts, actions, assumptions, choices, and desires to be challenged and changed by what God says in His Word? This is the posture toward biblical authority we need to cultivate and champion in a new generation of disciples. May God empower us by His Spirit and grace to do just that.

Jonathan Morrow is the director of cultural engagement and student discipleship at Impact 360 Institute and an adjunct professor of apologetics at Biola University. He is the author of several books, including *Welcome to College: A Christ-Follower's Guide for the Journey* and *Questioning the Bible: 11 Major Challenges to the Bible's Authority.* He created the online course *Refresh: A Practical Guide for Christian Parents on Smartphones and Social Media.* He is at Jonathanmorrow.org and on YouTube.

NOTES

Introduction—Apologetics for an Ever-Changing Culture

1. James Davis and Michael S. Graham with Ryan P. Burge, *The Great Dechurching: Who's Leaving, Why Are They Going, and What Will It Take to Bring Them Back?* (Grand Rapids, MI: Zondervan, 2023), 5.

2. Davis et. al., *The Great Dechurching,* 5.

3. Sean McDowell & John Marriott, *Set Adrift: Deconstructing What You Believe Without Sinking Your Faith* (Grand Rapids, MI: Zondervan, 2023).

4. Alisa Childers and Tim Barnett, *The Deconstruction of Christianity: What It Is, Why It's Destructive, and How to Respond* (Carol Stream, IL: Tyndale, 2023).

5. The Barna Group in partnership with Alpha, Biblica, and World Vision, *The Open Generation: How Teens Around the World Relate to Jesus,* Vol. 1 (2022).

6. For example, Gary Habermas is completing a four-volume defense of the resurrection, William Lane Craig is writing a multi-volume philosophical theology, Frank Beckwith is updating his academic defense of the unborn, and J.P. Moreland has published a sophisticated, academic defense of the existence of the soul. And on the topic of near-death experiences, there are a number of peer-reviewed publications that have appeared in recent years. For instance, see John C. Hagan III ed., *The Science of Near-Death Experiences* (Columbia, MO: University of Missouri Press, 2017).

Chapter 2—Truth Never Gets Old

1. This is a loose, modern-day translation of a quote from Friedrich Nietzsche's book *Thus Spoke Zarathustra,* translated by Walter Kaufmann (New York: Penguin Books, 1966), 195. The original quote reads like this: "'This is *my* way; where is yours?'—thus I answered those who asked me 'the way.' For *the* way—that does not exist."

2. See *Gen Z: Volume 1* (2018) and *Gen Z: Volume 2* (2021), published by The Barna Group and Impact 360 Institute.

3. Jonathan Morrow, "Moral Relativism is One of the Defining Characteristics of Gen Z," *Impact 360 Institute,* available online at: https://www.impact360institute.org/articles/moral-relativism-one-defining-characteristics-gen-z/.

4. Edmund Bourne and Lorna Garano, *Coping with Anxiety* (Oakland, CA: New Harbinger Publications, 2003), viii.

5. Carl Trueman, *Strange New World: How Thinkers and Activists Redefined Identity and Sparked the Sexual Revolution* (Wheaton, IL: Crossway Books, 2022), 22.

6. For your students, be clear on the distinction of knowing or being certain a statement to be true (epistemological issues) and its ontological status as true (a metaphysical issue). A statement can be objectively true even if we could not know it as such.

7. Francis Beckwith and Gregory Koukl, "Truth Is a Strange Sort of Fiction—Part V: Christianity and Post-modernism: The Emerging Church," *Solid Ground*, July 2007.

8. Peter Berger, *Facing Up to Modernity: Excursions in Society, Politics, and Religion* (New York: Basic Books, 1977), 133.

9. Nancy Pearcey, *Total Truth: Liberating Christianity from Its Cultural Captivity* (Wheaton, IL: Crossway Books, 2004), 20. Pearcey's book provides an in-depth analysis of the public/private split. It is a must-read for Christian leaders who want to understand the thought forms that dominate American culture.

10. Christian Smith, *Soul Searching: The Religious and Spiritual Lives of American Teenagers* (New York: Oxford University Press, 2005), 73.

11. C.S. Lewis, *Mere Christianity* (San Francisco: HarperSanFrancisco, 2001), 32.

12. Consider taking your students on one of MAVEN's life-changing Immersive Experiences. You can find more information at https://maventruth.com/immersive-experience.

13. Blaise Pascal, *Pensées*, trans. A.J. Krailsheimer (Harmondsworth, Middlesex: Penguin, 1972), 34.

An Interview with Hillary Morgan Ferrer

1. Brad M. Griffin, "Why Doubt Needs to Have a Place in Your Youth Ministry This Year." *Fuller Youth Institute* (August 18, 2016), at https://fulleryouthinstitute.org/blog/why-doubt.

Chapter 3–A Fresh Apologetic: Relationships That Transform

1. "Modeling the Future of Religion in America," *Pew Research Center* (September 13, 2022), at https://www.pewresearch.org/religion/2022/09/13/modeling-the-future-of-religion-in-america/.

2. "Openness to Jesus Isn't the Problem – The Church Is," *The Barna Group* (April 30, 2023), at https://barna.gloo.us/articles/spiritually-open-issue-3.

3. "Openness to Jesus Isn't the Problem – The Church Is," *The Barna Group*.

4. Commission on Children at Risk, "Hardwired to Connect: The New Scientific Case for Authoritative Communities," *Institute for American Values* (2003). This commission was a joint initiative of YMCA of the USA, Dartmouth Medical School, and the Institute for American Values.

5. "Back to School 1999—National Survey of American Attitudes on Substance Abuse V: Teens and Their Parents," The Luntz Research Companies and QEV Analytics, August 1999, 4; quoted in Lori Lessner, "Dads Key Against Drugs, Study Finds," *Dallas Morning News* (August 31, 1999), 9A.

6. Melanie Warner, "Two Professors Found What Creates a Mass Shooter. Will Politicians Pay Attention?," *POLITICO* (May 27, 2022), at www.politico.com/news/magazine/2022/05/27/stopping-mass-shooters-q-a-00035762. See also *The Violence Project: How to Stop a Mass Shooting Epidemic* by Jillian Peterson and James Densley.

7. Caroline Thomas and Karen Duszynski, "Closeness to Parents and the Family Constellation in a Prospective Study of Five Disease States: Suicide, Mental Illness, Malignant Tumor, Hypertension, and Coronary Heart Disease," *Johns Hopkins Medical Journal* (May 1974), vol. 134, no. 5, 251-70.

8. Dan Kimball, *They Like Jesus but Not the Church* (Grand Rapids, MI: Zondervan, 2007).

Chapter 4–Apologetics and Culture: Four Challenges of Our Age

1. See "The Parable of the Madman" from Friedrich Nietzsche, *The Gay Science* (1882, 1887) para. 125; ed. Walter Kaufmann (New York: Vintage, 1974), 181-82. Available online at https://sourcebooks.fordham.edu/mod/nietzsche-madman.asp.

2. Available online with commentary at https://www.gutenberg.org/files/1998/1998-h/1998-h.htm.

3. Carl R. Trueman, *The Rise and Triumph of the Modern Self: Cultural Amnesia, Expressive Individualism, and the Road to Sexual Revolution* (Wheaton, IL: Crossway, 2020).

4. Steven H. Woolf and Heidi Schoomaker, "Life Expectancy and Mortality Rates in the United States, 1959–2017," *JAMA* 2019; 322(20): 1996–2016. doi:10.1001/jama.2019.16932. See also John Stonestreet and Kasey

Leander, "American Life Expectancy Continues to Fall," *Breakpoint* (January 25, 2023), at https://www.breakpoint.org/american-life-expectancy-continues-to-fall/.

5. See, for example, David Introcaso, "Deaths of Despair: The Unrecognized Tragedy of Working Class Immiseration," *STAT* (December 29, 2021), at https://www.statnews.com/2021/12/29/deaths-of-despair-unrecognized-tragedy-working-class-immiseration/.

6. Peter L. Berger, Brigitte Berger, and Hansfried Kellner, *The Homeless Mind: Modernization and Consciousness* (New York: Vintage Books, 1974), 78.

7. For a summary of modern gnostic views of the body, see John Stonestreet, "You Are Your Body," *Breakpoint* (August 22, 2023), at https://www.breakpoint.org/you-are-your-body-2/.

An Interview with Adam Davidson

1. Kalam is a discipline of theological and philosophical study in Islam originating in the Middle Ages. Its initial purpose was to develop defenses to the Islamic faith in response to surrounding religions and philosophies.

2. The Kalam Cosmological Argument argues for the existence of a Creator of the universe based on three statements of logic: (1) Whatever begins to exist has a cause of its beginning. (2) The universe began to exist. (3) Therefore, the universe has a cause of its beginning. William Lane Craig, "The *Kalam* Cosmological Argument," lecture given at the University of Birmingham (2015), at https://www.reasonablefaith.org/writings/popular-writings/existence-nature-of-god/the-kalam-cosmological-argument.

Chapter 5–Effective Apologetics in the Local Church

1. Norman L. Geisler, "Need for Apologetics," *Baker Encyclopedia of Christian Apologetics* (Grand Rapids, MI: Baker Books,1999), 37.

2. Norman L. Geisler, *Systematic Theology, vol. 4: Church, Last Things* (Minneapolis, MN: Bethany House, 2005), 294-318.

3. "Vision and Values," *Transformation Church*, at https://transformationchurch.tc/vision-values/.

4. "The Bible Says What?!," *Transformation Church*, at https://transformationchurch.tc/series/the-bible-says-what/.

Chapter 6–Doing Apologetics in the Home

1. Author J. Warner Wallace has compiled a helpful summary here: J. Warner Wallace, "Updated: Are Young People Really Leaving Christianity?" *Cold-Case Christianity* (October 30, 2021), at https://coldcasechristianity.com/writings/are-young-people-really-leaving-christianity/.

2. I responded to her entire post in my article "A Christian Response to a Viral Deconversion Post," *Natasha Crain* (August 25, 2023), at https://natashacrain.com/a-christian-response-to-a-viral-deconversion-post/.

3. Part 1 of my book *Talking with Your Kids about God: 30 Conversations Every Christian Parent Must Have* (Grand Rapids, MI: Baker Books, 2017) offers conversation outlines for kids of all ages on this subject.

4. Natasha Crain, *Faithfully Different: Regaining Biblical Clarity in a Secular Culture* (Eugene, OR: Harvest House, 2022).

5. My books cover 100 questions and answers for parents to discuss with kids: *Keeping Your Kids on God's Side: 40 Conversations to Help Them Build a Lasting Faith* (Eugene, OR: Harvest House Publishers, 2016); *Talking with Your Kids about God: 30 Conversations Every Christian Parent Must Have* (Grand Rapids, MI: Baker Books, 2017); and *Talking with Your Kids about Jesus: 30 Conversations Every Christian Parent Must Have* (Grand Rapids, MI: Baker Books, 2020).

Chapter 7–Storytelling and Persuasion

1. A proposition is a statement that affirms or denies something and is either true or false.

2. See also Proverbs 22:21-25; Zechariah 7:9-10; Romans 12:20.

3. Of course, most of the propositional content and imagery are integrated with each other, so a strictly

scientific separation is not possible. Both are necessary to God's revelation, but the sheer comparison of volume is revealing.

4. I am indebted to N.T. Wright for his awesome explication of this in his two volumes *The New Testament and the People of God* (Minneapolis, MN: Fortress Press, 1992) and *Jesus and the Victory of God* (Minneapolis, MN: Fortress Press, 1996).

5. Wright, *The New Testament and the People of God*, 77.

6. Wright, *The New Testament and the People of God*, 78.

7. Kenneth E. Bailey, *Jacob and the Prodigal: How Jesus Retold Israel's Story* (Downers Grove, IL: InterVarsity Press, 2003), 51.

8. Kevin J. Vanhoozer, *The Drama of Doctrine: A Canonical-Linguistic Approach to Christian Theology* (Louisville, KY: Westminster John Knox Press, 2005), 50.

9. Robert Gallagher and Paul Hertig, eds., *Mission in Acts: Ancient Narratives in Contemporary Context* (Maryknoll, NY: Orbis Books, 2004), 224-25.

10. Xenophon, *Memorabilia*, ch. 1. See also Plato, *Apology* 24B-C; *Euthyphro* 1C; 2B; 3B.

11. Scripture quotations are NASB 1995.

12. Sophocles, *Oedipus Tyrannus*, 260; Pausanias, *Description of Greece*, 1.17.1, quoted in Charles H. Talbert, *Reading Acts: A Literary and Theological Commentary on the Acts of the Apostles* (Macon, GA: Smyth and Helwys, 2001), 153.

13. Explained of Zeno by Plutarch in his *Moralia*, 1034B, quoted in Juhana Torkki, "The Dramatic Account of Paul's Encounter with Philosophy: An Analysis of Acts 17:16-34 with Regard to Contemporary Philosophical Debates," (Helsinki, FI: Helsinki University Printing House, 2004), 105.

14. Euripides, frag. 968, quoted in F.F. Bruce, *Paul: Apostle of the Heart Set Free* (Cumbria, UK: Paternoster Press, 2000), 240.

15. Seneca, *Epistle* 95.47; Euripides, *Hercules* 1345-46, quoted in Talbert, *Reading Acts*, 155.

16. Seneca, *Epistle* 95.52, quoted in Michelle V. Lee, *Paul, the Stoics, and the Body of Christ* (Cambridge, UK: Cambridge University Press, 2006), 84.

17. Seneca, *Epistle* 44.1, quoted in Talbert, *Reading Acts*, 156.

18. Dio Chrysostom, *Oration* 30.26, quoted in Talbert, *Reading Acts*, 156.

19. Epictetus, *Discourse* 1.14, quoted in A.A. Long, *Epictetus: A Stoic and Socratic Guide to Life* (Oxford, UK: Oxford University Press, 2002), 25-26.

20. Dio Chrysostom, *Olympic Oration* 12:28, quoted in F.F. Bruce, *The Book of the Acts*, New International Commentary on the New Testament, rev., ed. Gordon D. Fee (Grand Rapids, MI: Eerdmans, 1988), 339.

21. Seneca, *Epistle* 41.1-2, quoted in Talbert, *Reading Acts*, 156.

22. Quoted in Bruce, *The Book of the Acts*, 338-39.

23. Bruce, *The Book of the Acts*, 338-39.

24. Epictetus, *Discourses* 2.8.11-12, quoted in Gallagher and Hertig, *Mission in Acts*, 232.

25. Dio Chrysostom, *Discourses* 12.27; cf. 12.12, 16, 21, quoted in Gallagher and Hertig, *Mission in Acts*, 229.

26. Epictetus, *Discourses* 2.8.11-14, quoted in Gallagher and Hertig, *Mission in* Acts, 229.

27. Ben Witherington III, *The Acts of the Apostles: A Socio-Rhetorical Commentary* (Grand Rapids, MI: Eerdmans, 1998), 524.

28. Witherington, *The Acts of the Apostles*, 526.

29. Aeschylus, *Eumenides*, 647, quoted in Bruce, *Paul: Apostle of the Heart Set Free*, 247.

30. Curtis Chang, *Engaging Unbelief: A Captivating Strategy from Augustine to Aquinas* (Downers Grove, IL: InterVarsity Press, 2000), 26.

31. Chang, *Engaging Unbelief,* 29.

32. Chang, *Engaging Unbelief,* 30.

33. Wright, *The New Testament and the People of God,* 42.

An Interview with Lee Strobel

1. Jeffrey M. Jones, "Belief in God in U.S. Dips to 81%, a New Low," *Gallup* (June 17, 2022), at https://news .gallup.com/poll/393737/belief-god-dips-new-low.aspx.

Chapter 8—Capturing the Imagination Before Engaging the Mind

1. Eusebius of Caesarea, *Demonstratio Evangelica,* book III, chapter 5, in *The Proof of the Gospel Being the Demonstratio Evangelica of Eusebius of Caesarea,* vol. 1, trans. W.J. Ferrar, Translations of Christian Literature, Series I: Greek Texts, eds. W.J. Sparrow Simpson and W.K. Lowther Clarke, (New York: The Macmillan Company, 1920), 131-32.

2. John Warwick Montgomery, *Tractatus Logico-Theologicus* (Bonn, Germany: Verlag für Kultur und Wissenschaft, 2002), 186.

3. J.R.R. Tolkien, "On Fairy Stories," quoted in Montgomery, *Tractatus Logico-Theologicus,* 187-88.

4. C.S. Lewis, *The Grand Miracle and Other Selected Essays on Theology and Ethics from God in the Dock* (New York: Ballantine Books, 1970), 41.

5. Douglas Wilson and Douglas Jones, *Angels in the Architecture* (Moscow, ID: Canon Press, 1998), 181.

6. Alister E. McGrath, *Intellectuals Don't Need God* (Grand Rapids, MI: Zondervan, 1993), 198.

Chapter 9—Emotionally Healthy Apologetics: Understanding Our Ways of Finding Meaning and Truth

1. These seven beliefs comprise Barna's Theolographic Profile for Evangelical Beliefs. See David Kinnaman, "Teens and Supernatural Report," 43. Available online at www.barna.org.

2. Kinnaman, "Teens and Supernatural Report."

3. Commission on Children at Risk, "Hardwired to Connect: The New Scientific Case for Authoritative Communities," *Institute for American Values* (2003).

4. Commission on Children at Risk, "Hardwired to Connect."

5. Dr. Hall is the editor of *The Journal of Psychology and Theology* and also the founder of Alidade Research. His "Furnishing the Soul" and other work can be found at alidaderesearch.com.

6. See Daniel J. Siegel, *The Developing Mind,* Third ed. (New York: The Guilford Press, 2020).

7. See Daniel J. Siegel, *The Developing Mind.*

8. Todd Hall, "Christian Spirituality and Mental Health," *Journal of Psychology and Christianity* 2004, vol. 23, no. 1, 66-81.

9. Will Slater, et al., "Measuring Religion and Spirituality," *Journal of Psychology and Theology* 2001, vol. 29, no. 1, 4-21.

Chapter 10—Making Apologetics Come Alive in Youth Ministry

1. Here are a few I recommend: Summit Ministries (summit.org); Frank Turek's events (crossexamined.org); Brett Kunkle's immersive trips (maventruth.org); Summer Family Bible Conference (awmi.net); Reasons for Hope camps (equipretreat.org); The Billy Graham Training Center (thecove.org); and I humbly include my ministry's own never-ending apologetics tour (https://alexmcfarland.com/events/).

2. See Francis Schaeffer, *He Is There and He Is Not Silent* (Wheaton, IL: Tyndale, 1972).

An Interview with Jeff Myers

1. A Research Report by George Barna, "Millennials in America," Cultural Research Center at Arizona Christian University (2021), 7.

Chapter 11–Defending the Faith Online: Becoming a Twenty-First-Century Online Apologist

1. The National Science and Media Museum, "A Short History of the Internet," *Science+Media Museum* (December 3, 2020), at https://www.scienceandmediamuseum.org.uk/objects-and-stories/short-history-internet.

Chapter 12–Helping People Through Doubt

1. The Barna Group, "Doubt & Faith: Top Reasons People Question Christianity," *Barna* (March 1, 2023), at https://www.barna.com/research/doubt-faith/.

2. Pseudonym.

Chapter 13–Taking the Other Perspective

1. Kenneth S. Wuest, "Hebrews" in *Word Studies of the Greek New Testament*, vol. 2 (Grand Rapids, MI: Eerdmans, 1970), 94.

2. While Nathan consented to this interview, for privacy's sake, I've changed his name and omitted personal information.

3. Dalai Lama XIV, *Spiritual Advice for Buddhists and Christians*, ed. Donald W. Mitchell (New York: Continuum, 1999), 17.

4. To read an introductory critique of today's popular form of pluralism, see my book cowritten with apologist J.P. Moreland—*The God Conversation: Using Stories and Illustrations to Explain Your Faith*, 2d ed. (Downers Grove, IL: InterVarsity Press, 2017).

5. For a deeper description of this method, see Sean McDowell and Tim Muehlhoff, *End the Stalemate: Move Past Cancel Culture to Meaningful Conversations* (Carol Stream, IL:Tyndale, 2024).

6. Robert Waldinger and Marc Schulz, *The Good Life: Lessons from the World's Longest Scientific Study of Happiness* (New York: Simon and Schuster, 2023), 113.

7. Patrick Stokes, "Wounded Stories," *New Philosopher* (June-August 2022), 36.

8. Anna Deavere Smith, *Fires in the Mirror* (New York: Anchor Books, 1993), 80.

9. R.C. Sproul, *Enjoying God: Finding Hope in the Attributes of God* (Grand Rapids, MI: Baker Books, 2017), 88-9.

10. Kenneth Burke, *A Grammar of Motives* (Berkeley, CA: University of California Press, 1969), 100.

11. In today's divisive age, we need to practice perspective-taking. To work on engaging diverse views, I've created an interactive website that will help you learn the finer points of perspective-taking: endthestalemate.com.

12. As communicated in Jack Michael Antonoff's song "Everybody Lost Somebody," RCA Records, 2017.

Chapter 14–Urban Apologetics–Two Tensions

1. *A New Kind of Apologist*, ed. Sean McDowell (Eugene, OR: Harvest House, 2016).

2. Pew Research Center Report, "Jewish Americans in 2020," section 12, *Pew Research Center* (May 11, 2021), at https://www.pewresearch.org/religion/2021/05/11/people-of-jewish-background-and-jewish-affinity/.

3. Morf Morford, "Do Blacks have Souls?" *Red Letter Christians* (February 22, 2019), at https://redletterchristians.org/2019/02/22/do-black-people-have-souls/.

4. Willie James Jennings, "Can White People Be Saved?," *Can "White" People be Saved?*, eds. Love L. Sechrest, Johnny Ramírez-Johnson, and Amos Yong (Downers Grove, IL: InterVarsity Press, 2018), 27-43.

5. J. Kameron Carter, *Race: A Theological Account* (New York: Oxford University Press, 2008).

6. "Being Antiracist" *National Museum of African American History and Culture*, at https://nmaahc.si.edu/learn/talking-about-race/topics/being-antiracist.

7. George Yancey, *Beyond Racial Gridlock: Embracing Mutual Responsibility* (Downers Grove, IL: InterVarsity Press, 2006), 24.

8. George Yancey, *Beyond Racial Division: A Unifying Alternative to Colorblindness and Antiracism* (Downers Grove, IL: InterVarsity Press, 2022), 9.

9. Yancey, *Beyond Racial Division*, 14.

Chapter 15–Homosexuality: Truth and Grace

1. Cleon L. Rogers Jr. and Cleon L. Rogers III, *The New Linguistic and Exegetical Key to the Greek New Testament* (Grand Rapids, MI: Zondervan, 1998), 317.

2. Bernadette Brooten, *Love Between Women: Early Christian Response to Female Homoeroticism* (Chicago: University of Chicago Press, 1996), 59-60; Thomas K. Hubbard, "Peer Homosexuality," in *A Companion to Greek and Roman Sexualities*, ed. Thomas K. Hubbard, (Chichester, UK: Blackwell Publishing, 2014), 128-49, as cited in Preston Sprinkle, *People to Be Loved: Why Homosexuality Is Not Just an Issue* (Grand Rapids, MI: Zondervan, 2015), 91.

3. An obvious exception is mentioned in 1 Corinthians 5:9-12. This, however, is in the context of a church setting and refers to self-professed Christians who are unrepentant in their sexual sin.

Chapter 16–Defending Femininity: Why Jesus Is Good News for Women

1. I will be using *femininity* as a synonym for any biological or soul difference that distinguishes women from men, not merely culturally conditioned differences. For a detailed explanation of the unique aspects of the feminine soul, see my book *Ruby Slippers: How the Soul of a Woman Brings Her Home* (Grand Rapids, MI: Zondervan, 2007).

2. I will be using *gender* to mean all differences between the sexes, not as the academy uses "gender" to refer exclusively to socially conditioned differences.

3. Thomas Webster, *Woman: Man's Equal* (New York: Nelson and Phillips, 1873), introduction by Bishop Simpson. Available online at https://www.gutenberg.org/cache/epub/11632/pg11632-images.html.

4. Mishkat 13, 3; Ehsan Yar-Shater, ed., *The History of al-Tabari*, vol. 9 (Albany, NY: State University of New York Press, 1990), 131; Quoted in William E. Phipps, *Muhammad and Jesus: A Comparison of the Prophets and Their Teachings* (New York: Continuum, 1996), 142.

5. Qu'ran 2:223; 4:34; Mishkat 26, 651, as quoted in Phipps, *Muhammad and Jesus*, 111, 140, 148-49.

6. Samuel Bereholz and Sherab Chodzin Kohn, eds., *Entering the Stream: An Introduction to the Buddha and His Teachings* (Boston: Shambhala, 1993), 7, 9-10.

7. Karen Armstrong, *Buddha* (New York: Penguin, 2001), 1-2.

8. Lucy Walker Kimball, autobiographical sketch from the church archives of The Church of Jesus Christ of Latter-day Saints; quoted in Richard Lyman Bushman, *Joseph Smith: Rough Stone Rolling: A Cultural Biography of Mormonism's Founder* (New York: Alfred A. Knopf, 2005), 490-91.

9. Bushman, *Joseph Smith: Rough Stone Rolling*, 492-493.

10. Joseph Smith, *Doctrine and Covenants*, 132:37, 52-54.

11. J.J. Ross, *Some Facts and More Facts About the Self-styled Pastor Charles T. Russell* (Santa Ana, CA: Westminster Press, 1920), 25-31.

12. My husband and I have found women confused, lost, and even homeless about their femininity. But we are convinced that men are equally lost. We've seen that men tend to define their masculinity through competition, control, and disdain for women rather than through measuring themselves to Christ. The popularity of John Eldredge's books and the like indicate a vacuum in both sexes and a longing for clarity about their gender.

13. See David Murrow, *Why Men Hate Going to Church: Completely Revised and Updated* (Nashville, TN: Thomas Nelson, 2011); Leon J. Podles, *The Church Impotent: The Feminization of Christianity*, 2d ed. (Moscow, ID: Canon Press, 2024); Holly Pivec, "The Feminization of the Church," *Biola Connections* (February 28, 2006), available online at https://www.biola.edu/blogs/biola-magazine/2006/the-feminization-of-the-church. *Biola Connections* is the former name of *Biola Magazine*.

14. See Julia O'Faolain and Lauro Martines eds., *Not in God's Image: Women in History from the Greeks to the Victorians* (New York: Harper Torchbooks, 1973).

15. Dorothy L. Sayers, *Are Women Human?* (Grand Rapids, MI: Eerdmans, 1971), 68-69.

16. Dan Kimball, *They Like Jesus but Not the Church* (Grand Rapids, MI: Zondervan, 2007), 121.

17. To develop a better understanding of these verses, see *The IVP Women's Bible Commentary* (Downers Grove, IL: InterVarsity Press, 2002); Sarah Sumner, *Men and Women in the Church: Building Consensus on Christian Leadership* (Downers Grove, IL: InterVarsity Press, 2003).

18. To read up on these movements I recommend Ronald Pierce and Rebecca Goouthius eds., *Christians for Biblical Equality: Complementarity Without Hierarchy* (Downers Grove, IL: InterVarsity Press, 2005), 23-75.

19. Here are some good sources for understanding these verses: *The IVP Women's Bible Commentary*, *Women and Men in Ministry: A Complementary Perspective* (Chicago: Moody Press, 2001), and *Christians for Biblical Equality*.

20. Not until my postgraduate work, when I began researching God, femininity, and imagery in Scripture, did I realize that it was not Jesus' maleness that saved humans, it was His divinity. For more on this see Sumner, *Men and Women in the Church*.

21. Renée Altson, *Stumbling Toward Faith: My Longing to Heal from the Evil that God Allowed* (Grand Rapids, MI: Zondervan Youth Specialties, 2004), 11, 15.

22. Altson, *Stumbling Toward Faith*, 155, 156.

23. See Gordon D. Fee and Mark L. Strauss' excellent guide to translations, *How to Choose a Translation for All Its Worth: A Guide to Understanding and Using Bible Versions* (Grand Rapids, MI: Zondervan, 2007), 97-108.

24. Simone de Beauvoir, *The Second Sex* (New York: Vintage Books 1989), 131, 170.

Chapter 17—Wading into the Abortion Debate: Making the Controversial Civil

1. UN General Assembly, Resolution 2200, International Covenant on Civil and Political Rights, A/RES/2200(XXI), (December 16, 1966), Article 6.5, at https://treaties.un.org/doc/treaties/1976/03/19760323%2006-17%20am/ch_iv_04.pdf.

2. A resource I recommend as a starting point is Perinatalhospice.org.

3. These resources can be found on my website at www.loveunleasheslife.com.

4. Cara Buckley, "Man Is Rescued by Stranger on Subway Tracks," *The New York Times* (January 3, 2007), at https://www.nytimes.com/2007/01/03/nyregion/03life.html.

5. CBS New York, "5 Years Later, New York City Subway Hero Wesley Autrey Is Still the Man," *CBS News* (February 21, 2012), at https://www.cbsnews.com/newyork/news/5-years-later-new-york-city-subway-hero-wesley-autrey-is-still-the-man/.

Chapter 18—Critiquing Critical Theory

1. Scott Alexander, "New Atheism: The Godlessness That Failed," *Slate Star Codex* (October 30, 2019), at https://slatestarcodex.com/2019/10/30/new-atheism-the-godlessness-that-failed/.

2. Simon Moya-Smith, "Your Fancy New Brunch Place Is Probably Colonialist and You're a Colonizer," *NBC News* (February 24, 2019), at https://www.nbcnews.com/think/opinion/your-fancy-new-brunch-place-probably-colonialist-you-re-colonizer-ncna974971.

3. Marina Watts, "In Smithsonian Race Guidelines, Rational Thinking and Hard Work Are White Values," *Newsweek* (July 17, 2020), at https://www.newsweek.com/smithsonian-race-guidelines-rational-thinking-hard-work-are-white-values-1518333.

4. Black Lives Matter, "What We Believe," archived July 1, 2020. Accessed on archive.org.

5. Jonathan Weisman, "A demand to define 'woman' injects gender politics into Jackson's confirmation hearings," *The New York Times* (March 23, 2022), at https://www.nytimes.com/2022/03/23/us/politics/ketanji -brown-jackson-woman-definition.html.

6. James A. Lindsay and Mike Nayna, "Postmodern Religion and the Faith of Social Justice," *Areo* (December 18, 2018), at https://areomagazine.com/2018/12/18/postmodern-religion-and-the-faith-of-social-justice/.

7. Ibram X. Kendi, *How to Be an Antiracist*, 1st ed. (New York: One World, 2019), 197.

Chapter 19—Church of Invisible Diseases: Apologetics and Mental Health

1. Pseudonym.

2. C.S. Lewis, *God in the Dock*, ed. Walter Hooper (New York: HarperOne, 1994), 199.

3. Bob Smietana, "Mental Illness Remains Taboo Topic for Many Pastors," *Lifeway Research* (September 22, 2014), at https://lifewayresearch.com/2014/09/22/mental-illness-remains-taboo-topic-for-many-pastors/.

4. Sarah Eekhoff Zylstra, "1 in 4 Pastors Have Struggled with Mental Illness, Finds LifeWay and Focus on the Family," *Christianity Today* (September 22, 2014), at https://www.christianitytoday.com/news/2014/ september/1-in-4-pastors-have-mental-illness-lifeway-focus-on-family.html.

5. Lisa Rudolfsson and Glen Milstein "Clergy and Mental Health Clinician Collaboration in Sweden: Pilot Survey of COPE," *Mental Health, Religion and Culture*, vol. 22, issue 8 (October 29, 2019), 805-818, at https://doi.org/10.1080/13674676.2019.1666095.

6. Jeremiah Johnston, *Unleashing Peace: Experiencing God's Shalom in Your Pursuit of Happiness* (Grand Rapids, MI: Bethany House, 2021), 26.

7. Will Durant, *The Story of Philosophy* (New York: Simon and Schuster, 1961), 20.

8. *American Foundation for Suicide Prevention*, https://supporting.afsp.org/index.cfm?fuseaction=cms .page&id=1891&eventID=9707.

9. *Mental Health America of Wisconsin*, at https://www.mhawisconsin.org/suicide.aspx.

10. At several points, this chapter is dependent on my prior publications on the subjects of shalom and peace. See Jeremiah J. Johnston, *Unleashing Peace: Experiencing God's Shalom in Your Pursuit of Happiness* (Grand Rapids, MI: Bethany House, 2021) and Jeremiah J. Johnston, *The Peace Bible* (Nashville, TN: Thomas Nelson, 2025).

11. "Mental Health Issues Increased Significantly in Young Adults Over Last Decade," *American Psychological Association* (March 14, 2019), at https://www.apa.org/news/press/releases/2019/03/mental-health-adults.

Chapter 20—Engaging the Transgender Debate

1. Pseudonym.

2. Anna Brown, "About 5% of Young Adults in the U.S. Say Their Gender Is Different from Their Sex Assigned at Birth." *Pew Research Center* (June 7, 2022), at https://www.pewresearch.org/short-reads/2022/06/07/ about-5-of-young-adults-in-the-u-s-say-their-gender-is-different-from-their-sex-assigned-at-birth/.

3. A few great resources include Abigail Shrier's *Irreversible Damage* (Washington, DC: Regnery, 2020) on transgenderism as a social contagion. For parents hoping to resist medical and cultural pressure to "transition" struggling kids, check out *Lost in Trans Nation* by Miriam Grossman, MD (New York: Skyhorse, 2023). On understanding the transgender phenomenon as a whole, you can read Ryan Anderson's somewhat-banned *When Harry Became Sally* (New York: Encounter Books, 2018). To contrast the gender paradigm vs Genesis paradigm, see *The Genesis of Gender* by Abigail Favale (San Francisco: Ignatius, 2022).

4. Lisa Littman, "Rapid-Onset Gender Dysphoria in Adolescents and Young Adults: A Study of Parental Reports," *PLOS One*, vol. 13, (August 16, 2018), at https://www.researchgate.net/publication /327065646_Rapid-onset_gender_dysphoria_in_adolescents_and_young_adults_A_study_of_parental _reports.

5. Bibi Masala, Amy Love, Polly Carmichael, and Una Masic, "Demographics of Referrals to a Specialist Gender Identity Service in the UK between 2017 and 2020," *Clinical Child Psychology and Psychiatry*, vol. 29, issue 2, (September 12, 2023), at https://journals.sagepub.com/doi/10.1177/13591045231202372?icid=int .sj-abstract.citing-articles.15.

6. Lisa Littman, "Rapid-Onset Gender Dysphoria in Adolescents and Young Adults: A Study of Parental Reports."

7. "Binding Safety," *Gender Minorities Aotearoa* (accessed December 1, 2023), at https://genderminorities .com/resources/transgender-health-directory/binders-2/binding-info/.

8. OHSU Doernbecher Children's Hospital Gender Clinic, "Safe Tucking," at https://www.ohsu.edu/sites/ default/files/2022-03/Gender-Clinic-Safe-Tucking-Handout.pdf.

9. Stephen B. Levine and E. Abbruzzese, "Current Concerns About Gender-Affirming Therapy in Adolescents," *Current Sexual Health Reports*, vol. 15, 113-123 (April 14, 2023), at https://doi.org/10.1007/ s11930-023-00358-x.

10. American College of Pediatricians, "Transgender Interventions Harm Children," at https://acpeds.org/ transgender-interventions-harm-children.

11. Ana Costa-Ramon, Ana Rodríguez-González, and Meltem Daysal, "The Oral Contraceptive Pill and Adolescents' Mental Health," *Vox EU—Centre For Economic Policy Research* (August 26, 2023), at https://cepr .org/voxeu/columns/oral-contraceptive-pill-and-adolescents-mental-health.

12. American College of Pediatricians, "Transgender Interventions Harm Children."

13. Hannah Barnes, "Why Disturbing leaks from US gender group WPATH ring alarm Bells in the NHS," *The Guardian* (March 9, 2024), at https://www.theguardian.com/commentisfree/2024/mar/09/ disturbing-leaks-from-us-gender-group-wpath-ring-alarm-bells-in-nhs.

14. "Information on Estrogen Hormone Therapy," *UCSF Transgender Care* (July 2020), at https://transcare .ucsf.edu/article/information-estrogen-hormone-therapy.

15. "Practical Guidelines for Transgender Hormone Treatment," *Boston University Chobanian and Avedisian School of Medicine: Department of Medicine Endocrinology, Diabetes, Nutrition and Weight Management*, at https://www.bumc.bu.edu/endo/clinics/transgender-medicine/guidelines/.

16. Silvana Zito, Guido Nosari, et al., "Association Between Testosterone Levels and Mood Disorders: A Minireview," *Journal of Affective Disorders*, vol. 330 (June 1, 2023), 48-56, at https://www.sciencedirect.com/ science/article/abs/pii/S0165032723002768.

17. "Reasons For Transgender Men to Get a Hysterectomy," *Hysto.net* (updated March 2, 2022), at https:// www.hysto.net/reasons-transmen-get-hysterectomy.htm.

18. Lindsey Tanner, Associated Press, "Transgender Kids Tend to Maintain Their Identities as They Grow up, Study Suggests," *PBS News* (May 4, 2022), at https://www.pbs.org/newshour/nation/ transgender-kids-tend-to-maintain-their-identities-as-they-grow-up-study-suggests.

19. Peggy T. Cohen-Kettenis PT, Henriette A. Delemarre-van de Waal HA, and Louis J G Gooren, "The Treatment of Adolescent Transsexuals: Changing Insights," *Journal of Sexual Medicine*, (July 2008), 1892-7, quoted in Michelle Cretella MD, et al., "Gender Dysphoria in Children," *American College of Pediatricians* (November 2018), at https://acpeds.org/position-statements/gender-dysphoria-in-children.

20. Aleksandr Solzhenitsyn quoted by *Concord Monitor*, (January 17, 2021), "Solzhenitsyn Quote on Front Page of Concord Monitor," *The Aleksandr Solzhenitsyn Center*, (January 29, 2021), at https://www.solzhenitsyn center.org/whats-new/2021/1/29/solzhenitsyn-quote-on-front-page-of-concord-monitor.

21. "Five Lies of Our Anti-Christian Age (with Rosaria Butterfield)," *The Great Awokening Podcast*, (October 16, 2023), at https://www.youtube.com/watch?v=zs-prEzu7E4.

An Interview with John Marriott

1. Pew Research Center Report, "America's Changing Religious Landscape," *Pew Research Center* (May 12, 2015), at https://www.pewresearch.org/religion/2015/05/12/chapter-2-religious-switching-and-intermarriage/.

2. Pew Research Center Report, "Modeling the Future of Religion in America," *Pew Research Center* (September 13, 2022), at https://www.pewresearch.org/religion/2022/09/13/modeling-the-future-of-religion-in-america/.

3. Pinetops Foundation Report, "The Great Opportunity: The American Church in 2050," *Pinetops Foundation* (2018), 9.

4. Pew Research Center Report, "Modeling the Future of Religion in America."

Chapter 22—Nothing New Under the Sun: Engaging New Age

1. Steven Bancarz and Josh Peck, *The Second Coming of the New Age: The Hidden Dangers of Alternate Spirituality in Contemporary America and Its Churches* (Crane, MO: Defender Publishing, 2018), 3.

Chapter 23—Recentering Biblical Authority

1. For more about Impact 360 Institute's life-changing experiences that help students live out their faith with confidence and our latest next-generation research, visit www.impact360.org.

2. Charles Taylor, *A Secular Age* (Cambridge, MA: Belknap Press, 2007).

3. Carl R. Trueman, *The Rise and Triumph of the Modern Self: Cultural Amnesia, Expressive Individualism, and the Road to Sexual Revolution* (Wheaton, IL: Crossway, 2020). 42-45. See also, Carl Trueman, "How Expressive Individualism Threatens Civil Society," *The Heritage Foundation* (May 27, 2021), at https://www.heritage.org/civil-society/report/how-expressive-individualism-threatens-civil-society; and the helpful summary here: "Expressive Individualism And Civil Society," *Pioneering Minds*, at https://www.pioneeringminds.com/pqposts/expressive-individualism-civil-society/.

4. Jonathan Morrow, "Only 4 Percent of Gen Z Have a Biblical Worldview," *Impact 360 Institute*, at https://www.impact360institute.org/articles/4-percent-gen-z-biblical-worldview/. This research and much more is published in *Gen Z: The Culture, Beliefs and Motivations Shaping the Next Generation* (Ventura, CA: Barna Group, 2018).

5. Jonathan Morrow, *Questioning the Bible: 11 Major Challenges to the Bible's Authority* (Chicago: Moody Publishers, 2014).

6. John R.W. Stott, *The Authority of the Bible* (Downers Grove, IL: InterVarsity Press, 1974), 32.

7. Find free downloads and other "Grids for Growth" at jonathanmorrow.org. See some in action on my YouTube channel at https://www.youtube.com/@jonathan_morrow. Here are a couple of them: Jonathan Morrow, "Bible vs Culture (Who Wins?)," (July 14, 2024), at https://www.youtube.com/watch?v=7Py3ApU5fQ; and Jonathan Morrow, "How to Deal with Worry, Fear, and Anxious Thoughts," (November 30, 2023), at https://youtu.be/sHXJXVym5ZA.

SCRIPTURE COPYRIGHT NOTIFICATIONS

Unless otherwise indicated, all Scripture quotations are taken from the *Holy Bible*, New Living Translation, copyright © 1996, 2004, 2015 by Tyndale House Foundation. Used by permission of Tyndale House Publishers, Inc., Carol Stream, Illinois 60188. All rights reserved.

Verses marked NIV are taken from the Holy Bible, New International Version®, NIV®. Copyright © 1973, 1978, 1984, 2011 by Biblica, Inc.™ Used with permission of Zondervan. All rights reserved worldwide. www.zondervan.com. The "NIV" and "New International Version" are trademarks registered in the United States Patent and Trademark Office by Biblica, Inc.™

Verses marked ESV are taken from the ESV® Bible (The Holy Bible, English Standard Version®), copyright © 2001 by Crossway, a publishing ministry of Good News Publishers. Used with permission. All rights reserved. The ESV text may not be quoted in any publication made available to the public by a Creative Commons license. The ESV may not be translated in whole or in part into any other language.

Verses marked NASB1995 are taken from the (NASB®) New American Standard Bible®, Copyright © 1960, 1971, 1977, 1995 by The Lockman Foundation. Used with permission. All rights reserved. www.lockman.org.

Verses marked NASB are taken from the (NASB®) New American Standard Bible®, Copyright © 1960, 1971, 1977, 1995, 2020 by The Lockman Foundation. Used with permission. All rights reserved. www.lockman.org.

Verses marked NKJV are taken from the New King James Version®. Copyright © 1982 by Thomas Nelson, Inc. Used with permission. All rights reserved.

Verses marked NRSV are taken from the New Revised Standard Version Bible, copyright © 1989 National Council of the Churches of Christ in the United States of America. Used with permission. All rights reserved worldwide.

Verses marked CSB have been taken from the Christian Standard Bible®, Copyright 2017 by Holman Bible Publishers. Used with permission. Christian Standard Bible® and CSB® are federally registered trademarks of Holman Bible Publishers.

Verses marked HCSB have been taken from the Holman Christian Standard Bible®, Copyright © 1999, 2000, 2002, 2003, 2009 by Holman Bible Publishers. Used with permission. Holman Christian Standard Bible®, Holman CSB®, and HCSB® are federally registered trademarks of Holman Bible Publishers.

Verses marked RSV are taken from the Revised Standard Version of the Bible, copyright © 1946, 1952, and 1971 National Council of the Churches of Christ in the United States of America. Used with permission. All rights reserved worldwide.

Verses marked NET are quoted from the NET Bible®, https://netbible.com. Copyright ©1996, 2019. Used with permission from Biblical Studies Press, LLC. All rights reserved.

Verses marked KJV are taken from the King James Version of the Bible.